The Passion for Equality

The Passion for Equality

KENNETH CAUTHEN

Rowman & Littlefield Publishers

ROWMAN & LITTLEFIELD

Published in the United States of America in 1987
by Rowman & Littlefield, Publishers
(a division of Littlefield, Adams & Company)
81 Adams Drive, Totowa, New Jersey 07512

Copyright © 1987 by Rowman & Littlefield

All rights reserved. No part of this publication may
be reproduced, stored in a retrieval system, or transmitted
in any form or by any means, electronic, mechanical,
photocopying, recording, or otherwise, without the prior
permission of the publisher.

Library of Congress Cataloging-in-Publication Data

Cauthen, Kenneth, 1930–
  The passion for equality.

  Bibliography: p. 179
  Includes index.
  1. Equality. I. Title.
JC575.C38   1987   323.4′2   87-4301
ISBN 0-8476-7544-0

90 89 88 87
7 6 5 4 3 2 1

Printed in the United States of America

To
GLORIA:
She knows why.

Contents

PREFACE AND ACKNOWLEDGMENTS		ix
I /	A Defense of the Passion	1
II /	The American Tradition	31
III /	An Ideal Society: A Freedom-Equality Model	63
IV /	The Passion for Equal Opportunity	99
V /	The Passion for Economic Equality	129
VI /	The High-Minded Passion: Some Unconcluding Personal Reflections	168
BIBLIOGRAPHY		179
INDEX OF PERSONS		187
INDEX OF SUBJECTS		191

Preface and Acknowledgments

THE IDEA OF EQUALITY has fascinated me for a long time. It is a complex, subtle notion, with many nuances of meaning. Some of its mandates conflict with others. Equalizing some persons or groups in this or that way may create inequalities of a different sort. Moreover, equality may conflict with freedom or enlarging the common good. Different criteria come into play when the context shifts. When applied to a family, the rule of equality will have to be stated differently than when applied to society as a whole. Equality of opportunity may result in inequality of results. And so on it goes. No wonder its status as a principle of justice is judged so variously. I have known for a long time that I have a "passion for equality," as much equality as is possible or justifiable. Yet trying to figure out what that means and implies is a baffling task, and one is never sure all the complications have been taken into account and properly evaluated.

The occasion of a sabbatical leave from my teaching at Colgate Rochester/Bexley Hall/Crozer provided me an opportunity to explore this fascinating idea at some length. The result is the book that follows. It was an enormously profitable and enriching task.

Although I am a theologian by vocation, this is not a theological book in the usual meanings of that term. Yet from the standpoint of the methodology I set forth in a previous book, it can be regarded as an example of "Christian natural ethics."* This means that it is an essay in moral and social thought that uses methods and criteria appropriate to philosophy and the social sciences. Implicitly at work are norms and principles that I hold as a liberal Protestant Christian, although no appeal is made as such to the Bible or Christian tradition in any authoritative sense. It is a work (to use the traditional terms) based on "reason" and not on "revelation," even though my reasoning is shaped and guided at a primordial level by my Christian commitments. Hence, it is "natural ethics" but is "Christian" as well.

*See my *Process Ethics: A Constructive System*.

The book is also an expression of process philosophy in a sense peculiar to my own way of pursuing it. Many readers may consider it to be only marginally deserving of that description, since it contains little exegesis of specific texts and concepts derived from Alfred North Whitehead. Yet in the background are some of the motifs and perspectives that I learned from this seminal thinker.

I am grateful to President Larry Greenfield of the Divinity School for his concern to make a full year of research possible. The Trustees of the Divinity School also merit my gratitude for their generosity in providing support for an extensive leave.

The University of North Carolina at Chapel Hill and the Divinity School of Duke University gave me the title of Visiting Scholar, which made available to me the rich library resources of both institutions.

This year of study was made possible by grants from the Association of Theological Schools and from the Conant Fund of the Board of Theological Education of the Episcopal Church. I gladly take this opportunity to express my gratitude for this generous support.

My contact with Rowman & Littlefield has been a happy arrangement in every way, and I am deeply thankful for the enthusiasm the editors have shown for this project at every stage.

Finally, Chapter III was the basis of a paper prepared for the 1986 meeting of the American Academy of Religion, in particular for a subsection dealing with the the theme "Process Philosophy and Economic Organization." This paper will be published by the Center for the Scientific Study of Religion in a forthcoming volume edited by Drs. W. Widick Schroeder and Franklin I. Gamwell. I am grateful to Prof. Schroeder and to Rowman & Littlefield for making it possible for me to use this material in both places.

Rochester, New York

The Passion for Equality

CHAPTER ONE

A Defense of the Passion

There is no such thing as Jew and Greek, slave and freeman, male and female; for you are all one person in Christ Jesus (Galatians 3:28, *New English Bible*).
St. Paul

Inequality is natural. Equality is established by convention by the majority who are weak and fear being done injustice by the strong.
Callicles, in *The Gorgias*

According to natural law, all are equal.
Justinian, *Institutes*

God has ordained that some must be rich, some poor, some high and eminent in power and dignity, others mean and in subjection.
Governor John Winthrop (1630)

For really I think that the poorest he that is in England hath a life to live as the greatest he.
Colonel Rainborough, *The Putney Debates* (1647)

Let there be no longer any differences in mankind other than those of age and sex.
Manifesto of the Equals (1790)

Equality is slave morality.
Friedrich Nietzsche, *The Genealogy of Morals* (1857)

Most of the demand for equality springs from envy.
F. A. Hayek, *The Constitution of Liberty* (1960)

The passion for equality is an attribute either of the most high-minded or of those who are merely the most jealous and envious.
John Stuart Mill, "Diary" (1854)

Is "THE PASSION FOR EQUALITY" the supreme ideal of the "high-minded," or is it the morality of the weak, the fearful, the inferior, and the envious? Thousands of years of reflection have produced a complex set of disagreements about the matter. Issues old and new are still the subject of serious debate.

Equality is a peculiar idea as applied to human relationships. It has been thought to be the supreme ideal for society, as well as the epitome of muddled thinking. While it sounds simple, equality upon examination turns out to be a highly complex, slippery, and subtle concept. It would require an extensive analysis to explore all the underlying assumptions and practical implications about equality suggested in the quotations at the beginning of this chapter.

The idea of equality has been employed in various ways by different people with a variety of often conflicting meanings. It is hard for those who defend the ideal to use it in a consistent way, and to provide a moral justification for limiting or extending its applicability is not easy. Hardly anyone would assert that it has no application to human affairs, and few would deny that it must be qualified in some way. The problem is to decide in what respects human beings are or should be considered equal and in what respects inequality is appropriate both descriptively and normatively. Moreover, the meaning of equality may vary from one social setting to another. What is appropriate in the family or church may not be valid with respect to society as a whole. Trying to think clearly about equality is indeed like being tossed naked into a tangled thicket in the midst of a briar patch. Few emerge unscratched or unaffected by the experience.

Some moderns hold as the highest ideal the widest extension of liberty. Typically, such persons are in no way shaken loose from their commitment by the inequalities, no matter how enormous, that may result from its exercise. Yet many do at least admit that liberties should be equal for all. Others yearn for the widest extension of equality, even if this means that the liberty of some must be curtailed. How such basic life-stances are related to socioeconomic status is not always clear. Nonetheless, it does appear that frequently equality is the ideal of the poor, the outcast, the meek, the oppressed and their supporters. Political liberty is attractive to all, but economic liberty has a special appeal to the rich, the aggressive, the strong, the confident, those whose status is secure, and their defenders, that is, those in a position to benefit from it. Whether those of low status are moved by universally valid ideals or just jealous of their worthy superiors is debatable. Likewise, it is open to dispute whether the partisans of liberty are defending the most noble ideals imaginable or just being smug, arrogant, and self-righteous when they put down the aspirations of egalitarians.

It is important, however, not to oversimplify. The priority given to liberty by some and to equality by others is not determined merely by socioeconomic status or self-interest. Persons similarly situated may have very different outlooks. Beliefs and values have a measure of autonomy and are not reducible to functions of something else.[1] People have convictions and commitments based on what they hold to be true and right. How people come to formulate certain ideologies is a complex issue, doubtless involving the interplay of many factors. Perhaps temperament and predisposition arising out of genetic factors play a role, as well as cultural indoctrination, life history, self-interest, autonomous reasoning and valuing, and who knows what else.

Equality is frequently thought to be a beautiful notion of transcendent splendor but out of place in the real world of brutal facts. The Stoic philosophers imagined a Golden Age in which all were free and equal in a time of peace in which no coercion spoiled the glory of it all. But human folly and frailty brought about the present divisions between those of high and low status, accompanied by struggles for power and the rule of force. Christian theologians from the early centuries and afterward looked back to an Edenic Paradise characterized by freedom, equality, peace, and righteousness. But the primeval parents fell from grace, so we now are equal only in sin and unworthiness. The evil passions of this "mass of perdition" (Augustine) make it necessary for some to rule over others to curb the wickedness that would otherwise make things even worse. Hobbes, Locke, and Rousseau variously described the equalities they believed prevailed in the state of nature prior to the advent of human government, but the arrangements generated by the social contract create numerous inequalities acceptable to good judgment.

Even when a place has been made for equality in some sphere, its legitimacy has frequently been limited to certain areas of life or to special groups.[2] Athenian democracy granted equality to privileged citizens but denied it to slaves, barbarians, and other lesser persons. Christian theologians beginning with St. Paul and afterward attributed equality to all where the ultimate relationship of persons to God was concerned or even in the church, but then tolerated and justified all sorts of inequalities in the secular arena. The Declaration of Independence proclaimed that all men (people?) are created equal, but subsequent practice made it clear that white property-owning males were the primary beneficiaries of this primordial endowment, with others having less status and no vote. The ideal of political equality has had a claim to orthodoxy in the United States, but appeals for economic equality have generally been tainted with the charge of heresy. Many male theologians have played it both ways, insisting that "man" includes woman when it does not threaten the privileged status they enjoyed as men, but denying the equality of the sexes when it comes to ordination to the sacred office of ministry. How often these limitations of the reign of equality reflect the corruption of ideals by self-interest and prejudice and how much they represent realism and perspicacity is a topic for extended discussion.

All in all, equality as applied to human relationships is a fascinating subject. This book examines the meaning of equality as a concept and norm. The intent is to discover its inner logic and to explore some of the reasons why great minds have differed widely in interpretations of the applicability of equality to society. Primarily, however, the intent is to state a position that is valid both descriptively and prescriptively. While the historical background is essential and will receive considerable attention, the book's main purpose is systematic. This chapter will examine the idea itself: its meaning, its justification as a norm of justice, and its relation to other ideals.

Exploring the Logic of the Idea

The *Oxford English Dictionary* sustains the proposition that the term "equal" always implies at least one respect in which something is the same (no more or no less) when two or more entities are under consideration or are being compared. It implies measurement by the same rule, whether the reference is to amount, level, degree, number, magnitude, intensity, proportion, quantity, quality, or whatever.[3] Things or persons that are equal in one or more respects, however, may be unequal in some or all other respects. Hence, it is essential to state the rule or principle by which the measurement is made in each instance.

If justice is the subject under consideration, a statement of Aristotle provides a good beginning point. "Now justice is recognized universally as some sort of equality . . . justice involves an assignment of things to persons . . . equals are entitled to equal things. But here we are met by an important question: Equals and unequals in what?"[4] Indeed, that is the important question: In what respects does justice require equality, and in what respects does justice permit or mandate inequality? Sometimes equality is attributed to human beings *qua* human beings. But people differ in nearly every particular that can be named. Do these differences, or some of them at least, make a difference as far as equality is concerned? Are human beings equal considered simply as human beings, or are there different levels of persons as persons? If people are equal as people, when are they to be treated by that rule, and when are they to be treated unequally because of some particular characteristic or action?

The minimal meaning of equality as a constituent of justice, recognized by all who make rationality a criterion of thought, is that it requires impartiality. But this implies nothing more than that equals are to be treated equally. While this is a tautology, it is a nontrivial one. More precisely, it means simply that all to whom a rule applies are to be treated by that same rule.[5] But to whom does a given rule apply, and what rules are to apply to a given group under what circumstances?

One rule (or set of rules) may apply to free citizens and another rule (or set of rules) may apply to slaves, as it did for Aristotle. By nature, he thought, some were capable of ruling, while others were fit only to obey. But, all other relevant things being equal, whatever rules apply to one slave apply to all slaves. This is all that impartiality means. With respect to voting for president of the United States, an age-requirement rule treats those who are twenty-one-years old differently from those who are twenty-one-days old. In this respect age makes these two groups unequal. Hence, they may be treated differently. We might agree that having one rule (or set of rules) for slaves and another for free citizens is unjust, while treating adults and children differently when it comes to voting is just. Yet in both cases impartiality is observed, as long as equals are treated equally.

One could insist that having different sets of rules for free citizens and slaves violates impartiality only by defining in advance as equals all those who are human beings, rather than all those who are free and all those who are slave. But the point here is that the rule of impartiality does not make that decision. Those who use the principle of impartiality make that determination. Impartiality comes into play only after the rules have been made and the equals to whom the rules apply have been designated. Even a silly rule like giving tall people five times as many votes as short people does not violate impartiality as long as all tall people are given five votes and all short people only one.[6] Impartiality is a formal norm that requires only that equals be treated equally, i. e., by the same rule.

Impartiality, then, is a necessary part of the meaning of equality in relationship to justice, but not a sufficient or entire definition. One must ask further what rules are to apply to what groups or persons under what circumstances and in what respects. Only when all these conditions are specified can one say what it is that is to be the same, i. e., in what way the concept of equality applies.

Suppose a 90-pound child and a 300-pound football player are given different amounts of food. Is this an equal distribution? The answer is obviously "no" if amount is meant, since the amounts are not the same. The answer is "yes" if one means that both are dealt with by the same rule, i. e., in accordance with need or desire. If a question about equality is involved, one always has to specify what is and is not to be the same.

"Suppose that society is allotting musical instruments to C and D, and that C prefers a banjo and D a guitar. If society gives C a banjo and D a guitar it is treating them *differently* yet *equally*."[7] Depending on what is meant, one could also say that society treated them the same and therefore equally. Strictly speaking, in the respect in which the term "equally" applies, C and D were not treated *differently* but *the same*, i. e., according to their preferences.[8] To be treated equally (by the same standard), they would have to be treated differently (given different instruments). The seeming paradox in the statement disappears once we recognize that a shift in reference occurs between the first term and the second.

Distribution according to need has been called a "maxim of equal distribution" and "the most perfect form of equal distribution."[9] Both statements may be true if the meanings intended are clearly and precisely defined, i. e, if it has already been agreed that the respect in which people are to be treated the same is their need. This would require an equal distribution in the sense of the same amounts of the same things only if needs are the same.

Does the statement really claim that the highest form of *just* distribution is according to need? Just distribution may sometimes require a distribution of an equal number of units of the good in question on the basis of some agreed upon principle. Suppose a group has been given tickets to a concert and decides to distribute them on the basis of the principle of one person, one ticket. Need, as such, initially does not enter into consideration. But if one member (A) cannot attend, and another member (B) wants to take a friend, it would be appropriate, if all were agreeable, to shift the standard from the one previously agreed upon (one person, one ticket) to need (where need means "desire"). Then A might receive no ticket at all, while B would receive two. They are treated unequally in one sense (given different units of the good) and equally in another (provided in accordance with need). Would it have been unjust if A had insisted on her ticket so she could give it to a friend who could attend in her place? Would not A have a better claim to one ticket, even if she gave it away, than B would have for two? Distribution according to need, then, is not always or necessarily a maxim of just distribution, although it may be in some circumstances. It is a maxim of equal distribution only if what is the same is the principle used (need) rather than the things distributed (which might be unequal, or at least different).[10]

The Limits of Egalitarianism

So far it has been established that equality always implies one or more respects in which something is the same. The reference can be either to the individuals or groups who are to be considered as equals and who are to be assigned some right or good, or it can be to the right or good that is to be assigned. Precision of statement is important to prevent ambiguity, for "equality" is a subtle term. For example, the attribution of equal rights to individuals or groups can mean either (a) equal rights to x (reference to individuals or groups assigned rights) or (b) rights to equal x (reference to the good that is to be distributed).[11]

Moreover, it has been established that a minimal normative meaning of equality is that once the rules have established which persons/groups are equal and which goods (including liberties, privileges, rights, etc.) are to be assigned equally, impartiality must prevail. All equals (persons/groups) are to be dealt with according to the same rule.

But how much further should equality be taken as a normative concept? This point can be approached from the other extreme. Should the norm or goal be radical egalitarianism—the equality of all in all respects? Hardly anyone has seriously proposed this kind of unqualified, absolute egalitarianism, for reasons that become obvious upon a moment's reflection.[12] Yet it does provide an ultimate limit in the light of which a more reasonable position can be developed and defended.[13]

In working this out, it will be helpful to begin with the conventional distinction between natural and social inequalities. Natural inequalities are those differences rooted in the biological endowment of individuals: size, sex, looks, intelligence, talents, personality traits, bodily health, and the like. We are born with these characteristics, or at least their genetic base. Social inequalities are those differences that arise in humanly organized institutions and arrangements: status, role, authority, influence, wealth, rights, opportunities, privileges, honor, and the like.[14] With this distinction in mind, three qualifications of radical egalitarianism are essential.

1. Some inequalities are unavoidable. In particular, differences rooted in and dependent upon genetic endowment can be changed only within limits and with prohibitive costs and consequences. Medical procedures can modify our looks, surgery can modify sexual organs, and environmental influences may actualize to a greater or lesser degree the genetic potential of intelligence, and so on. It is not necessary to settle the ancient dispute between nature and nurture to make the essential point: while social influences and human interventions can mold and modify what we are born with, people are destined to live within limits set by their biological inheritance. Gifts and

talents, as well as many other capacities and characteristics of body and spirit, are rooted in nature. What is not given there cannot with present technology be supplied. Hence, natural inequalities beyond the human ability to change are unavoidable.

This point can be made clearer by conducting a thought experiment. Suppose it were possible through genetic engineering to provide every individual with whatever potential he or she wanted. Then inequalities rooted in biology could be avoidable, if we chose. Should we eliminate them? Here a distinction should be made between eliminating differences and eliminating inequalities. If one person had little musical talent and another had much, they would be unequally gifted in that sense. But two people might have different degrees of different gifts, talents, and capacities in specifics such that each would have a total ensemble that equaled the other in value. Equal here would mean equivalent. Those who had little musical talent might have athletic abilities or manual skills or a talent for politics, or some other characteristic equal in dignity and desirability. Great diversity would be possible and much to be desired. If a situation in which people were gifted differently (not the same talents) but equally (a total package that was the equivalent of all other genetic packages in worth) were conceivable in theory and possible in practice, it would be desirable. This assumes, of course, that the level at which the equality occurs is sufficiently high. Such a situation would be preferable to the random lottery that now prevails in which people are gifted both differently and unequally (in terms both of specific characteristics/aptitudes and of the total ensemble).

But if the inequalities rooted in nature are (presently) unavoidable, can all social inequalities be eliminated? The answer is "no," because some social inequalities come about as a result of unavoidable biological inequalities of physical skill, mental capacity, and traits of personality.[15] Moreover, some social inequalities may be unavoidable because eliminating some would inevitably produce others, at least provisionally. Making incomes more equal between whites and blacks might increase inequalities within each race. Making incomes more equal between women and men may increase inequalities between whites and blacks.[16]

2. Some social inequalities are necessary. "Necessary" here means inequalities that are essential to the very existence and functioning of society. While this is a conditional necessity, the alternative is to forego altogether the creation of political institutions, the means of producing and distributing economic goods, and other essential social arrangements. Some inequalities will inevitably accompany the organization of human beings into working groups to sustain essential functions and achieve cooperative goals. If there is to be a division of labor

with any chain of command, inequalities will emerge between those who give orders and those who obey. If there are to be governing institutions, then laws must be made and enforced, creating—even in pure democracies—some divisions between those who have more authority than others. If educational institutions are established, inevitably there will be teachers and students. If religions require a set-apart priesthood to impart sacramental grace, then inequalities appear between clergy and laity. In families the roles and functions of parents and children cannot be exchanged or equalized. While some anarchists believe that orchestras could do without conductors, most people agree that leaders are at some points desirable, if not necessary. In short, if there is to be a multiplicity of social roles, then some will have more authority, more status, and more influence than others.[17]

Let it be said at once, however, that social institutions can be organized in an enormous variety of ways, some of which will magnify, and some of which will reduce, inequalities while allowing for needed differences of role. Forms of authority can be established based on the consent of the governed. Power can be concentrated among the few, or it can be distributed widely among the many. There are absolute monarchies, and there are pure democracies. There are bureaucracies with a pyramidal chain of command working from top to bottom; there are also horizontal arrangements in which the flow of authority runs back and forth with numerous feedback loops. Power can be shared among mutually influencing parts of the whole. Some churches affirm the priesthood of all believers. In short, governments, economies, churches, schools, families, and all other institutions can be organized with the aim of preserving essential diversities of function while minimizing, as much as possible, inequalities of authority, status, wealth, influence, and so on.

Egalitarians need not insist that all social inequalities be eliminated at the cost of destroying society as such. Inequalities of authority, for example, need not even be offensive if positions are legitimately attained, are merited, are exercised justly, and are used for the good of all concerned. Egalitarians do contend, however, that many unnecessary inequalities could be eliminated without harming anything worth preserving. But before concrete blueprints could be devised for the reorganization of the social order in accordance with the maximal egalitarian ideal, numerous empirical questions would have to be answered and a good many trade-offs would have to be calculated. The fundamental issue is: What are the minimal and least objectionable inequalities that are necessary for the functioning of the most desirable society, i. e., one that is just and most productive of human well-being?

3. Some social inequalities are justifiable. This means that certain inequalities are either just or result in the achievement of a larger good

for all than would have otherwise been possible.[18] Justifiable, then, is a moral category. Morally mandated or permitted inequalities can be justified either deontologically or teleologically.[19] Absolute social equality for all in all respects would run into conflict with other values that sometimes take priority and that must always must be taken into account.

To begin with deontological considerations, merit, need, or previous agreements may lead to unequal outcomes. Those who work longer, harder, or make a greater contribution deserve more reward than others. At least in some contexts, this rule is morally just. In some other settings, contribution might be mandated in terms of ability and distribution made according to need. In the family or other groups where love is the reigning motif, this arrangement is appropriate. But whether merit or need is the principle, justifiable inequalities may result. Or people may enter voluntarily into contracts that produce higher incomes or other rewards for some than others.

On teleological (utilitarian) grounds, one can argue that rigid equality in all relationships prevents the realization of a larger good that would benefit all, or at least would benefit some while not harming others. Economists have frequently argued that there is an inevitable trade-off between equality and efficiency.[20] Granted the likelihood of some trade-off, one will still have to decide how much inequality of what sorts for whom will be permitted for the sake of what kinds and amounts of efficiency gains. Doubtless, many equality-efficiency bargains could be struck, some of which would be preferable to others in that they require less inequality for given efficiency increases.[21]

Sometimes the argument is put in terms of a conflict between equality and excellence. Holding everyone at the same level in all respects would necessarily mean equality at the lowest common denominator. This would prevent valuable achievements in science, art, literature, technology, and in every phase of culture. Some inequalities are justifiable for the sake of promoting all the arts and sciences of civilization by which the human race is improved materially, morally, culturally, spiritually, and so on. Or it may be claimed that the self-development of individuals is a reason for permitting all to realize their potential for achievement and happiness in ways that will leave some at a different place than others. Would even the most enthusiastic egalitarian want to inhibit the moral development of a Socrates or Jesus? It would be desirable if all could be equal at the level of moral perfection, but under present earthly conditions that hardly seems possible.

Liberty and equality can be justified on either deontological or teleological grounds or a combination of both considerations. Utilitarians would insist that no conflict ever arises between them, since the final criterion is utility. What kinds of freedom and what kinds of equalities result in the largest net good? Yet on deontological grounds it is widely agreed that sometimes a conflict may arise between the two values. The antagonism is not resolved merely by insisting that all have equal freedom. Equally free persons may engage in just interactions with others that result in great inequalities. For example, thousands of people buy tickets to baseball games, making the owners and players wealthier than most fans. But to prevent such inequalities from occurring, the freedom of people to enter into voluntary arrangements would have to be curtailed. One might argue convincingly that wealth and income should be partially redistributed to restore the balance, but can one insist on a complete equalization of outcomes without unjustly violating the freedom of individuals? Moreover, if one combines deontological and teleological considerations into an inclusive ethical perspective, it seems impossible to avoid complex tensions among freedom, equality, and maximizing the good—a situation that necessarily requires trade-offs.[22]

However, inequalities at one level can be justified only if they preserve the equality of persons in a more fundamental sense.[23] To allow distribution according to merit or need that produces inequalities of outcome is mandated by the principle of treating all persons (who as persons are equal) with the appropriate moral seriousness. All morally justifiable inequalities are a consequence of honoring equally the worth and dignity of persons and acknowledging equally their just aspirations for the greatest possible happiness. Hence, even inequalities must be validated by an egalitarian rule!

The foregoing analysis is not exhaustive and certainly does not resolve all the issues raised. The aim has been simply to refute radical egalitarianism and to provide a framework in which a more reasonable view can be elaborated and defended. To work out all the particulars will require all the rest of the book (and more). Here it is sufficient to emphasize that the goal of equality for all in *all* respects is an indefensible proposition, since some inequalities are unavoidable, some are necessary, and some are justifiable. All inequalities that are avoidable, unnecessary, and unjustifiable should be eliminated. Nonetheless, the ideal of equality for all in all respects does stand in the background as a transcendent reference point. Although not possible of full concrete realization and not desirable for good and sufficient reasons, it nevertheless is relevant to all societies. It stands forever as an ultimate limit toward which all social orders should be lured as possibility and desirability mandate. Radical egalitarianism is the background norm that serves as judge and guide in terms of which we assert that all inequalities that are avoidable, unnecessary, and unjustifiable should be eliminated.

Before leaving this point, it may be worth considering whether the idea of equality for all in all respects, taken literally and absolutely, is even a coherent notion. It is impossible to conceive a situation in which this ideal could be carried out totally. The sheer fact that physical objects have location in different portions of space is a limiting factor. In some places in California the distance between snow-capped mountains to the east and beaches to the west is not very great. But not everyone could live equidistant between them, even assuming they wanted to. Not everyone can attend the World Series, and not all who do can have the best seats. Not everyone can live far enough away from a major airport to avoid the noise and smell of jet engines but close enough for maximum convenience.

Is the notion of equal opportunity for all in all respects a coherent idea? Taken literally that would mean that everyone would have to be born with an identical set of aptitudes and capacities, have exactly the same training and environmental influences in every relevant aspect, have made the same effort to learn and prepare with exactly the same results, and be an equally qualified applicant for every available opportunity of every sort, everywhere. Even if anyone is concerned about equal opportunity in all ways relevant to justice, the notion of equality in *all* respects is not a practical idea.[24]

Yet while one must relinquish the absolute extremity suggested by *all respects*, one need not abandon completely the ideal of equality if there are *some respects* in which equality for all is both possible (conceivable in theory and actualizable in practice) and desirable. While not all can live in any particular good place, could not everyone live, taking everything into account, in some place equally as good, at least as subjectively judged (i. e., that suits everyone equally well)?[25] Many different places may be equally desirable, given the various interests and tastes of people. Not everyone wants to attend the World Series. While not everyone can have an equal chance at every opportunity, one might hope that over a lifetime, everyone could have an equivalent set of chances at some equally good possibilities for an equally fulfilling life, given the genetic endowment she or he brings into the world.

What all of these probes have shown is that equality enters at some level of generality in every case involving what is right and best for people. Justice *always* involves some form of equality, though more than equality is required for a full definition. At a minimum, justice requires impartiality. At most, all persons should be treated equally in all respects, except when inequalities are unavoidable, unnecessary, or justifiable. Even when inequalities are allowed under one or more of these rubrics, the revised norms must include an aim at equality for all in some fashion. The maximal form of this more limited form of egalitarianism, which allows only those inequalities which are unavoidable, necessary, and justifiable, will have as its ultimate operating goal the achievement of social arrangements conducive to the maximum and equal happiness of all.[26] A similar thesis will be stated and defended in this book. Maximal egalitarianism holds out the hope that all can and will be equally loved, equally respected, have their basic needs equally met, be given equal consideration as human beings, and be provided with equal opportunities to pursue their own self-defined self-realization in a community of persons who, as persons, are equal in worth.

While by definition inegalitarians would not subscribe to this maximal form of limited egalitarianism, presumably everyone—libertarians, egalitarians, inegalitarians, capitalists, socialists, anarchists, monarchists, elitists, democrats, and so on—could agree with the general principle that equality should prevail except when inequalities are unavoidable, necessary, and justifiable. At least all persons who believe that morally relevant and sufficient reasons must and can be given for social philosophies would presumably agree to this proposition. Nevertheless, the categories involved are purely formal, that is, have no specific content. The disagreements that inflame the passions and separate out the various ideologies have to do with *what it is* that is avoidable, unnecessary, and unjustifiable. All can agree—all good and worthy people anyway—that a just society is desirable. But what is justice? Everyone—all rational persons anyway—wants to believe only the truth. But what is true? Hence, the task of stating a full-orbed egalitarian philosophy has only begun. A description of what is both desirable and possible, practical and just, conceivable and enactable—this is still lacking. The ideal that could be actual—if enough people were sufficiently committed to it—has yet to be stated, though numerous hints have already appeared.

The same considerations attach to another way of stating a formal egalitarian principle: treat everyone equally unless sufficient reason can be given for treating them unequally. Obviously, the crucial issue here is what constitutes "sufficient" reason.[27] Even if "sufficient" is further defined in terms of reasons that (a) satisfy all the rules of logical discourse, (b) are morally relevant, and (c) are factually accurate, the formality remains. Many conflicting interpretations could satisfy these criteria in the minds of some rationally competent persons.[28] Moreover, it is not beyond dispute that exceptions to equality must be justified by the principle of sufficient reason. It is possible to oppose rules just because they are rules. Instead of rules we should perhaps be guided by the immediate inspirations of some charismatic leader or by the "spirit" of some group—the church, the race, the nation, the family, the tribe, and so on. It is not self-evident that this kind of irrational romanticism is always inferior to the rationality that demands that there be rules and that exceptions to rules be justified.[29]

To make one final statement of the point, we may distinguish between a "weak principle of equality," which urges that people are to be treated equally unless sufficient reason can be given for treating them otherwise, and a "strong principle of unconditional equality," which requires equality for all in all respects.[30] Here it has been argued that radical egalitarianism or the principle of unconditional equality has to be rejected in favor of the view that equality is required except when inequalities are unavoidable, unnecessary, and justifiable. These three qualifying categories turn out to be the same ones that are required to enumerate the subcategories of the requirement of sufficient reason demanded by the weak principle or conditional equality. Either way it is put, Aristotle's question remains: Equals and unequals in what? It will require the rest of the book to answer that question, but a beginning can be made in this chapter. Before this question is addressed, one more analytical or formal question must be dealt with.

The Context of the Equality Norm

In what contexts is the norm of equality relevant? Does it apply to all human relationships or only to some? Beyond the fact that the question of equal treatment arises in all cases where justice is at issue, what more needs to be said? Consider the following situations:

1. Susan walks down the street, glancing at some people walking past her but not at all.
2. James wants to marry Mary, but Mary decides to marry John instead.
3. A small private social club admits new members solely on a vote of the ten original founders. Joe complains that he was the only one of a circle of close friends who did not receive a letter of invitation.
4. Twins come in from play and ask their mother for the four remaining goodies in the cookie jar. She gives Joan three and Joanna one.
5. A factory employing 5000 people, the major employer in the county, pays equally qualified women less than men for doing the same job equally well and openly refuses to hire blacks, Jews, or Hispanics, though there are qualified applicants in each of these categories.
6. The law permits women to vote but denies the franchise to men.
7. As required by the constitution of a small country, all persons born with blue eyes become slaves for life.

In (1) no question about equal treatment would arise. One is not bound to give reasons for not glancing at all pedestrians while walking down the street. The rights and well being of no one are at stake. Even if some male wants Susan to look at him, he has no claim on her attention.

In (2) Mary might well be able to give good and sufficient reason why she preferred to marry John instead of James. If she appeals to intuitions beyond articulation, to her heart rather than to her head, no one would fault her. Her subjective decision, on whatever based, is final and sufficient. Is she does not care to, she is under no obligation even to give them equal consideration before she rejects one.

In (3) no would deny a small group the privilege of choosing companions to be with for purposes of having a good time. The membership committee has no obligation to explain to anybody outside the club why some were chosen and others not.[31] With respect to all three of these cases, there is no appeal beyond private evaluation and subjective decision. The liberty of the deciding subjects is the only relevant reference point. Those not favored have no just claims requiring equal treatment, no matter how disappointed they might be.[32]

The remaining four examples are of a different order, although it may not be easy to say exactly why. Moreover, the division between the first group and the second may be gradual and not sharp or discrete. But some features that mark the transition can be noted. Questions about unjust treatment involving equality typically arise in relation to practices affecting the rights, claims, and well-being of persons and/or groups who (normally) have membership in a given community. Community as used here does not necessarily imply the inclusion of everyone within a certain geographical area. Neither does it necessarily imply formal membership in an explicitly or highly organized group. The essential thing is that a system of relationships exists that binds the relevant persons together in certain particular morally obligating ways.

The qualification "normally" modifies community membership in the above sentence to accommodate the exceptional case of an alien who might end up in a foreign land (or in any kind of nonmembership situation). If the alien happened to be blue-eyed and fell into the hands of a tribe that enslaved blue-eyed people, the appeal would be to transcendent norms that invest all persons with the right to "life, liberty, and the pursuit of happiness." In that sense the relevant community is made up of all human beings. In that context an order of mutual rights and responsibilities arises. The fact that the blue-eyed enslavers refuse to recognize this appeal does not undermine its ultimate moral validity.

While even one breach of justice is wrong, the inequalities most open to condemnation have to do with general patterns of policy or violations of policy related to institutions, laws, or other social practices. Hence, they have an objective and public dimension. In some such context when persons who are equal in a way that is relevant to the question at issue are treated unequally, protest is justified. Three features, then, seem to be present in situations in which unequal treatment may wrongly occur. Involved are (a) institutions, laws, customs, or other public arrangements or social practices (b) affecting the rights and well-being of individuals or groups (c) belonging to some relevant community (order of mutually bonding, justice permeated relationships). Within this framework, two or more claimants must stand in relation to some community of relationships in a status of equality with respect to some legitimate expectation.

In case (4), if twin girls come into the house and ask their mother for a treat, justice requires (all else being equal) that mother divide the four remaining cookies equally. The twins are related to their mother in a family context such that claims of equal treatment rightfully arise. A parent who favored one child over another in the absence of good and sufficient reasons would certainly merit our condemnation. But, if the customs of a group required that children with light hair always be given preference over dark-haired offspring, the protest would better be directed against that pattern of group behavior. Perhaps most frequently, egalitarian movements have directed their attention toward social structures or patterns of relationships that affect groups or classes of people.

When discrimination is made among persons related to pay or employment (5), to voting (6), or to basic liberty (7) when the persons involved are equal in the relevant respects, the unequal treatment noted is not justified or justifiable: it is not based on sufficient reason. The irrelevance of sex to voting (6) seems so obvious that it is incredible that women were so long denied this basic right. The only explanation is that males who had the power were blinded by some deep-rooted prejudice that is no compliment to their alleged superior wisdom! Presumably, in the cases at hand, the discrimination in question is neither unavoidable nor necessary.

Three points need to be made or emphasized in order to complete this interpretation. First, the judgments that (4), (5), (6), and (7) involve offensive and indefensible inequalities of treatment are, of course, based on certain value assumptions regarding the equal worth of persons and their equal rights as members of families, of economic systems, or of political orders. While these values would be widely shared in contemporary America, they are not universal in that many persons and societies have operated on other premises. The point here is that every judgment about indefensible unequal treatment is based on some set of beliefs and values, that is, on an ideology. What constitutes a sufficient reason for differential treatment depends on the assumed set of convictions about the real and the ideal. The social values operating at a specific time are relative to a given society at a particular period in history.³³ Nonetheless, norms transcendent to any society but relevant to all may be invoked as a standard of judgment in light of which changes are mandated. But even these norms have a dimension of historical relativity about them.

Second, the claim that a practice is unfair is based on the fact that it treats people unequally who are equal in the respects that are relevant in each case. With regard to (4), for example, we would expect the mother to have a good and sufficient reason based on some objective fact to justify her preferential treatment of Joan. In this instance there are no pertinent differences between the two girls, although one could imagine a situation in which there might be. But on this occasion her arbitrary decision is not enough. In (5) sex and race, religion, and ethnic background are irrelevant grounds for lower pay or refusing to hire. Females, blacks, Jews, and Hispanics are equal as human beings and, assuming all have the same ability to do the job involved, this is all that matters. Being female is different from being male, but this difference is also irrelevant to the issue at hand.

Finally, two different settings may be envisioned as occasioning a valid protest against unequal treatment. (a) The actual practices, whether legal or illegal, may be held to be in conflict with the fundamental laws or values of the society otherwise acknowledged. For example, segregated schools, while legal in some states, were held by the Supreme Court in 1954 to be inherently unequal and thus in violation of the Constitution of the United States. Discrimination against women and blacks in the labor market violates the constitutional guarantee of equal rights.

(b) The fundamental laws and underlying values of a society, as well as its prevailing legislation and actual practices, may be held to be in conflict with some transcendent norms or values, which take precedence. Positive law may be said to contradict natural law and thus be invalid. Appeal may be made to God, to the Bible, to reason, to conscience, to human decency, or to other authoritative sources of normative morality. Slavery, even of blue-eyed people, could conceivably be in line with the basic values and laws of a certain society. Yet one could protest against this inequality by appealing, for example, to natural law or to the divine will. In any case, whatever is thought to be the ultimate ground of rights or justice may be called on to justify criticism of a given unauthorized inequality.³⁴

In the light of this analysis, the dividing line is clearer between (1), (2), and (3), on the one hand, and (4), (5), (6), and (7), on the other hand. In the latter group, those treated harmfully and unequally (although equals in the relevant particulars) are bound together in some definable community of relationships in which rights and claims are valid. Membership in a common order of morally infused relationships is lacking in (1), (2), and (3). Instead, the actors are bound by ties of random contiguity (1) or personal acquaintance (2) and (3), but by no bonds that establish claims to equal treatment with the particular others specified. The fact that they live in the same town, county, or country, or even attend the same church does not in these three cases constitute the system of rights and obligations that is required. They are related as individuals in associations that are established by accident or personal initiatives and responses, but are not bound by rules and expectations grounded in a justice-authorizing order of relationships.

Everyone making decisions that affect the well-being of others is, of course, obligated to treat them justly as individuals with equal worth and dignity. Hence, Susan is obligated not to trip up elderly people carrying bags of groceries, and she ought to tell the truth if asked for the time. Mary ought to deal with both John and James individually in an honest and caring way, but she is not under obligation to consider them as having a right to her affection. That can only be freely given in love, not demanded on the basis of justice. But neither the casual passersby nor the competing suitors have the right to equal treatment in the respects in question as do Joan and Joanna as children of the same mother in a common family. The social club ought not to make false promises to prospective members, nor insult inquirers, nor inflict deliberate harm on anyone. But the members are free to discriminate based on personal likes and dislikes or even on eccentric whims.

Case (5) is an interesting test of the hypothesis that participation in a relevant structure of justice-infused relationships provides the essential framework in which claims to equal treatment are established.[35] Some libertarian employers have argued that since they own the store or the factory, they should be free to hire whomever they choose and to pay them whatever they can voluntary contract for. On this basis no grounds can be cited for giving women and blacks equal opportunity with white males. A job is something the employer, who holds all the rights to the gift, is free to bestow on whomever he or she pleases, just as the worker is free to refuse the job when offered. This claim suggests that employers are under no more obligation to treat whites and blacks equally than was Susan to glance equally at all pedestrians who walked past her.

The contrary argument presupposes that the economic order is a public arena in which the rules of justice come into play with its requirement that inequalities be justified. Participants in an ongoing joint enterprise of this sort incur rights and responsibilities in relation to each other. Employers and workers are bound together in a set of interdependent relationships within a society in which they have common membership. Those who buy and sell, or hire and fire, in a complex economy are involved in more than simple individual contracts. Systemic or organic features in the economy are essential and not merely accidental. Something more is present than the sum total of individual transactions. In fact, all who engage in business are interlocked structurally and are thus bound to community standards that define the common good. It can be argued within this framework that it is a breach of rightness for equals (in ability to do the job) to be treated unequally (paid less for the same work or denied employment altogether). Good and sufficient reason cannot be provided to justify differential treatment based on sex or race when these factors are irrelevant to the issue at hand.

But are all economic transactions subject to this principle? Some difficult lines have to be drawn between private transactions, in which the freedom of individuals to make voluntary contracts with whomever they please is valid, and public transactions, in which special rules of equalitarian justice come into play. Two factors are crucial to the admittedly vague transition points between the private and the public realms. The first element has to do with the size of the operation. Here importance is the criterion. Units that take on significance because large numbers of people are affected are in a different category from individual arrangements that affect only those immediately involved. Firms that are large enough to matter to the community at large must be responsible to community standards of justice and well-being. A company that holds a monopoly on employment in an area is the clearest example of a unit that must be held publicly accountable for its acts, since its behavior is crucial to the good of the whole.[36]

The second ingredient has to do with the relative strength of the negotiating units. Only those employers whose power (as a unit) is sufficiently disproportionate to the power of the applicant (as a unit) should be so bound. More precisely, significantly large employers take on a public or social function that is not on a par with the power or importance of an individual applicant. In these situations the employer and the single job-seeker are not equals as economic actors. In a somewhat analogous way, parents and children are not equal in social role or power and hence have a different order of responsibilities, liberties, and privileges. But if there were plentiful and equally good opportunities elsewhere for blacks in companies that welcomed them, then no legislation forbidding discrimination would be justifiable.[37] The liberty of each party to make purely voluntary contracts would take precedence over racial equality.

To cross the line in the other direction, if a white individual with a business that required only one employee offered a black who sought employment a good job with good pay, would we insist that the black should be forced to take it if she/he happened to dislike white people and for that reason alone did not want the job? Would we, then, insist that the same employer be obligated to provide equal opportunities to blacks and whites if he/she were prejudiced against blacks? Precise lines marking the transition between cases where public rules or private preferences ought to prevail are not easy to draw, though general guidelines, as suggested here, are relevant.

Closely related to the above framework is the fact that different spheres of human relationships have their peculiar logic. Each area has its particular rules for defining claims and establishing equalities and inequalities.[38] Justice-equality norms enter in many contexts, but the point may be illustrated by comparing the family and the economic order. In the family the rule may well be: from each according to ability, to each according to need. Parents and children are treated equally (according to the same rule) if they contribute what they are able and receive what they require in light of the total resources of the family. This rule works well in small groups where strong commitment to the common good and to the equal good of each can be presupposed and where love is the dominant motive uniting the group. A small religious order or a community of highly committed communal egalitarians might also successfully follow this norm.

A large, complex economic order is another matter. While some level of commitment to the common good and to meeting the minimal needs of all is a mandate of justice, a much larger scope must be given for individuals and families to seek their private good within a framework of fair opportunity for all with special help to the handicapped and socially disadvantaged. Love is too intimate and personal a motive to be directly relevant to the operation of an impersonal, complex market economy involving millions of people.[39] Christian ethics holds, however, that love (*agape*) can express itself as social justice. This would mean at least mutual respect among all, along with commitment to the common good and the equal rights of others. Given the interdependent nature of the economy today, justice requires that a measure of equality of results complement equal opportunity.[40] That task will require extensive treatment later. Here it is sufficient to repeat that the rules of justice-equality are internal to each particular area of social life.

Maximum Desirable Equality

A maximal egalitarianism will favor those conditions that will tend to make all as happy as possible and as equally happy as possible within the constraints of the inequalities that are unavoidable, necessary, and justifiable.[41] Stated differently, the aim is to maximize happiness and to maximize justice, recognizing that each of these norms limits the other.

Idealistic egalitarianism affirms the goal that every human being should have the best life that is possible for him or her.[42] But even at this very general level, equality may be compatible with or even require various inequalities in many other ways.

The quest for greater equality usually arises both as a protest and as a demand. The protest is against certain obnoxious and curable inequalities prevailing at a given time and place. The demand is that the specific inequalities be removed, or at least reduced, for the sake of a more humane, just, and desirable social order. A feature common to the most notable historical protests is that inequalities are opposed that enabled some to have rights, privileges, opportunities, and the good things of life at the expense of others. Even if no oppression as such is involved, idealistic egalitarians would like to see everyone healthy, happy, wise, and reasonably well-off, regardless of the reason why some are not.[43] The intent is not to deprive those who have more of something when it has been justly attained, but to let those who have less share in what ideally would be distributed more widely. The yearning that as many as possible participate as widely and fully as possible in as many of the good things of life as possible is at the root of what Mill called the "high-minded passion" for equality. The egalitarianism that is worthy and noble has simply wanted everyone to have equal access to the means of happiness and equal participation in the good that is common to all.

For libertarians, however, the important point is whether state coercion is used to achieve equality in accordance with some pattern. They might approve greater equality in principle as a personal preference and lend support to any voluntary efforts to achieve it. Libertarians believe that individual freedom must not be violated.[44] Equal freedom for all and equality before the law will result in many kinds of legitimate inequalities, which justice has no stake in trying to correct. This book will advocate limited state action as well as voluntary efforts to achieve greater social equality for the sake of justice, because equality is then held in balance with freedom instead of being subordinated to it. This balance is not simply a personal preference, but is a corollary of the interdependence of people in modern society. This communal fact creates a claim in the direction of an equal sharing of the total social good.

Egalitarianism is at its finest when it champions the cause of the poor, the oppressed, the weak, and the meek—those who have been left out or shut out or permitted to stay out of the green pastures of life. Its best impulses spring from the belief that God or justice or natural law, or whatever it is that makes for righteousness and goodness, mandates a wider rather than a narrower distribution of what is good in this life.[45] It is rooted in the conviction that everyone matters when measured by what ultimately matters, that all persons are equal in value in the light of whatever is ultimately valuable and value-giving. Egalitarianism arises out of the intuition that when somebody has less of something good (and appropriately or justly desired) than others, it would be better if she or he had as much as those who have more.[46] Only when persuaded that inequalities which affect the good life are absolutely unavoidable, fundamentally essential, and thoroughly justifiable are they reluctantly willing to accept what must be but what they wish could be otherwise somehow.

Perhaps it is just an idle fantasy that everyone should have much of what is good and as much as anyone else. The egalitarian (for example, the author of this book) at heart may be merely a dreamer and an idealist who feels strongly that in the best of all worlds, heaven would be real for everybody and no more and no less for anybody, and if that kind of world is not possible, something is wrong somehow. Or at least it is too bad that the dream cannot be realized in the world that is and not merely in the world of thought. At the same time, the idealistic egalitarian is sure that many kinds of equality would be both possible and desirable if only the political realities were such that the better, if not the perfect, social order could be made real. Whatever equalities there would be at whatever levels in the best of all possible worlds, the egalitarian is certain that there could be many fewer inequalities of many kinds in the best of all real worlds.

To summarize and conclude this long analysis, the maximal egalitarian thinks and works in the space defined by four points of reference:

1. the real world at a given time and place with a given set of inequalities
2. inequalities that are unavoidable, necessary, or justifiable
3. the greatest possible happiness for each and all
4. equality for all in all respects.

The egalitarian takes a stance in the real world in some particular society at some specific time in its history and asks whether the inequalities that prevail are indeed unavoidable, necessary, or justifiable in light of the goal of achieving the greatest possible happiness for each and all. The activist egalitarian will accept only those inequalities that meet this test and will seek to eliminate those that do not. The ideal as stated—the greatest possible happiness for each and all—assumes that the full actualization of the potential for enjoyment is sought within the framework of justice. No good is sought for anyone at the expense of another. Maximizing happiness (well-being, satisfaction, enjoyment) is pursued under the restraint of justice. An alternate expression is self-realization in community. The same meaning can be expressed in terms of maximizing the good, maximizing freedom, and maximizing equality within the constraints each places on the others.[47] Since society cannot guarantee happiness, social policy can aim only at creating those institutions, laws, and practices that provide the objective framework in which the common good and individual good can be sought justly by persons and groups. The idea of equality for all in all respects stands as a lure toward maximal egalitarianism, that is, achieving at every level all the kinds of equalities that are mandated by the governing ideal of maximizing happiness and justice equally for all.

All of this is stated in highly formal and abstract terms. The actual work of achieving the egalitarian goal takes place in innumerable practical situations by human beings using their best judgment in the midst of all the complexities, ambiguities, and changing circumstances of actual life. It is a never-ending task that is carried on in blood, sweat, and tears, enduring many compromises, trade-offs, and frustrations. Equality is a complicated ideal never fully realizable without compromise—not only because of the lack of commitment by enough people, but also because some of its aims frequently conflict with other aims, at least in the immediate context. Yet under the lure of achieving the greatest possible happiness equally for each and all, the everlasting task goes on in the hope that what cannot be made perfect and entirely harmonious can at least be improved by achieving less objectionable conflicts and trade-offs.

The Justification of the Equality Ideal

Some inegalitarians have objected that the legitimacy of greater equality is often assumed but seldom argued for.[48] Therefore, it is important to state the moral and metaphysical assumptions that give rise to egalitarian claims for a given system of thought. Many value claims have been made already, but the philosophical foundation on which they rest has been largely implicit. In very brief fashion, some of these presuppositions will be made explicit.

It is necessary but not sufficient to make equality a procedural assumption. It may be stated as follows: all persons are to be treated equally unless good and sufficient reason can be given for treating them unequally.[49] It is unarguable that human beings *qua* human beings, as measured by whatever criteria make individuals members of that class, are equal. Hence, this procedural assumption would hold that the burden of proof rests on the proposal that persons are to be treated unequally. In particular, they must be shown to be unequal in the respect that counts with regard to the distribution at hand, for example, need or merit. But if the issue in question demands treatment of human beings as human beings, then they must be treated equally. This would seem to be no more than a spelling out of the nontrivial tautology: treat equals equally, treat unequals unequally. This still does not answer Aristotle's question: Equals and unequals in what?

Moreover, this abstract and purely formal analysis needs concrete content and substance. This requires a theory of value to give grounding to the meaning of justice and happiness. A version of process philosophy informed by (but not necessarily identical with) the ideas of Alfred North Whitehead is useful for this purpose.[50] According to this outlook, reality consists of systems and sequences of lifelike events. Life, seen most clearly in plants and animals, is the process by which an organism appropriates relevant aspects of its environment in quest of internally guided ends. Put differently, it is the actualizing of potential in an organism, such as, for instance, the way in which an acorn becomes an oak tree. At the animal level, an organism has a unified or dominant center of experience with a complex potential for enjoyment. Enjoyment is the accompaniment of the actualizing of potential in these living centers of experiencing. Even at the simpler levels of molecules, atoms, and down to the most primitive occasions, the element of subjectivity involving selectivity of aims is present in rudimentary form. In this sense reality is made up entirely of experiencing subjects or organisms. Gross material objects knowable through the senses, like typewriters and stones, are not as such experiencing subjects, although they are composed of them.

The world, then, consists of series and societies of these lifelike happenings in quest of relevant aims at varying levels of organized complexity. The elementary subjects are incorporated into larger systems and systems of systems composing in their widest extension the cosmic organism itself. The cosmos and all of its component societies are lured into creative advance by an All-Inclusive Persuasive Purpose (God). Creative advance takes place as more complex forms of richer, more intense, qualitatively superior experiences of satisfaction occur and as these experiences are integrated into more inclusive systems of harmonious meaning and enjoyment.[51] For purposes here, creative advance at the human level operationally means increases in happiness and in justice.[52]

Value is connected with the experience of subjects. Good is the experience of enjoyment and, by extension, whatever contributes to such experience. Any experiencing subject with potential for enjoyment (happiness, satisfaction) has some degree of intrinsic value. The greater the complexity, range, depth, intensity, and fullness of experience, the greater the intrinsic value. Human beings have more inherent worth than any other beings known to us, but all experiencing subjects have intrinsic value in proportion to their capacity for enjoyment. Hence, plants and animals have more intrinsic value than molecules and atoms. Typewriters and stones, as such, are objects and thus have only instrumental value, but even they have within them the intrinsic value of their component molecular subjects. Hence, everything has at least minimal inherent worth in some sense. This is a philosophical version of the biblical notion of the goodness of the whole creation (Gen. 1). A person is an experiencing subject with an enormous potential for high-level enjoyment and hence has great intrinsic value.

Within this framework two moral imperatives arise. (a) The deontological imperative is: honor the intrinsic value of human beings and, in proportion, of all sentient beings. (b) The teleological imperative is: promote the enjoyment of human beings and, in proportion, of all sentient beings. Persons have rights because they have intrinsic value. They have intrinsic value because they are experiencing subjects with a capacity for enjoyment. The basis for justice is found in the deontological imperative. The basis for increasing the happiness of all is found in the teleological imperative.

The moral imperative, then, requires acts and rules that maximize justice for all and that promote the equal happiness of all. Put differently, the two norms are justice and happiness, each to be sought within the constraints each places on the other. Within this framework, the formal procedural assumption regarding equality holds. Persons as persons are equal in intrinsic value and hence have equal rights based on this natural fact. Moreover, persons are to be treated equally unless there are good and sufficient reasons from treating them unequally. But persons differ in all sorts of ways. When any of the ways in which persons are different is the relevant reference, inequalities may legitimately arise.

How is a person to be defined? A full answer to this question is not necessary here. All that need be said is that, given the definition of "person" anyone provides, all beings who qualify are members of that class. Imagine a circle filled with dots at various places within the circumference. However much the dots differ in position from one another, they all are within the circle. Imagine a circle that contains all beings who meet the definition of person. No matter how much they may differ from one another in whatever ways, as long as each meets the minimal or threshold requirements of the essential attributes that constitute personhood, they are all equally persons. A more precise and sufficiently inclusive definition should state that all that is required is that one have or have had the capacity for personhood, whether that capacity has yet to be developed (as in normal new-born infants) or has been lost (in the case of accident, disease, or tragic circumstance). Borderline cases there will be, of course, but normally we have no practical problems in deciding who is to be, or at least who should be, regarded and treated as a person.[53]

Included in the definition of "person" might be the capacity to have a conception of one's own good and a capacity to understand and honor the rights and promote the good of others.[54] Beyond that a certain degree and kind of intelligence, self-consciousness, rationality, moral freedom, and the like might be presupposed as the necessary basis for conceiving of justice and goodness in relation to self and others. One might also include at least minimal potential for some or all of the following: the capacity to entertain meaning as related to the purpose of human existence, to have hope for the future, to love and be loved, to see life as related to some ultimate purpose or framework of meaning, to worship God, and the like. The point is that, however conceived, all members who stand within the required range of the necessary capacities are to regarded as human beings and equally so with all others in that category. This is the case regardless of how much they may differ in the degree to which they embody the essential capacities or attributes, or differ in any other nonessential ways, such as race, sex, hair color, height, weight, and so on.

The philosophical perspective suggested here is not an essential basis for egalitarianism. Indeed, many philosophers simply begin with equality as a procedural assumption without grounding it in any metaphysical outlook. Moreover, other philosophical positions could equally well support the moral views set forth above. What is maintained is that an egalitarian ideology is supported plausibly and adequately by these metaphysical principles. The connection between the metaphysics and the ethics is organic but does not necessarily exclude other options. Not all process thinkers would hold to the kind of egalitarianism espoused here, nor would all who accept this egalitarianism find the process metaphysics credible or convincing.

Conclusions

To conclude, it is necessary to point out that equality itself and as such is not the ultimate norm or goal. An idolatry focused on this single value must be avoided. What finally counts is people—the meaning and fulfillment of which they are capable and which the Creator intends. The ultimate reference, then, must be to human happiness and social justice. Equality acquires validity only when it arises from obedience to the twin mandates of observing justice and increasing happiness. For just that reason, it has a large role to play. Subsequent chapters must give substance to that claim.

The next task is to examine briefly the idea and ideal of equality in American life and history. This will form the background against which an ideal model of the just and good society can be developed. The remainder of the book will look at some matters pertaining to equality in the economic sphere.

Notes

1. See Sidney Verba and Gary R. Orren, *Equality in America*, pp. 2–3, 248–52.
2. Richard McKeon contends that the history of the idea reveals a twofold long-run tendency: "increase in the number of those who are considered 'equal' and the diversification of what is sought as 'equal.' " See "Justice and Equality," *Nomos VI: Justice*, p. 45.
3. *The Compact Edition of the Oxford English Dictionary* (Oxford: Oxford University Press, 1971), Vol. I, pp. 885–86.
4. Aristotle, *Politics*, p. 86.
5. As Isaiah Berlin points out, this is merely to spell out "the conception of rules," namely, that they allow no exceptions ("Equality," *Proceedings of the Aristotelian Society, 1955–1956*, p. 306). This article is one of the finest brief expositions of the idea of equality available. See pp. 301–26.
6. Ibid., pp. 301–11.
7. W. K. Frankena, "The Concept of Social Justice," p. 11.
8. In this section I am very dependent upon the analysis provided by Hugo Adam Bedau, "Egalitarianism and the Idea of Equality, *Nomos IX: Equality*, ed. J. Roland Pennock and John W. Chapman, pp. 3–27.
9. Gregory Vlastos, "Justice and Equality," in Brandt, ed., *Social Justice*, p. 40.
10. While I have not in every case followed the definitions and conclusions of Bedau in this section, I acknowledge with gratitude his insightful analysis.
11. Richard Wollheim, "Equality," *Proceedings of the Aristotelian Society, 1955–1956*, p. 282. Cf. Bedau, "Egalitarianism," p. 6.
12. Felix Oppenheim says that some 19th-century anarchists did sponsor this notion. See "Egalitarianism as a Descriptive Concept," *American Philosophical Quarterly*, p. 144, and his article "Equality," *International Journal of the Social Sciences* 7: 105. Rees, however, says that the closest thing to radical egalitarianism he knows about is *The Manifesto of the Equals*, which seems at least to allow different treatment in terms of age and sex, e. g., nourishment, though at one point it does urge that since all are alike, all should have the "same portion and quality of food." See John Rees, *Equality*, pp. 96–97.
13. Sir Isaiah Berlin notes that the ideal of "extreme equality" in which everyone is maximally similar to everyone else has never been defended by any serious thinker, but it "possesses the central importance of an ideal limit or idealized model at the heart of all egalitarian thought." See "Equality," p. 315.
14. This distinction has a long history and in one of its forms can be found in *The Dialogues* of Plato. The modern distinction was given its classical form by Rousseau, who referred to natural or physical inequalities as opposed to moral or political inequalities (see his *Discourse on Equality*). John Rees, *Equality*, pp. 11–27, offers a helpful discussion.
15. John Rawls, of course, acknowledges that some social inequalities will result from biological inequalities. But he urges us not to worry, since society can be organized so that these inequalities work out for the benefit of all, especially the least fortunate. See *A Theory of Justice*, pp. 100–108.
16. See Verba and Orren, *Equality in America*, pp. 246–66.
17. This point is made well in Rees, *Equality*, pp. 80–90.
18. The divisions between the categories of unavoidable, necessary, and justifiable are not always clearcut. Some overlapping is present. Some inequalities are justifiable (in some sense) because they are necessary to the function-

ing of society. And are some inequalities necessary (in some sense) because they are unavoidable, or unavoidable (in some sense) because they are necessary, or just necessary and unavoidable (in some senses)? The effort here has been to relate unavoidable inequalities primarily, but not exclusively, to differences that are rooted in given and (presently) unchangeable genetic factors. Necessary inequalities are those that are essential to the very existence and functioning of any organized society. "Justifiable" as used here is strictly a moral category. Justifiable inequalities are those necessary to the realization of the highest moral values.

19. For a definition of these terms, see Kenneth Cauthen, *Process Ethics: A Constructive System*, pp. 36–82, or William Frankena, *Ethics*, pp. 12–60, or any standard textbook or dictionary of philosophical ethics. Briefly put, in deontological ethics rightness inheres in an act or rule itself (It is just wrong to lie or kill) and/or is mandated by some authority (God or natural law or custom or reason, etc. requires it). Something other than consequences is determinative of right and wrong. In teleological ethics rightness is determined by consequences alone and consists in whatever is productive of the highest or largest good.

20. See, for example, Arthur M. Okun, *Equality and Efficiency: The Big Trade-off*.

21. This is the thesis of Robert Kuttner, *The Economic Illusion: False Choices Between Prosperity and Social Justice*.

22. See Cauthen, *Process Ethics*, pp. 263–310, esp. 295–305.

23. Bedau cites Wolfgang von Leiden and Gregory Vlastos as philosphers who have made a version of this case. See Bedau, "Egalitarianism," p. 25.

24. Cf. Rees, *Equality*, pp. 96–106, and Berlin, "Equality," pp. 312–15.

25. Such statements are made deliberately in full recognition of the difficulties of making comparisons of interpersonal utility. If one person announces a preference for Minnesota while another prefers Florida, I would assume that if the first can live in Minnesota and the latter in Florida the criterion would be met. Whether all persons can have their stated preferences equally met is another question. Given a sufficiently large population, it is obvious they could not be equally met for everybody. Yet the ideal can guide practice within the limits of practical possibility.

26. I regard this as another way of speaking of the ideal as "self-realization in community"—the norm of the just and good society that I defended in *Process Ethics*, pp. 195–230.

27. This rather obvious point has been made by many thinkers, including Felix Oppenheim, Isaiah Berlin, J. R. Lucas, and J. W. N. Watkins. See Rees, *Equality*, p. 195.

28. See Rees, ibid, pp. 106–22, for a convincing statement of this proposition.

29. See Berlin, "Equality," pp. 325–26.

30. The phrases come from J. W. N. Watkins. See Rees, *Equality*, pp. 95–96.

31. This case could be controversial. If an alleged social club is also a place where important business discussions take place and thus has a public character, the situation might be different. Women have protested some private men's clubs on this basis, and with good reason. This assumption here, however, is that the club is small and really for social purposes only, and serves no public economic or political function.

32. One might argue that the distinctive point here is that those excluded

from favor have no claims for any kind of treatment in the regard at issue, rather than just an unequal claim. That is, of course, correct and will be implied in the analysis that follows.

33. Michael Walzer stresses this point and criticizes John Rawls for using an ahistorical and thus false method for discerning justice. Walzer stresses that one cannot deal with equality apart from a consideration of the social meanings that have developed historically in a particular society. See Walzer, *Spheres of Justice*.

34. Berlin notes that protests against inequalities can be based on two considerations: rules are being violated, or appeal is made to a wider or more general rule. The first is the most direct plea for equality. The second appeals to a more general form of equality which takes precedence over the inequalities justified under some more specific rule. He also notes that all rules can be rejected simply because they are rules. This is an attack on the idea of equality itself. See "Equality," pp. 301–11.

35. This sentence illustrates how slippery, subtle, and ambiguous a term like "equal treatment" is. Individuals as individuals are equal to each other in dignity and worth and so should be treated as equals—when that is the point of relevant reference. The cases under consideration have to do with other kinds of equalities that are humanly established in group contexts.

36. Complex issues arise here. Large labor unions also have great power for good or ill and are also publically accountable. But even persons who belong to unions are usually hired one at a time in separate transactions. A union that could prevent large numbers of people from working for particular firms it did not like would also have power that would have to be socially controlled for the common good. Many discriminating judgments would have to be made to account for all the many types of circumstances that would affect whether individual liberty or social control for the sake of justice and the common good should prevail. Labor unions as socially important actors should not be free to exclude otherwise qualified persons because of race, sex, religion, and other prejudices.

37. More precisely, no legislation would be needed on grounds of economic justice. A majority might well decide, however, that it was not in the common good for major elements of the economic order to be organized on a segregated basis, and forbid racial discrimination for some such reason. Laws are a means of expressing social values as well as an instrument of justice. The problem always arises, however, regarding the point at which the line should be drawn between unregulated individual freedom and social control for the sake of the common good.

38. This point is the major burden of Walzer, *Spheres of Justice*.

39. This is what Proudhon argued against St. Simon and others who said that the moral basis for socialism was not justice but love. Love, Proudhon maintained, applied only in the family. What was called for in the larger society was respect for the dignity of other people. Society was based not on love but on mutuality and reciprocity. See Robert C. Tucker, "Marx and Distributive Justice," *Nomos VI: Justice,* ed. Pennock and Chapman, p. 310.

40. This point is argued for in *Process Ethics,* pp. 278–90, 295–310.

41. Perhaps one should speak more precisely of creating a set of social arrangements that would facilitate the achievement of fulfillment for all justly. Society, no matter how just or good its institutions and practices, cannot guarantee happiness for anyone, but it can seek to create those objective conditions most conducive to the flowering of the good life equally for all. See

ibid., pp. 231–62, for a discussion of the good life, and good person, and the good society.

42. I am indebted to William Frankena, *Ethics,* p. 53, for this way of putting it. However, see the criticism that Rawls makes of this notion in *A Theory of Justice,* pp. 510–11. Rawls points to the old, familiar difficulty of measuring the goodness of life, but I argue that there are ways of dealing with this without abandoning the utilitarian dimension, which must be connected with the deontological concern for justice.

43. It should be noted that some libertarians express the private sentiment that more equality among persons might well be desirable. But the priority they give to liberty does not allow them to approve coercive efforts to increase equality as a mandate of justice, since such actions would infringe upon individual freedom. For example, see F. A. Hayek, *Constitution of Liberty,* pp. 87–88.

44. Ibid.

45. This is the spirit that pervades one of the classic works of egalitarian thought. See R. H. Tawney, *Equality.*

46. Strictly speaking, this does not mean that all distribution should be equal regardless. It only means that idealism holds that it would be better if all could be equal, but equal on terms that do not violate justice. That is, if some have more because they deserve more, the idealist would not contravene the rule of merit, but wishes that those who have less were now or could become more or equally meritorious. If there are steps that can be taken to help people have more merit, then such would be desirable.

47. All of this is spelled out in detail in my *Process Ethics.*

48. See Robert Nozick, *Anarchy, State, and Utopia,* p. 232.

49. Cf. Rees, *Equality,* pp. 124–38, and Rawls, *A Theory of Justice,* pp. 504–12.

50. See my *Process Ethics,* pp. 37–76, for a more extended discussion of the views that are to follow. For the metaphysics involved, see my *Science, Secularization and God.* In the background is Alfred North Whitehead, *Process and Reality,* although I do not claim merely to reproduce his ideas.

51. Cf. Henry Nelson Wieman, *The Source of Human Good,* and Alfred North Whitehead, *Adventures of Ideas,* pp. 251–56.

52. For a more detailed discussion and elaboration of the metaphysical scheme presupposed here, see my *Science, Secularization and God,* pp. 90–194.

53. Cf. Rawls, *A Theory of Justice,* pp. 504–12.

54. Cf. the definition of moral person given by Rawls, ibid.

CHAPTER / TWO

The American Tradition

> Two major traditions of belief, capitalism and democracy, have dominated the life of the American nation from its inception.
> Herbert McClosky and John Zaller
> *The American Ethos*

> America's key values—equality and achievement—stem from our revolutionary origins.
> Seymour Martin Lipset
> *The First New Nation*

> Liberty and equality—the two central commitments of the American Republic.
> J. R. Pole
> *The Pursuit of Equality in America*

"A NATION, CONCEIVED IN LIBERTY, and dedicated to the proposition that all men are created equal" was Abraham Lincoln's way of stating the American creed. Whether equality is linked with liberty or with achievement, or whether democracy is joined with capitalism, a central core of beliefs and values is suggested that comes close to the heart of the matter. When equality and liberty are further connected with individualism, the major components of the paradigm are present, needing only to be connected to the presuppositions that give life and substance to these ideas.[1]

One important assumption surrounding liberty and equality has been a belief in the open future—the confidence that the new and the better can be created by purposive human action. The idea of progress has been at work both in the churches and in the secular mentality. From the millennial expectations of the coming of the Kingdom of Christ on earth generated by the Great Awakening a generation before the

Revolution, to the "I have a dream" aspirations of Martin Luther King, Jr., hope of a fully redeemed social order has been a recurring theme. Even when Americans have doubted that things can be made perfect, they have insisted that at least they can be made better. In more secular terms, they believed that human beings, freed from the shackles of the past by the enlightenment of reason and science, can make improvements in both the material and moral dimensions of life. Such hope has created a powerful dynamic for change. Frequently an increase in equality has been at the center of sought-for reform.

This chapter will examine how the idea (and ideal) of equality was viewed at various times in the American tradition. The aim here is to look to the historical past to illuminate various ways in which equality has been praised and damned, affirmed and denied, lifted up in profession but only partly actualized in practice. In particular, four slices of American history will be examined: (a) the formation of an ethos of equality (1740–1840), (b) the controversy over slavery and racial equality (1820–1875), (c) the women's rights movement and sexual equality (1848–1920), and (d) the assault on equality by Social Darwinists and other libertarians and the reaffirmation of equality by egalitarians (1859–1918).

The Formation of the American Tradition

In the 17th and 18th centuries a revolution occurred in social philosophy, just as it did in the natural sciences. The modern mind, as it came to expression in Europe and America, developed conceptions of both nature and society that stood in sharp contrast to views of reality common to previous ages. In medieval times the cosmos had been viewed as a hierarchical system of purposes in which each component had its proper end that guided its behavior. Unsupported stones fell because they sought to find their place at the downward limit of things. At the center of the universe was the gross earth, surrounded by the planets and stars made of purer stuff, whose substance became increasingly more ethereal as the outermost spheres were approached. At the apex of reality and value was God—an absolute and perfect Being whose will determined and ruled all.[2]

In the new view expressed by Sir Isaac Newton, the machine, not the organism, was the illuminating metaphor of the natural world. The new view described physical reality as tiny particles of matter operating in accordance with inexorable laws that could be stated with mathematical exactitude. The heavens were made of the same stuff and exhibited the same discoverable patterns of motion and change as did earthly objects. A kind of cosmic equality prevailed in that everything everywhere was part of one system of nature, composed of the same elements and obeying the same laws. God served—for Newton and others—as the Original Designer and Creator of the world machine.[3]

The Great Chain of Being also provided a metaphor for social relations prior to the 18th century. According to this metaphor, a series of graded ranks ran from God in the Highest to the lowliest form of brute matter.[4] Humanity was located between angels and animals, somewhat similar to each but having its own proper place in the scheme of things. The notion of hierarchy with its levels of authority and value pervaded the paradigm. A place for everything and everything in its place—this gave the clue to order, harmony, and a sense of aesthetic beauty and rightness. A perfectly reasonable analogy suggested that human society should exhibit a like hierarchy of grades running from kings to the humblest subjects. The unequal distribution of wealth, wisdom, and privilege seemed quite proper as did the unequal distribution of authority and honor. A similar view was held by the original European settlers of what was to be the thirteen colonies. As Governor John Winthrop put it in 1630, "God Almighty, in His most holy and wise Providence, hath so disposed of the condition of mankind that, as in all times, some must be rich, some poor; some high and eminent in power and dignity, others mean and in subjection."[5] This theological claim could be supported secondarily by an appeal to nature. Human inequality was "in conformity with the rest of His works," Winthrop said.

Christian theology had long operated on a distinction between the natural law that prevailed in the pre-Fall Paradise of Eden and the relative natural law (or positive law) that governed humanity in the state of sin.[6] Eden was characterized by peace, harmony, and equality; contemporary life was dominated by conflict, greed, force, violence, and inequality. All the oppressive institutions—male domination, private property, slavery, and the coercive state—were the result of sin and had been instituted by God to ensure peace and order. The relative natural law expressed in those institutions was therefore both the result of sin and the remedy for sin. Once lawlessness and injustice had entered the world, natural law could become effective only in the form of an order of law and compulsion that would combat corruption. Inequalities of rank, authority, wealth, and political power were necessary, since the "continuance of the natural equality of Eden would result only in the slaughter of all good Abels by the wicked Cains."[7] As mediated through John Calvin, Puritan thought expressed by Winthrop accepted the social and political inequalities of the natural order as ordained by God for the purpose of controlling the lawless impulses of sinful humanity.

By 1776 a new vision of humanity and society, resting on quite different assumptions, was making its way in the world. Capitalism was the economic expression of this outlook. Adam Smith described the newly emerging economy around him and found in it the clue to social order and material prosperity. Individuals are organized by a division of labor, he stated, for the sake of an efficient system of production, a procedure that multiplies many times what each can accomplish alone. Property owners, manufacturers, wage laborers, professionals, and artisans all use their own resources to improve their lot. Self-interest, not charity, motivates the butcher, the baker, and the manufacturer to provide services and goods to the community. As each economic actor seeks to maximize private gain, an "invisible hand" coordinates all these separate actions into an efficient means of increasing the general wealth.[8]

Democracy was the expression of the new ideology in the political order. Thomas Hobbes, Jean-Jacques Rousseau, and John Locke—among others—developed the notion of the social contract to explain in principle (if not in historical fact) the origin of government. Their theory: free and equal individuals existing in the state of nature experience various inconveniences and threats to life, property, and the pursuit of well-being. Hence, they contract with each other to create a central authority, to whom all are bound, to guard their rights and interests and to create a framework in which they may realize their chosen ends to the fullest degree possible. Not all versions of the social contract resulted in a democratic theory of the social order, for example, that of Hobbes. But this was the wave of the future for the American experiment. Governments, which have their authority solely by the consent of the governed, arise to coordinate the aims of individuals and to promote the common good. Moreover, individuals have rights prior to the advent of human governments. These rights both limit the power of the governing authorities and direct the purposes of government toward providing a framework in which these rights can be justly exercised with the least impediment.

That these ideas of European origin were abroad in the revolutionary period in America can be documented by numerous examples. Note, for instance, the words of George Mason in the Virginia constitution: "All men are by nature equally free and independent, and have certain inherent rights, of which, when they enter into society, they cannot by any compact deprive or divest their posterity; namely the enjoyment of life and liberty, with the means of acquiring and possessing property and pursuing and obtaining happiness and safety."[9] The preamble to the Massachusetts constitution states: "The body politic is formed by a voluntary association of individuals: It is a social compact, by which the whole people covenants with each citizen, and each citizen with the whole people, that all shall be governed by certain laws for the common good."[10]

Thomas Jefferson was chosen to write the Declaration of Independence because of his "peculiar felicity of expression." He penned the familiar words that have provided a primary frame of reference for all subsequent discussions of human equality in the American tradition: "We hold these truths to be self-evident: that all men are created equal, that they are endowed by their Creator with certain inalienable rights, that among them are life, liberty, and the pursuit of happiness."[11] To claim that "these truths are self-evident" apparently is to assert that all persons have a rational and moral consciousness that enables them to grasp intuitively these universal propositions. The egalitarian implications are obvious. No external authority—the Bible, the church, cultural tradition, or anything else—is needed to establish these declarations. They can be known directly and immediately by all. The natural law basis of these assertions is skillfully put in words that both orthodox Christians and the rationalistic deists could accept on their own terms.[12]

The historical consciousness that came into prominence in the 19th century still lives on in the 20th and reminds us how much this way of thinking was characteristic of the 18th century. "Nature" and "reason" were key terms in the climate of opinion that provided the background for the rhetoric of the American Revolution. Just as scientific reason was laying out the patterns and laws that governed the natural world (Newton), so social and philosophical reason was setting forth the principles that were normative for society (Smith, Locke). (Montesquieu, who was not unknown to American thinkers, had set forth a version of historical relativism, according to which political ideas and practices were conditioned by a variety of geographical and climatic factors. His was not the point of view that entered into the American canon, however.)

Missing from this account so far is the contribution of evangelical religion to the democratic and egalitarian impulses of the era. One line of historical interpretation has it that the triumph of democratic theory awaited the overcoming of the view of human depravity espoused by benighted Calvinists still in the grip of an outmoded orthodoxy.[13] Enlightenment, optimism, and rationalism produced the rhetoric and reality of the revolution, aided and abetted by the liberal preachers who lifted up the virtues of a religion based on reason. The more convincing version of the 18th century maintains that equalitarian and democratic motifs evolved in Calvinistic orthodoxy itself.[14] Moreover, the liberal exponents of rational religion in the churches generally were politically conservative. They were usually more concerned with preserving order than giving power to the unpredictable masses of people who might use their equality to threaten established privileges and practices.[15] While affirming the right of the people to rule and to resist tyranny, the exponents of rational religion were thus reluctant rebels, hesitant to make a break with Britain because of their fear of anarchy. Jonathan Edwards and the other Calvinist evangelicals who generated the enthusiasms of the religious revivals of the Great Awakening (1734–1744) "provided pre-Revolutionary America with a radical, even democratic, social and political ideology."[16]

Among the many religious factors that had an equalitarian, democratic, even revolutionary, potential, the following are frequently cited. The belief in the natural equality of humanity before the Fall justified protest against British power when it became unjust and destructive of human rights. (Never mind that the Fall could also be used to justify social inequalities and the use of coercive power by government to restrain the unruly passions of the degenerate masses.)[17] The revivals appealed to the direct and immediate experience of the Spirit in ways that enhanced the authority of individuals.[18] They also produced a millennial enthusiasm that foresaw the perfection of society coming not in a sudden and catastrophic ending of history at the Second Coming of Christ, but in the gradual transformation of the whole of national life as the newly regenerated individuals produced good works in the world.[19] Calvinist political theory argued not only that government must serve the common good or lose its mandate, but that the authorities were accountable to the will of the people, who could remove them if necessary.[20] A congregational or democratic polity had increasingly become the rule in the churches and provided a model for the governance of society as a whole.[21] Equalitarian themes were central to the understanding of the social norm commended by Edwards and his successors. They spoke of the "happy equality" of all citizens, noting that happiness depended on keeping everyone in a "middling condition of life," and that by "bringing down the haughty, we restore our race to its natural order."[22] Suffice it to say, then, that one product of the Great Awakening was "the spirit of American democracy."[23]

A brief illustration of the rich mix of thought in the revolutionary period is provided by Calvinist preacher Nathaniel Niles, who argued (1774) against the Lockean notion of the social contract. He took issue with the idea that individuals have prior private interests that governments must honor and protect; rather, governments arise as an expression of the social nature of humanity. The interdependence of each and all requires a coordinating central authority. The purpose of the state is to promote the common good; a private interest disconnected from the well-being of all is an expression of sin and the source of disorder. Moreover, individuals are to do all they can to promote the highest good of the whole body. In fact, so strong was Niles's subjection of private interest to the common welfare that one might wonder whether individualism had yet taken firm root. Nonetheless, he was quite clear that governments are responsible to the people, that they can be dismissed by them, and that majority rule—though fallible—offers the best means of achieving the good of the whole.[24]

In sum, the American scene in the last quarter of the 18th century contained diverse winds of doctrine. Many swirling currents, some flowing against others, were in evidence. But the result of the interplay of creative thought and the social setting was an increasingly democratic outlook in which the equality of free and independent individuals was a prominent theme. Piety and reason, evangelical religion and Enlightenment rationalism, challenged and reinforced each other in what all agree was a crucial period of transformation.[25] Perhaps no one knows just how theological motifs interacted with appeals to reason, nature, and the social contract theory of Locke to produce the new paradigm. Nevertheless, the infant nation entered into the post-revolutionary period with a fresh ethos centering on the equal rights of all to exercise their liberty in the pursuit of happiness and the governance of society.

But does this imply that all (adult) human beings have the inalienable rights of citizenship guaranteeing them the privilege to consent to their governance, plus equal liberty to pursue opportunities of their own choosing? This was to be the subject of much controversy from 1776 onward. In general, the ideal of equal liberty that was emerging as the core belief of the new republic was assigned fully only to white, property-owning males. Women, African slaves, and Native Americans were assigned a status of inferiority in different ways. A number of the signers of the Declaration of Independence, including Thomas Jefferson, owned slaves. The Constitution specified that slaves counted only for three-fifths of a person in determining how many representatives each state would have in the Congress; Indians counted for nothing. Women were not eligible to vote. Many state constitutions required ownership of property as a condition for voting and holding office. Indentured servants underwent a kind of temporary slavery.

Hence, political equality was not universal, even among males or whites. Religious freedom—or equality of conscience—was won only after a long, hard struggle.[26] The first amendment of the Constitution guaranteed the free exercise of religion and forbade Congress to make laws regarding "an establishment of religion." It was ratified by three-fourths of the states in 1791, and by 1833 disestablishment had occurred in all the states.

Numerous observers noted the feeling of equality prevalent in early America. William Eddis, a young Englishman living in Maryland, commented in 1772, "An idea of equality seems generally to prevail, and the inferior order of people pay little but external respect to those who occupy superior stations."[27] Better known are the observations of

Alexis de Tocqueville, who was impressed by the fact and the ideal of equality. "No novelty in the United States struck me more vividly during my stay there than the equality of conditions."[28] The realities of high and low status and the great discrepancies in economic well-being contradicted in considerable measure his notion of "equality of conditions." Nevertheless, much in the new nation did stand in sharp contrast to the more rigid and stable hierarchies and the inherited positions of wealth, power, and esteem characteristic of Europe and of de Tocqueville's France.

The conditions of life on the ever westward-moving frontier were equalizing opportunities for all who had the ability and the will to work. Confronting the wilderness and an untamed land tended to put everyone on the same footing. What one could do took priority now over inherited position.[29] A democratic spirit was abroad and grew during the Jacksonian era—the age of "the common man." By 1860 universal suffrage for adult white males had been achieved and property qualifications, essentially eliminated.[30] Other moves such as the advent of direct primaries and the civil service spread political power among more people in equalizing ways.[31] At the same time, growing concentrations of wealth in the North produced a labor movement with commitments to, but not much accomplishment of, greater economic equality.[32] Aside from a few radicals such as Thomas Skidmore of New York, not many serious proposals were made for government action to equalize wealth and property.[33] Equality of opportunity was the standard, while inequality of result was to be expected. Said Andrew Jackson, "Distinctions in society will always exist under every just government. Equality of talents, or education, or of wealth cannot be produced by human institutions."[34]

So far an attempt has been made to explore the place of equality among the ideals of early America. Obviously, the actual stood in considerable contradiction to the ideal, even as then proclaimed. But the theme had been introduced in ways new to the history of nations, even though only rarely has "the idea of equality dominated American debates on major questions of policy."[35] Nevertheless, the ideal has persisted tenaciously as the rallying cry of the underdogs, the oppressed, the outsiders. The remainder of this chapter will highlight a few of the significant moments in the continuing struggle over who is to be regarded as equal and in what respects.

Equality and Slavery

It is shocking to be reminded how recently otherwise kind and learned people defended the proposition that it was morally permissible for one person to own, buy, and sell another. An examination of the reasoning that led to the abandonment or the reinterpretation of the doctrine of human equality in defense of slavery is particularly instructive with respect to its place in the American tradition. In the long run this cruel practice could not withstand the logic of equality as embedded in the early American tradition and in the continuing reflections of those hungry for truth and justice. But at the time it was linked to noble human values and was defended on the basis of the highest authorities. Aristotle and the Bible were quoted, along with pragmatic appeals insisting that both master and slave, both South and North, were better off with this peculiar institution than without.

The moral reasoning employed to justify slavery seems thoroughly spurious—even silly—today.[36] So lacking in cogency are the arguments that they are hardly worth refuting. Whatever plausibility some of the particular propositions may have had in the context, they by no means yielded the vindication that was sought. Yet some of the best minds of the period were committed to a pro-slavery sentiment that is difficult to account for. Moreover, so thoroughly does the mode of reasoning reflect the circumstances of the time that our faith in the transcendent validity of human ideas and values may be sorely tested. On what basis can we believe that our confidently held doctrines are any less relative to our own time and place or any less subservient to our own needs and interests? Yet unless the struggle for equal liberty has some autonomy in relation to the historical forces that shape us, the only criterion for the validity of ideas is that they survive. And unless we have some capacity to make valid judgments about truth and right, we are but actors in a play whose lines are written for us by an Ultimate Author whose motives we cannot surmise. Fortunately, confidence that good causes may be greater than ourselves is partially renewed by the recognition that high ideals outlive both their defenders and detractors, to challenge us to ever-fresh but always incomplete interpretations of their truth. We must hope that some winnowing of wheat from the chaff takes place in the process, so that we can claim that we see more clearly the deeper meaning of justice than did our predecessors.

Until the 19th century was well under way, leading thinkers in both North and South agreed that slavery must be ended. The invention of the cotton gin in 1793 and the emergence of an aggressive abolitionist movement in 1831 were primary factors leading to the most sustained and systematic apologetics in its behalf. It may not be stretching the point to say that the movement of thought proceeded over the decades from the idea that slavery was an unnecessary evil, through its defense as a necessary evil, to the final triumphant proclamation that it was a positive good. In the process the idea of human equality was first qualified and then rejected altogether.

The arguments on behalf of slavery can be summarized under four headings:

1. *Economic.* The economic well-being of both North and South was much dependent on slave labor. The cotton gin enabled large quantities of cotton to be sold and exported profitably. With money made from the sale of cotton, the South bought products from other parts of the country and fueled the economy in the whole country. For example, raw materials produced in Georgia led to employment in New England textile mills. One modern interpreter concludes, "The first hundred million pounds of exportable cotton made slavery a defensible institution in spite of its admitted evils. The first billion pounds made it the 'corner-stone' of progress, civilization, republicanism, and Christianity. Cotton was king."[37] Advocates claimed that only blacks could withstand the hot sun in the cotton fields and that only slave labor was economically feasible.[38]

2. *Scriptural.* Despite whatever general principles of human equality one might draw on theological grounds, the most literal reading of the Holy Book seemed to favor the defenders of slavery rather than the abolitionists. In this instance, as in others, the most humane exposition of Scripture required some way to invalidate numerous specific texts, which, unfortunately, could be quoted in favor of many evils, including slavery. The equalitarian themes could, with some plausibility, be limited by pro-slavery enthusiasts to pre-Fall Eden, the ultimate status of persons before God as sinners or recipients of saving grace, or to the afterlife. "Show me a passage anywhere in the Bible that unequivocally condemns African slavery" was the audacious challenge of the apologists. Slavery is an accepted institution in the Old Testament, nor is it rejected as such in the New Testament, either by Jesus or by the Apostles. Instead, slaves are enjoined to serve their masters with a glad and humble spirit (for example, I Peter 2: 18–20; Ephes. 6:5–8; Col. 3:22–25; I Tim. 6:1–2; Titus 2:9–10; Philemon). Numerous theologians in the South made the case from Scripture over and over, in great detail and in large volumes.[39] They were supported in this endeavor by an impressive list of respected scholars and preachers in prestigious northern seminaries and churches.[40]

3. *Social.* The fundamental premise of a large set of arguments was the innate and permanent inferiority of the natives of Africa. This led to the conclusion that their subordination to the white race was in the best interests of everyone. The character of blacks suited them for dependence and servitude. Moreover, the arguments continued, they were better off in America under the care and tutelage of benevolent masters than those who remained in the barbarous darkness of Africa or who lived free in the North. The supreme advantage to the African was the opportunity for eternal salvation through God's design to bring these lost souls to the missionaries. Besides, the consequences of

freeing such large numbers of slaves would be disastrous. (Whites, fearing massacres by uncontrollable masses of blacks, anxiously cited the horrors following emancipation in Haiti and Jamaica.) Remaining as slaves, blacks could profit from all the humanizing benefits the white race had to offer; freed, they would be menace both to themselves and whites. Finally, slavery elevated the character of the master. Freed from menial labor, the superior race could devote itself to the finer things of life. Among the blessings of slavery was counted a sense of equality among whites, since race alone sufficed to guarantee dignity. Did not the achievements of the great civilizations of the past rest on the foundation of slave labor?[41]

4. *Philosophical.* The opponents of slavery invariably rested their case on the equality of all human beings, a status sanctioned by nature or God or both. The Declaration of Independence was, of course, quoted as a primary authority. The philosophical argument was that while blacks were admittedly unequal to whites in numerous particulars, they were actually equal in certain ways more fundamental than the observable inequalities. In those specifications that make a person a person, blacks are equal to whites. Moreover, rights are conferred by God or nature, not by society; hence, it is wrong for society to deprive any human being of liberty. Christians could base their opposition to slavery on principles of justice, love, and kindness derived from Scripture. They were at considerable disadvantage, however, when it came to quoting specific texts relating to slavery. Science and higher criticism had not yet undermined the theory of verbal infallibility or demonstrated the historical relativity of biblical morality.

The defenders of African servitude followed two lines of reasoning. (a) One strategy was to accept the premise of Jefferson that all are created equal and have certain inalienable rights. But immediately they noted that no one had ever supposed that all people were equal in *all* respects. Moreover, everyone recognized that sometimes the rights of individuals had to be limited for the greater good of society as a whole. Then they proceeded to demonstrate the economic and social benefits for master, slave, and the whole country that required slavery as the necessary means. Such enormous gains took precedence, they said, over the natural rights of the slaves, whose own best interests were, after all, being served.[42]

(b) As the abolitionist attacks grew more fierce, the defenders of slavery simply tended to abandon the doctrine of human equality. Slavery then became an institution remarkably fitted to relate the superior to the inferior race. They substituted Aristotle for the authority of John Locke and Thomas Jefferson. The ancient and revered philosopher had discovered long ago that some were by nature suited to command, while others had mentality sufficient only to obey. As already noted, Scripture offered no unambiguous refutation of Aristotle and was often quoted in support of the great thinker.

John C. Calhoun argued that slavery was good in itself—*bonum in se*. Accepting nature as the norm and Aristotle as the authority, he argued for the natural inequality of the races and for slavery as the appropriate corollary of that fact. Contrary to Locke, there was no "state of nature" prior to human society; society itself is the natural condition. We are born into a group as a dependent social being. People are unequal in every particular, there being no created status or fundamental essence that establishes some primordial equality. The races sprang from different origins, not from one source, and display varying capacities. Present observation confirms the natural inferiority of the Negro, who shows up everywhere in history as a hewer of wood and drawer of water for more favored races.[43]

George Fitzhugh, thoroughly untypical but perhaps the most interesting of the apologists for slavery, rejected with vehemence and moral indignation the fundamental values of the American tradition. He attacked individualism, freedom, and industrial capitalism as well as equality. Fitzhugh lambasted, with a ferocity hardly exceeded by that of Karl Marx, the "free society" of the North and its cruel exploitation of wage labor. The main thing wrong with socialism is that it shares too many values of the capitalist order it attacks. The true form of socialism, he said, is based on slavery. In essence, his argument was that freedom and equality beget a ruthless competition motivated by selfishness to improve one's lot. The result is destructive for the poor, the weak, and the helpless. People are not equal, and to grant them all liberty is a license for the powerful and rich to grind the faces of the defenseless in the dirt. Conflict, hatred, and oppression by the strongest are inevitable. Capitalists are "cannibals all," exploiting their workers by making profit on their labor. Workers are "slaves without masters," enriching their employers while they are healthy workers but abandoned to a life of pauperism when they are old, sick, or injured.

In its place Fitzhugh proposed an organic, hierarchical, paternalistic society based on love and the mutual dependence of races and classes. Slaves would work for their masters but in turn would be cared for by them from infancy to the grave for the greater good of all. True democracy would equalize the burdens in which the weak and the strong would serve each other. Peace, security, harmony, love, and prosperity would flourish when, in a hierarchy of unequals, each race and class found its proper place. All would serve according to capacity to the mutual benefit of each participant.[44]

In the North, meanwhile, Stephen Douglas maintained that equality as proclaimed in the Declaration of Independence referred only to

European whites and not to African blacks, Asian immigrants, or Indians. Abraham Lincoln contended against him that equality included blacks as far as their natural rights to life, liberty, and the pursuit of happiness were concerned. He doubted whether blacks were his intellectual or moral equals. Lincoln's personal feelings resisted the idea of full social and political equality; in his view the actualization of equality for all was a goal to be sought as circumstances permitted. Numerous Americans wanted slavery abolished and for blacks to be able to make their own way in the world, but at the same time they did not want to share with the African race the political institutions that would guarantee these rights. The 1857 Dred Scott decision of the Supreme Court denied that free blacks were citizens of the country, since Negroes had not been citizens at the time the Constitution was adopted.[45]

Other voices among blacks and whites called for immediate emancipation and movement toward the granting of full civil and political rights. Dr. Martin Delaney, a black physician, spoke for those who had given up hope for improvement in this country. He gave early expression to intense black pride as well as black separatism and proposed voluntary emigration. Frederick Douglass continued to believe in the possibility of racial amalgamation. His second marriage, to a white woman, put into practice what he preached. A few among the abolitionists saw in the black race better qualities in some respects than those possessed by whites. Theodore Tilton, also a feminist, thought that in terms of those intellectual and moral qualities relative to intuition and instinct, blacks were superior to white men and equal to white women. Moncure Daniel Conway held that the European advantage in intellect and energy was balanced by African superiority in goodness and "affectionateness"; the mixture of races would produce better character than either group possessed separately. Few whites thought that blacks had the competitive drive and ability to succeed in the economic world. For this reason, after emancipation it was easy to overlook the overwhelming social disadvantages that blacks suffered in the struggles to get ahead.[46]

So stood the main lines of opinion as the Civil War approached. The Emancipation Proclamation of 1863, the Civil War, and the Thirteenth Amendment to the Constitution settled the question of slavery. The Fourteenth Amendment gave citizenship to all persons born or naturalized in the United States. The Fifteenth Amendment established the right of citizens to vote without regard to race, color, or previous condition of servitude. These were major steps toward establishing political equality. Nevertheless, the southern states found all sorts of constitutional reasons to prevent voting, or at least effective voting, by blacks, and it was not until the Voting Rights Act of 1965 that this fundamental act of democratic citizenship came to be more or less enforced everywhere by the federal government.

Meanwhile, the Supreme Court in 1896 (*Plessy v. Ferguson*) gave constitutional sanction to the notion of separate but equal in the provision of services to different races. Hence, in the southern and border states segregation followed upon slavery as still another way to deny full and equal rights and benefits to blacks. The tragic truth was that the effective rule was generally separate and unequal. In the rest of the country, equal rights before the law prevailed in principle but by no means always in practice. Widespread prejudice and discrimination often meant that denial of equal opportunity was as effective *de facto* as that which occurred in the South *de jure*. A half-century later, in 1954 (*Brown v. Board of Education*), segregation finally lost its legal status. In combination with other legislation, mainly a series of civil rights acts in the 1950s and 1960s, this led to important steps toward political equality and equal rights before the law. But racism is deep, pervasive, and persistent; its poison remains potently effective. Full equality between the races is still a goal, not a reality, mandated by law but often denied in fact.[47]

Equality and the Rights of Women

If it is startling to recall that slavery was abolished only a century and a quarter ago, even more astonishing is the fact that women were not given the right to vote until 1920. That the ballot was so long denied is eloquent testimony to the power of custom, cultural prejudice, and vested self-interest to resist the simple logic of equalitarian principles. As Lucy Stone and others pointed out, a thoroughly ignorant man, totally lacking in manners or morals, could vote, while the male guardians of civilization denied this privilege to their own wives, mothers, and daughters no matter what their character or intelligence.[48] During the debates over the Fourteenth and Fifteenth Amendments, those campaigning for woman suffrage found to their dismay that Congress was willing to grant the ballot to black men—whose cause the suffragists sponsored—but not to women of either race. In part their opposition came from black males, who shared with white men a like bias against equal rights for women. Moreover, only a minority of women supported the struggle for even as basic a privilege of democracy as the franchise. Altogether, it is a curious part of our past.[49]

The ironies and moral ambiguities that accompany the struggle for justice are seldom revealed more vividly. The quest for sexual equality was a thoroughly just cause, yet the strongest opposition came from Bible-quoting clergy and pious church people. Yet it is also true that, later, more clergymen supported the women than did men from other professions. (Women who had wanted to join the fight against slavery often had been shunned by male abolitionists.)[50] At the same time some of the male supporters were racial bigots—George Train, for example.[51] This created antagonism with black activists like Frederick Douglass, otherwise a strong supporter of equal rights for women. During Reconstruction feminists had been told by reformers like Horace Greeley and Wendell Phillips, "It is the Negro's hour. Woman suffrage must wait." But Elizabeth Cady Stanton, Susan B. Anthony, Lucretia Mott, and others found it necessary to oppose suffrage for black males unless women were given the vote. As Stanton put it, they feared that black men "would be more despotic with the governing powers than even our Saxon rulers are."[52]

In the beginning when there was little hope of soon gaining their ends, feminists tended to be more idealistic and more universal in their egalitarianism. When they began to win and lose battles, they made compromises for the sake of particular gains. As the 19th century moved toward an end, the suffragists were caught up in turbulent currents of thought that threatened their early proclamation that all human beings were equal and had certain basic rights. Notions of racial and national superiority were rampant. Many middle-class, Anglo-Saxon, Protestant women prominent in the suffrage movement shared these views, agreeing that the inferior should not rule the superior. One consequence was that the pre–Civil War idealism degenerated by the 1890s into a "pact between woman suffrage and white supremacy."[53] Humiliated and hardened by the fact that white males would make "former slaves the political superiors of their former mistresses," feminists began to exploit racial and class prejudice to their own advantage.[54] In her opening testimony before a Senate committee in 1880, Mary A. Stewart said, "The negroes are a race inferior, you must admit to your daughters, and yet that race has the ballot."[55] The alliance with racism was heightened by the view that Democratic votes from the South were essential in Congress to the success of the suffrage movement.

Suffragists also resented the fact that multitudes of immigrants from all over the world were entering the country, many of them ignorant and quite traditional in outlook. Yet male immigrants could vote, while educated native women could not.[56] They also suspected that these foreign-born men would oppose woman suffrage. In 1894 Carrie Chapman Catt warned of the menace posed by the men in the slums and by the ignorant foreign vote. The Rev. Anna Howard Shaw spoke in 1914 of the unique humiliation American women experienced in being ruled over by men of every color and nationality, whereas in other nations, at least they were subject to men of their own race and country. (A bias against the lower classes and working men had always hovered about the movement.)[57] In 1902 the aged Stanton expressed support for a literacy test that would "abolish the ignorant vote" among men and women alike.[58] An educational requirement appealed to the suffragists because it would allow middle-class women to vote while preserving white supremacy and the dominance of native-born citizens over the new immigrants. These alliances with racism and nativism did not go unchallenged and were the occasion of bad conscience among many who embraced them for the sake of winning. In the last years before enfranchisement, a more open attitude developed when it was discovered that the immigrant and working-class vote could be won to the cause.[59]

As with slavery, so here too—especially in the early days—the debate frequently centered around what nature and Scripture taught.[60] A pastoral letter from the Council of Congregationalist Ministers of Massachusetts typified the opposition by invoking both the Bible and nature:

> The appropriate duties and influence of woman are stated in the New Testament. . . . The power of woman is in her dependence, flowing from the consciousness of the weakness which God has given her for her protection. . . . When she assumes the place and tone of man as a public reformer . . . she yields the power which God has given her . . . and her character becomes unnatural.[61]

"Woman's place is in the home" was the supposed truth about a normative natural order that defined the heart and center of the opposing position.[62] Theological, biological, and sociological arguments supported this thesis.[63] (a) God ordained that women perform different functions from men. (b) Biology taught that women were not fitted physically or mentally to engage in political affairs: women were emotional and intuitive and not logical and practical in the ways that politics demanded.[64] (c) Sociological considerations decreed that the best interests of society were served when women stayed at home to raise their children, a duty that outside activity would corrupt. Political participation would mean "pretty girls buttonholing strange men on Election Day in behalf of the 'handsome candidate' " and women, locked in jury rooms with males, subjected to tales of shocking behavior.[65] In this scheme women in effect had the right not to vote, the privilege of being free from the burden of politics.

Moreover, was not the superiority of men demonstrated by disproportionate accomplishment of the sexes in the arts, sciences, and all other public arenas? The women faced a dilemma. If they admitted their present social inferiority, as some did, then their claims to make political and cultural contributions as equals was weakened. If they denied it, as others did, male oppression was not as damaging as they had claimed.⁶⁶ All, of course could insist on the essential equality of women with men and that what women lacked was opportunity, although they dealt differently with the effects of the environment as it related to whether women were presently fit for public roles.

The argument from nature was used by both sides. Particularly in the earlier period, a fundamental appeal of the women reformers was to the equality of all persons grounded in nature itself. This was a self-evident truth that sanctioned certain inalienable rights. The 1848 Seneca Falls convention, called by Lucretia Mott, Elizabeth Cady Stanton, and others, authored a Declaration of Sentiments that followed the form of the Declaration of Independence. The wording was changed to make clear that "all men and women are created equal." The list of grievances spelled out the various inequalities and oppressions women had suffered at the hands of men. The resolutions were prefaced with "the great precept of nature" that "man shall pursue his own true and substantial happiness." Hence, any human laws or customs that do not recognize the full equality of women with men in this regard are invalid. The demand for equal rights for all—men and women alike—based on "the law of nature" and "dictated by God himself" was a constant appeal throughout the struggle.⁶⁷ Here, as has been case in all American history, the Declaration of Independence provided a bedrock authority for those who sought to overcome intolerable inequalities.

In effect, the rationale for women's rights was based on the indivisibility of equality: natural law is universal, applying to all persons. Nineteenth-century feminists argued that the principle of equal natural rights that justified European males in revolting against Britain and that invalidated the enslavement of blacks also supported the claims women made for themselves. Women were being taxed without being represented in government; women were subordinated in a kind of slavery; equality cannot be divided up and parceled out to some human beings to the exclusion of others. This logic was not lost on some of the opponents of woman suffrage, who then contended that the vote must not be given to black men, since there would then be no reason not to extend it to women, as well.⁶⁸

The contrary argument depended on a division of spheres according to sex as determined either by God, nature, or society. While all human beings might be equal in some respects, they were unequal, or at least different, in others. Natural law or divine ordinance takes both into account and thus allocates to each order of humanity its proper sphere, granting status, rights, privileges, and duties accordingly.⁶⁹ Or they argued that voting is a privilege granted by the state, not a right sanctioned by nature. To this Stanton simply replied that women refused to accept any longer the judgment of men about what their proper place in nature or society was, and assumed for themselves that prerogative.[70] Harriet Burton Laidlaw in 1912 summed it up by insisting that insofar as women were like men, they should have the same rights; insofar as they were different, women should speak for themselves.[71] So the debate raged.

Women had argued from the beginning that equal rights were necessary to them for self-protection, for self-development, and for the sake of the common good; but reference to the equality of the sexes rooted in natural law had dominated the earlier period. By the turn of the century primary argumentation shifted from grounds of justice to an appeal to expediency.[72] National attention had become focused on the differences among people and on the inequalities among races and nationalities. Suffragists and anti-suffragists alike were concerned that the best people should rule. Many middle-class Anglo-Saxons were not sure that the principle of "the consent of the governed" should apply to the new immigrants, workers in the cities, and natives in the islands acquired by the United States in 1898. Hence, the new appeal was to the good that would result to society if at least educated women were given the vote.

The Bible presented a special kind of obstacle to sexual equality. Its authority was so highly respected that it could hardly be ignored. Unfortunately for the suffragists, the Bible is in many ways a sexist book. Numerous passages teach the subordination of women (Gen. 3:16; I Cor. 11:1–12, 14:34–35; Ephes. 5:22–24; Col. 3:18; I Tim. 2:11–15; Titus 2:3–5). The Bible also contains egalitarian passages, but many of these can plausibly be interpreted—by those whose interests so dictate—as referring to the status of all before God without necessarily implying any reformation of society (Gen. 1:27; Gal. 3:28). Feminists, like the abolitionists, made their best case for equality by appealing to general moral principles or grand religious themes rooted in Scripture. The defenders of male privilege could more often quote chapter and verse, and did not hesitate to do so.

In response, the advocates of equality took a variety of approaches.[73] The conservative position was represented by Antoinette L. Brown, who boldly asserted that the Bible taught the equality of the sexes in every respect. She quoted Scripture with good effect, but had to resort at times to dubious exegesis to neutralize the offensive texts most often cited to demonstrate female subordination.[74] Ernestine Rose, taking issue with Brown, contended that it was best not to appeal to the Bible, since it could equally well be used against the claims of women as in their behalf. Lucretia Mott agreed, urging women to rely on the self-evident truths of nature that established the equality of women and required no external authority.[75] The Tenth National Woman's Rights Convention (1860) adopted resolutions that whatever any book may teach, equal natural rights for all persons are not invalidated. Stanton, Rose, Anthony, and others observed, also in 1860, that while "the general principles of the Bible are in favor of the most enlarged freedom and equality of the race, isolated texts have been used to block the wheels of progress in all periods."[76]

Elizabeth Cady Stanton and others produced *The Woman's Bible*, in two parts, which presented a feminist critique of Scripture.[77] The result showed that some passages were indeed oppressive (for instance, Gen. 2–3), while other parts of the Bible (such as Gen. 1) established the equality of the sexes. Stanton concluded that one should use the Bible like any other book, "accepting the good and rejecting the evil it teaches."[78] *The Woman's Bible* was a scandal to most women in the movement. Stanton's own Suffrage Association, but not Susan B. Anthony and others, repudiated it out of fear that it would damage their efforts beyond repair. After Stanton's anti-clericalism ceased to be an issue, the biblical issue tended to fade, and the arguments shifted to other concerns. By the 20th century, more enlightened views of scriptural authority became prevalent in many quarters, so that the earlier literalist dogmatism had lost some of its punch.

While the struggle for the vote was central, it was not the only plank in the platform of the women crusaders. Especially in the liberal wing led by Stanton and Anthony, a thoroughgoing critique of the oppression of women in every sphere of life animated the movement.[79] Elizabeth Oakes Smith, at the 1852 Syracuse National Convention, asked rhetorically, "Do we fully understand that we aim at nothing less than an entire subversion of the present order of society, a dissolution of the whole existing social compact?"[80]

In particular, marriage was attacked as an institution riddled with inequities by which the wife was without rights regarding her own person, her property, and her children.[81] Susan B. Anthony said in 1860 that "nearly all the wrongs of which we complain grow out of the inequality, the injustice of the marriage laws, that rob the wife of the right to herself and her children—that make her the slave of the man she marries."[82] The reformers demanded that women should be equal partners in marriage, not submerged in the person of their husbands, and that marriage and property laws should reflect that equality in every respect. Moreover, divorce should be available where no true union in love exists. (Conservatives like the Rev. Antoinette Blackwell Brown fought this proposal.)

Other complaints followed. Women were denied education, were limited to the most menial pursuits outside the home, and were paid a mere pittance in comparison to men. All the professions should be open to either sex. Women should be allowed to develop their talents in every realm and participate in business and public life for their own self-fulfillment and the benefit of society. In short, men and women should be social and political equals: given the same esteem, offered the same privileges, judged by the same moral code, treated the same before the law, and in every sphere provided the same opportunities and rewards.[83]

Toward the end of the 19th century and into the 20th, the movement generally became more conservative and respectable, with a more single-minded focus on suffrage. In 1920 the Nineteenth Amendment, giving women the vote, was ratified. Now lacking a unifying theme, a number of reform efforts continued under a wide variety of separate banners.[84] In 1923 an Equal Rights Amendment proposed by Quaker Alice Paul of the National Women's Party was introduced into Congress. Most women's organizations opposed it because it would wipe out labor laws designed to protect female workers from abuse. The issue of protective legislation for women persisted as a point of controversy.[85] Not until the 1960s did a new feminist movement arise to pursue equality for women with a militancy that matched the fervor of earlier efforts.[86] While many gains have been made on a variety of fronts, the Equal Rights Amendment is still not law. The drive for sexual equality has come a long way since the days of Elizabeth Cady Stanton and Susan B. Anthony, but the revolution they undertook is far from finished.

The Assault on Equality: Social Darwinism and *Laissez-Faire*

The examination above of the slavery controversy and the women's rights movements has revealed a denial of social and political equality related to race and sex. The exaltation of liberty at the expense of equality (to be analyzed in this section) involves a more direct focus on individuals and classes of whatever race or sex. Those at the bottom of the economic order are allegedly there because of their failure and lack of merit; the successful have earned their status by making good use of their superior abilities. This way of viewing society was based on supposed facts of nature that "determine" how the world works. It involved the proposition that liberty and equality are in necessary and everlasting opposition to each other, so that one must choose between them. This intellectual vision claimed the authority of science as well as of political economy and philosophy. The result was that the 18th-century notion of human equality rooted in nature, guaranteeing to all people certain inalienable rights, was rejected in favor of an ideology based on inequality.

The Origin Of Species by Charles Darwin was published in 1859. The well-known thesis of this monumental work is that present-day species have evolved gradually over long periods of time by a process of "natural selection" involving a struggle for existence and the "survival of the fittest." Those organisms best suited to the environment live to perpetuate their kind, while the nonadapted perish. The variations thus introduced slowly but surely lead to all the forms of life that now inhabit the earth. Human beings, as part of this evolutionary scheme, spring from nonhuman ancestors that can be ultimately traced back to primitive types from which all living creatures have evolved. In Darwin's words, "man is descended from a hairy, tailed quadruped, probably arboreal in its habits." In a relatively short time this theory about the evolution of life in nature became for many the clue to the past and future of human society, as well as to its present functioning.

Darwinism was introduced into an America that was undergoing rapid and profound changes: the growth of cities, the rapid increase of population swelled partly by mass immigration, the expansion of industry, the coming of big business and trusts, increasing material wealth, the rise of huge personal fortunes, and so on. One result was economic inequalities on a scale the nation had never seen before. Before 1870, wealth, status, and power had been spread widely. For example, in 1840 not twenty millionaires lived in the whole country, but by 1910 probably that many sat in the Senate. In 1891 Thomas Shearman estimated that 120 men in the country each had a fortune greater than ten million dollars. The Census Bureau in 1893 suggested that 9 percent of the families owned 71 percent of the wealth of the country.[87] In 1906 Werner Sombart, a German sociologist, made a startling claim: "It may be said indisputably that the absolute contrasts between poor and rich are nowhere in the world anything like as great as they are in the United States."[88]

The late 19th century was also a time of widespread theories of racial and national superiority.[89] Most pervasive, of course, was the assumption that the colored races, especially blacks, were inferior to white. White native-born Protestants were fearful of the consequences for American democracy resulting from the influx of multitudes of immigrants from southern and eastern Europe and Asia, whose beliefs and values clearly did not measure up to theirs. Xenophobia was rampant.[90] Studies in eugenics emphasized the importance of heredity in determining racial and national character.[91] The upper classes were naturally thought to be the genetically "fit" and the lower classes the "unfit" in the social struggle. Numerous writers exalted the cultural superiority of the Anglo-Saxon and Teutonic races and confidently asserted that future progress depended on their continuing ascendancy.[92] In an era of expansionism and imperialism, it was taken for granted that the superior should govern the inferior.

Social thought found, in the biological theories of Darwin, a basis on which the inequalities that were both real and fanciful could be explained and justified. Social Darwinism saw a process of "natural selection" occurring in society as well as in nature, a "struggle for existence" among individuals, classes, nations, and races in which the "fittest" survive and prosper while the "unfit" fall behind. Poverty was justified as the judgment of the law of life on those who fail the competitive test. The rich, who have succeeded in the social struggle, reap the deserved benefits of their superior abilities and efforts. To interfere with these outcomes would be futile. Progress would be thwarted by any such attempts to violate the fundamental laws of the natural order. And inequalities are an inevitable fact of life, the necessary accompaniment of the advance of civilization toward higher stages of material and moral existence.[93] As mediated through Herbert Spencer of England and his American followers, these ideas made a powerful impact on America. It is no wonder that business tycoons such as Chauncey Depew, James J. Hill, John D. Rockefeller, and Andrew Carnegie found in them a philosophy congenial to their achievements and outlook on life.[94]

The most prominent advocate of Social Darwinism in America was William Graham Sumner. He was a student of theology in his youth and at one time rector of the Episcopal Church in Morristown, New Jersey. When he was a professor at Yale, he propounded a body of doctrines whose major premises he had derived from Herbert Spencer. With Malthus, Darwin, and Spencer in the background, Sumner argued that the clue to human society is found in the struggle for existence in the context of the "man-land ratio." When people are few and land is abundant, equality and democracy may thrive; but when soil is in short supply, conflict ensues and aristocracy prevails. Competition for resources and rewards must not be interfered with, since it is the law of life by which the successful are selected out to shape the future. The accumulation and hereditary transfer of capital are the keystones of progress; huge fortunes are the legitimate reward for the introduction of efficiency. The wealthy are the competent who do a necessary work for society, and the poor deserve their status, since they have failed to meet the conditions of success. Nature is a hard task-master, but its judgments in distributing wealth and poverty are accurate and fair.

Sumner's attitude toward equality is clear. "That all men should be alike or equal, by any standard whatsoever, is contrary to all the facts of human nature and all the conditions of human life."[95] Beyond the principle that chances should be equal in all areas of the competitive struggle insofar as state action is relevant, equality has little place in this scheme. Equal chances will rightfully and beneficially produce unequal results in proportion to merit. The yearning for equal outcomes is the product of envy and can be achieved only by robbing A to reward B. Every such effort involves a sacrifice of liberty. Charity and mutual helpfulness in one-to-one relationships are duties, but the attempt of society to legislate equality of results is disastrous. The struggle for survival inevitably generates inequalities as it selects out the fit from the unfit. This process is as universal and as basic as the law of gravitation. The stern but just sorting-out of the competent from the incompetent must be acknowledged as the price of the advance of civilization.[96]

Other conservatives took a similar, although not always as harsh, line. The central point of many was the inevitable conflict between liberty and equality,[97] with liberty receiving clear and total priority. Nicholas Murray Butler argued that the cornerstone of democracy is "natural inequality, its ideal, the selection of the most fit."[98] True democracy requires the development of an elite core of leaders based on intellect and service. Equal opportunity is necessitated by liberty itself and is thus legitimated. But equal liberty leads to inequalities of attainment in accordance with merit and virtue. Liberty is far more precious than equality, he claimed, and in everlasting antagonism with it.

Abbot Lawrence Lowell spoke of the "exploded doctrine of the natural rights of man" and contended that the aim of government is to promote "personal liberty and private right."[99] The flowering of individual enterprise requires freedom from governmental restraint and the confidence that the successful can enjoy the unmolested fruits of their labor. Arthur Twining Hadley observed that few would now subscribe to the broad statement of human equality and natural rights asserted in the Declaration of Independence. He favored liberty, understood as the power, free from state control, to use intelligence to guide conduct. Private property provides a system of incentives and rewards and a means to compensate those whom one harms. The danger in the present-day (1925) industrial democracy is that the masses will attempt to use Congress to redress economic inequalities and enforce a standardized conformity on all.[100] These thinkers frequently expressed a fear of the mob spirit of undisciplined and impulsive masses of people.[101]

The Social Darwinists and the *laissez-faire* enthusiasts, of course, had their opponents. Sociologist Lester Frank Ward, for example, challenged the monistic assumption that one set of laws is descriptive of strictly determined processes found in both nature and society alike. He proposed a dualism between genetic phenomena ruled by blind force (nature) and telic phenomena guided by conscious will and purpose (society). "If nature progresses through the destruction of the weak, man progresses through the protection of the weak."[102] Instead of *laissez-faire* he proposed deliberate state action to ameliorate the ills of society and to protect the poor and defenseless. Confident of the potential of ordinary citizens springing from his own lower-class background, he denied that the rich and powerful were necessarily the fit and the virtuous. Wealth might result from the accident of birth and ruthless schemes, rather than simply from industry or intellect. Between *laissez-faire* and socialism, Ward proposed "sociocracy," a planned society that would allow inequalities based on genuine merit, but that by equalizing opportunities would eliminate artificial inequalities based on "undeserved power, accidental position or wealth, or anti-social cunning."[103]

If Ward represented the middle ground with contrast the libertarians on the right, Edward Bellamy took a position on the egalitarian left. He wrote utopian novels in which he attacked the competitive order based on selfishness. In its place he envisioned a society in which all worked cooperatively in the service of the nation and shared equally in a common fund. Democracy rests on the equality proclaimed in the Declaration of Independence. This ideal will not be fulfilled until all experience an equality of material conditions.[104]

Other currents of thought and action flowed as well. Economists Richard T. Ely and Thorstein Veblen offered alternatives to *laissez-faire* conservatives.[105] Henry George, in *Progress And Poverty* (1879), proposed a "single tax" on land as a means to restore a more equitable distribution of resources that he thought prevailed at the time of the Revolution. Against the determinism of the Social Darwinists, philosophers William James and John Dewey contributed to the rise of pragmatism. This melioristic outlook described an open universe in which creative, problem-solving intelligence would shape the social environment in the interest of a better human future.[106] The Social Gospel movement in American Protestantism argued that the coming of the Kingdom of God on earth—its central theme—required the transformation of social structures and institutions as well as the conversion of the individual. Toward this end churches and clergy supported a variety of humanitarian causes with an egalitarian bent.[107]

In the political arena, Populism and Progressivism proposed governmental reforms on behalf of the average citizen and against the giant trusts, the vested interests, money power, the "machines," and the "bosses."[108] One result was an increase in the direct power of the people through mechanisms such as the initiative, the recall, the referendum, and the popular election of senators. The electorate itself was broadened by the granting of the vote to women in 1920. Yet the increase in political equality was not matched by an increase in economic equality, although the 1912 passage of the Sixteenth Amendment authorizing an income tax did provide at least that potential.[109] Herbert Croly, a Progressivist intellectual, advocated a modest redistribution of wealth through inheritance and progressive income taxes.[110]

By the end of World War I Social Darwinism had spent its force, although *laissez-faire* and libertarian thought with Sumnerian overtones remained strong.

Conclusion

The previous pages have made no attempt to tell the full story of equality in America. Instead, four areas (eras) have been examined to illustrate controversies and arguments in which the concept of equality has been a primary focus of attention. While the emphasis has been on ideas and not movements as such, the historical contexts and institutional settings in which the debates about equality occurred have been suggested. Moreover, the stress has been on ideals rather than on factual achievements The modest aim has been to exhibit the conceptual bases and particular claims that exponents and critics of equality as a norm for human relationships have made in some important parts of American life over the last two centuries. Many ideas other than these have been sponsored by individuals and small groups, ideas that lie outside the boundaries that more or less define the main lines of the American tradition. The picture presented here is selective and partial in a variety of ways, but does identify the key themes that have been prominent and persistent.

Some of the dominant features of this history can be summarized. A hundred years ago British commentator James Bryce made observations that have a great deal of validity for the century preceding and the one to follow. Noting that America is known worldwide as "preeminently the land of equality," he made some helpful distinctions. The equality that prevails *does not* refer to material conditions, education, intelligence, class, or to any kind of particular achievements. Here gradations and differences of considerable import are to be found; great fortunes have arisen introducing inequalities of wealth never seen before. Equality does pertain to two other areas, however. (a) Legal equality is present. By this is meant equal possession of civil rights, equality before the law, the right to vote and hold office, etc. (b) Equality of estimation is real, for in America no order of established rank, privilege, or preference is recognized. At bottom every citizen thinks of her/himself as being the same and as good as any other, despite differences of attainment.[111] If we recognize that Bryce is most accurate when the reference is to white European males, he is not far from describing something close to the center of the normative American tradition.

To approach the matter differently, equality in America has been understood within a framework of individualism. Individuals are the primary unit of society and the focal point of the assignment of rights, privileges, duties, opportunities, and rewards. All are declared to be equal as persons and as citizens. Liberty and equality have been primary values. But when individualism is dominant, it follows naturally that liberty will be given priority. In this context equality tends to be subordinated to, or at least interpreted within, an individualistic libertarianism. The result is that while equality has, in some respects, an independent and separate standing, much in the American tradition is explained if we recognize that the core value has been the equal *liberty* of all individuals to participate in their governance and to exercise their abilities in the pursuit of happiness.

To be more precise, equality in America seems primarily to mean sameness of status among individuals insofar as they are contracting or at least constitutive members of society. This yields the idea of equality of citizenship or political equality, which is characteristic of American democracy. This political equality is bound up with and completed by the ideal of equal liberty for all to achieve what they can in every sphere of life—economic, political, and cultural. The social order, then, is composed of free and equal individuals who can be governed only by their consent and who can make of themselves whatever their abilities and efforts allow in fair competition with others. This fits well with a capitalistic conception of the economy.

No inherited status or privilege carries automatic authority or validity. Careers are to be open to talent. Equality of opportunity is the norm in that no formal or legal or intrinsic barriers should impede advancement. Theoretically, success depends on what one does and can do, not on roles and rules determined by birth. But equality does not imply that all have the same ability or potential. Since human beings differ in every specific category that one can name, inequalities of wealth and status will doubtless abound. But persons are equal as persons, having the same God-given natural rights, and equal as citizens, having the same set of socially guaranteed liberties. As such they are to think of themselves as equal to others, not in native ability or attainment, but equal as a human being and as a social and political agent. In these respects everyone is on equal footing—the same as and as good as any other.

Yet even this is to make the paradigm clearer and purer than it actually was. Nowhere is the American creed officially laid out in such detailed precision. The preceding paragraph is a kind of abstracted ideal essence, imaginatively created from the multitude of often-conflicting beliefs, values, and social philosophies expressed over the last two centuries. Vague yearnings, unspoken impulses, and conflicting sentiments in the minds of ordinary citizens have existed alongside the consciously articulated philosophies of public voices. Minority voices have existed outside this consensus in every era. Yet if one persists in seeking for the heart of the main line tradition, the notion of a democratic republic of citizens with equal rights and privileges and with equal liberty to make of their abilities and opportunities whatever they can is not far from the mark.

Recent decades have witnessed new drives for equality. As a result a group of "neo-conservatives" has defined as a part of its agenda the criticism of the "new egalitarianism." They fear that equality has replaced liberty as the chief value.[112] Since the issues they raised are in the center of contemporary debates, they will be receive considerable attention in subsequent chapters. In particular, two complex and controversial matters should be noted: (a) the question of individual equality versus group equality and (b) equality of opportunity versus equality of outcome.

Equality is a subtle and complex idea, as this book will amply illustrate. Its concrete meanings and its presumed range of applicability depend on the cultural consciousness that prevails at a given time. Hence, signers of the Declaration of Independence with its proclamation of human equality held slaves, and not always with qualms of conscience or a sense of contradiction. Even white Anglo-Saxon women were denied the vote until 1920 by males who swore by their revolutionary faith. If there is a trend over the whole span of time from 1776 to 1986, it is that the circle of those held to be equal in ways that matter politically and socially has been greatly enlarged. Hence, today blacks and women are regarded as equal by law in terms of certain basic rights, freedoms, and opportunities that were unavailable to them in 1820. In many Protestant denominations women are increasingly accepted as equals in terms of ordination and other leadership roles. Denial of ordination in the more "catholic" churches, such as Roman Catholicism and Eastern Orthodoxy, is still a matter of official doctrine. Ordination for women did not become a legal possibility in the Episcopal Church in this country until 1977.

Moreover, in those spheres in which equality is officially normative—that is, the equal liberty of persons and citizens and equality before the law—progress has been made in making professed principles effective in policy and fact. Equality in the area of civil rights, in politics, and in the economic sphere is more real for blacks and women than ever before in our history. But the actual for many Americans still falls short of the professed ideal.

Also, the way in which equality functions normatively and functionally in some domains does not measure up to what full justice requires—or so this book will maintain. Economic inequalities, for instance, are greater than the highest ideals mandate. (This will be a major focus of attention in the chapters that follow.) A primary thesis is that justice requires as the highest priority of the moment societal moves aimed at (a) obliterating poverty as a fact of life for any Americans and (b) decreasing the inequalities of wealth and income that now separate the richest from the poorest segments of society.

The justification of these proposals will require (a) seeing equality as fully co-equal with liberty in the concept of justice and (b) setting liberty and equality within a conception of society in which individualism is balanced by communitarianism. The social order has organic features; that is, individuals are interdependent in ways that have not been recognized in the main line of the American tradition. New conceptions and new realizations of economic equality are essential to the fulfillment of the promise that this new nation "conceived in liberty and dedicated to the proposition that all . . . are created equal" offered to the world. It is a magnificent vision. Its finest hour, however, is not in the past, but will occur in the day when liberty and equality are made real in some constellation of justice—though rich with internal tensions—in which the pursuit of happiness for all has the best chance of yielding complex satisfactions of joy not yet envisioned.

The chapter to follow will outline an ideal model of society in which liberty and equality are appropriately balanced within a more organic conception of society.

Notes

1. Robert N. Bellah, Richard Madsen, William M. Sullivan, Ann Swidler, and Steven M. Tipton, *Habits of the Heart: Individualism and Commitment in American Life*, pp. 142–63.
2. See, for example, Alexandre Koyré, *From the Closed World to the Infinite Universe*.
3. Ibid. The literature on the transformation that modern science wrought is immense. For a brief discussion and reference to some of the literature, see Kenneth Cauthen, *Science, Secularization and God*, pp. 13–31.
4. A. O. Lovejoy, *The Great Chain of Being*. See also J. R. Pole, *The Pursuit of Equality in America*, pp. 3–12.
5. Quoted in Perry Miller, "Equality in the American Setting," *Aspects of Human Equality*, ed. Lyman Bryson, p. 239.
6. See Ernst Troeltsch, *The Social Teachings of the Christian Churches*, Vol. 1, pp. 150–54; Vol. 2, pp. 620–21.
7. Miller, "Equality in the American Setting," p. 241.
8. Adam Smith, *The Wealth of Nations* (1776).
9. Quoted in Pole, *Pursuit of Equality*, p. 49.
10. Ibid.
11. It appears that Jefferson had originally written that these ideas are "sacred and undeniable" and that the change to "self-evident" was suggested by Benjamin Franklin. See ibid., pp. 51–52, note 83.
12. For an exposition of the meaning of the Declaration, see A. J. Beitzinger, *A History of American Political Thought*, pp. 157–69.

13. An older example of this is Vernon Parrington, *Main Currents in American Thought,* Vol. 1. See also T. V. Smith, *The American Philosophy of Equality.* Smith says, "It is no accident, then, that those who incited and led the rebellion against King George were deists or deistically inclined persons who had first lead a quieter revolt against the Calvinistic God" (p. 17).

14. See Alan Heimert, *Religion and the American Mind.*

15. Ibid., pp. 16–17.

16. Ibid., p. viii. For a contrary view, see Pole, *Pursuit of Equality,* p. 68.

17. See Perry Miller, "Equality in the American Setting," pp. 246–50. Miller explains how the understanding of human depravity held by American Calvinists was itself capable of producing resistance to tyrannical power. Granted, humanity in its fallen condition can no longer enjoy the freedom and equality of Eden. In their fallen state the masses must be controlled by coercive power lest sinful lusts produce total havoc. Yet the governing authorities ordained of God who exercise restraining force against the unruly passions of the degenerate are themselves not free from corruption. Pride, greed, and the lust for power and glory persist stubbornly in the life even of the redeemed. The remedy for sin, then, can itself become the occasion of new outbursts of oppression that offend the natural equality of the governed. Hence, excesses of governmental power must be resisted by the people whose rights and well being are to be served. When confronted with the growing pressure of British tyranny, the Calvinist preachers needed only to work out the implications of their theology for the situation at hand. They found in their own religious heritage, which assumed the depravity of humanity, a basis for supporting the Revolution.

18. William G. McLoughlin, *New England Dissent, 1630–1833,* Vol. 1, pp. 336–38.

19. Alan Heimert and Perry Miller, *The Great Awakening,* pp. xxiii–xxiv, xliii–lxi; and Heimert, *Religion and the American Mind,* pp. 59–94.

20. Heimert, *Religion and the American Mind,* pp. 510–52.

21. Miller, "Equality in the American Setting," pp. 246–49.

22. Heimert, *Religion and the American Mind,* pp. 307–8.

23. Heimert and Miller, *The Great Awakening,* p. lxi.

24. Heimert, *Religion and the American Mind,* pp. 514–18.

25. For a brief account, see Martin Marty, *Religion, Awakening, Revolution.*

26. See Pole, *Pursuit of Equality,* pp. 59–111; and Marty, ibid., pp. 155–70. McLoughlin tells in great detail (in two large volumes) the story of the Baptist fight in New England for religious freedom. See his *New England Dissent.*

27. Quoted in Pole, *Pursuit of Equality,* p. 26.

28. Alexis de Tocqueville, *Democracy in America, 1835–1840,* p. 9.

29. See Smith, *American Philosophy,* pp. 1–18.

30. Chilton Williamson, *American Suffrage: From Property to Democracy, 1760–1860,* pp. 260–80.

31. Sidney Verba and Gary R. Orren, *Equality in America,* pp. 29–32.

32. Pole, *Pursuit of Equality,* pp. 130–40.

33. Ibid., pp. 126–30. In *The Rights of Man To Property* (1829), Skidmore proposed that all existing property be redistributed by the state and that inheritance of property be prohibited. At death all ones property reverts to the state. Slaves should be freed and given property.

34. Quoted in Verba and Orren, *Equality in America,* p. 31.

35. Pole, *Pursuit of Equality,* p. ix.

36. Most of the best ones can be found in E. N. Elliot, ed., *Cotton Is King and Pro-slavery Arguments*.
37. Henry Alonzo Myers, *Are Men Equal?*, p. 70.
1945), p. 70.
38. For a detailed presentation of the economic arguments, see Arthur Young Lloyd, *The Slavery Controversy, 1831–1860*, pp. 194–223.
39. Among many that might be cited are Josiah Priest, *Bible Defense of Slavery* (Glascow, Ky., 1852); and Fred Ross, *Slavery Ordained of God* (Philadelphia: J. B. Lippincott, 1857). For reference to numerous others, see Lloyd, *Slavery Controversy*, pp. 162–93.
40. Lloyd, *Slavery Controversy*, pp. 168–69.
41. Ibid., pp. 224–63.
42. See Smith, *American Philosophy*, pp. 57–71.
43. Ibid., pp. 69–79.
44. Fitzhugh's thought is found in three books: *Slavery Justified, Sociology for the South,* and *Cannibals All.*
45. Pole, *Pursuit of Equality*, pp. 148–213; Henry A. Myers, *Are Men Equal?*, pp. 68–97; and Beitzinger, *American Political Thought*, pp. 364–75.
46. Pole, *Pursuit of Equality*, pp. 166–68.
47. Ibid., pp. 177–292. It is no accident that a large portion of Pole's book on equality in America deals with the history of inequality as related to race.
48. Mari Jo and Paul Buhle, eds., *The Concise History of Woman Suffrage*, p. 123. This book contains selections from the classic documentary source of the suffrage movement edited by Elizabeth Cady Stanton, Susan B. Anthony, Matilda Joslyn Gage, and Ida Husted Harper, *History of Woman Suffrage*, 6 Vols., [1881–1922] (New York: Arno Press, 1969).
49. Brief histories of the women's movement can be found in Pole, *Pursuit of Equality*, pp. 293–324; Judith Hole and Ellen Levine, *Rebirth of Feminism*, pp. 1–14; and Buhle and Buhle, *Woman Suffrage*, pp. 1–44. See also June Sochen, *Herstory: A Woman's View of American History;* and Eleanor Flexner, *Century of Struggle: The Woman's Rights Movement in the United States.*
50. Buhle and Buhle, *Woman Suffrage*, pp. 78–87.
51. Ibid., pp. 18–23, 247, 257–58. With the help of Train's money, Susan B. Anthony and Elizabeth Cady Stanton published *"The Revolution,"* a militant feminist weekly devoted to the cause of sexual equality.
52. Ibid., p. 238. See also William L. O'Neil, *Everyone Was Brave*, pp. 14–21.
53. Aileen Kraditor, *Ideas of the Woman Suffrage Movement, 1890–1920*, p. 200. See pp. 163–218 for full documentation.
54. Quoted words were from a speech by Anna Howard Shaw to the National American Woman Suffrage Association in 1903 in New Orleans. Ibid., p. 70.
55. Ibid., pp. 69–70.
56. Ibid., pp. 123–62.
57. See ibid., p. 20, where Stanton is quoted as saying in 1869 that "the worst enemies of Woman's Suffrage will ever be the laboring classes of men."
58. Pole, *Pursuit of Equality*, p. 308.
59. O'Neil, *Everyone Was Brave*, pp. 74–75.
60. Smith, *American Philosophy*, pp. 85–129.
61. Quoted in Hole and Levine, *Rebirth of Feminism*, p. 3.
62. Buhle and Buhle, *Woman Suffrage*, pp. 100, 126.
63. Kraditor, *Woman Suffrage Movement*, pp. 14–42.
64. Women had no difficulty in holding up this notion to ridicule by pointing to political conventions and other events at which men behaved riotously,

expressing emotions far in excess of what characterized public female behavior. See ibid., pp. 108–9.

65. Ibid., p. 23.
66. Ibid., p. 103.
67. Buhle and Buhle, *Woman Suffrage*, pp. 91–98.
68. Pole, *Pursuit of Equality*, pp. 174–75, 301–5.
69. Smith, *American Philosophy*, pp. 92–93, note 1. Smith quotes a woman opponent of the women reformers who states the case well. She admits that before God and in terms of salvation, men and women are equal. But political inequality has been established by divine ordinance, since God said to Eve that man would rule over her (Gen. 3:16).
70. Hole and Levine, *Rebirth of Feminism*, p. 8.
71. Kraditor, *Woman Suffrage Movement*, p. 111.
72. Ibid., pp. 43–74.
73. Ibid., pp. 75–95.
74. Buhle and Buhle, *Woman Suffrage*, pp. 130–31.
75. Ibid., p. 135. Unfortunately for this position, however, the list of self-evident truths or, indeed, whether there are such in the political and social realm, is as controversial and subject to as much heated dispute as is the question of what the Bible *really* teaches. While it is apparent to us that the women had the better case on the issues, the dispute concerned just what it was that Scripture or nature did in fact disclose about the will and intention of God with respect to the equality of the sexes.
76. Ibid., pp. 98–103, exp. 100.
77. *The Woman's Bible* (New York: European Publishing Co., 1895, 1898), 2 Parts.
78. Hole and Levine, *Rebirth of Feminism*, pp. 12–13.
79. In 1869 a split occurred with the more liberal western New York group led by Stanton and Anthony forming the National Woman's Suffrage Association (NWSA). The Boston conservatives headed by Lucy Stone and Julia Ward Howe organized as the American Woman's Suffrage Association (AWSA). The liberals continued to follow an inclusive agenda embracing a whole range of sexual inequalities. Stanton campaigned for "free divorce" and became more militant in her attack on the Bible and the churches. In addition, Anthony and Stanton published their journal *The Revolution*, in which they promoted their own more inclusive and militant agenda. The AWSA concentrated on getting the vote. The two groups joined in 1890 to form the National American Woman's Suffrage Association (NAWSA).
80. Buhle and Buhle, *Woman Suffrage*, pp. 120–21.
81. Ibid., pp. 94–97, 170–89.
82. Ibid., p. 189.
83. O'Neil, *Everyone Was Brave*, pp. 3–48.
84. Sochen, *Herstory*, pp. 292–95; O'Neil, *Everyone Was Brave*, pp. 264–359.
85. Hole and Levine, *Rebirth of Feminism*, pp. 54–77.
86. See Sochen, *Herstory*, pp. 285–423, for an account of developments regarding women since World War I. Hole and Levine's *The Rebirth of Feminism* traces the revival of the feminist movement in the 1960s.
87. Richard Hofstadter, *The Age of Reform*, pp. 135–36.
88. Werner Sombart, *Why There Is No Socialism in the United States*, p. 8. Quoted in Herbert McClosky and John Zaller, *The American Ethos*, p. 167.
89. Pole, *The Pursuit of Equality*, pp. 222–45.
90. Hofstadter, *The Age of Reform*, pp. 173–84, 81–88.

91. Richard Hofstadter, *Social Darwinism in American Thought*, pp. 161–67.
92. Ibid., pp. 170–200.
93. Hofstadter gives a full account of this way of thinking in his *Social Darwinism in America*.
94. Ibid., pp. 44–50.
95. William Graham Sumner, *Folkways*, p. 43.
96. William Graham Sumner, *What Social Classes Owe to Each Other*.
97. Myers, *Are Men Equal?*, pp., 98–152.
98. Nicholas Murray Butler, *True and False Democracy*, p. 57.
99. Abbot Lawrence Lowell, *Essays on Government*, pp. 9, 10.
100. Arthur Twining Hadley, *The Conflict Between Liberty and Equality*.
101. See, for example, Butler, *True and False Democracy*, pp. 6–15, 24–25.
102. Quoted in Hofstadter, *Social Darwinism in America*, p. 79.
103. Ibid., p. 83.
104. Edward Bellamy, *Looking Backward, 2000–1887*, and *Equality* (New York: D. Appleton and Co., 1897).
105. Hofstadter, *Social Darwinism in America*, pp. 143–56.
106. Ibid., pp. 123–42.
107. Standard histories of this movement are: Charles Howard Hopkins, *The Rise of the Social Gospel in America, 1865–1915;* and Henry F. May, *Protestant Churches and Industrial America*.
108. Hofstadter, *The Age of Reform*.
109. Verna and Orren, *Equality in America*, pp. 36–41.
110. Herbert Croly, *The Promise of American Life*, pp. 22–23, 381–85.
111. James Bryce, *The American Commonwealth*, Vol. 2, pp. 514–24.
112. See Peter Steinfels, *The Neo-Conservatives*.

CHAPTER / THREE

An Ideal Society: A Freedom-Equality Model

IN THE AMERICAN TRADITION, liberty and equality stand in a double relationship. On the one hand, liberty (freedom) takes priority over equality, although the ideal of equal liberty for all is asserted. On the other hand, equality is an independent value standing alongside liberty. All persons are equal and have certain inalienable rights. The fact that individualism has been the ruling conviction has stood in the way of the full co-equality of equality in comparison to liberty, which is the more deeply held norm. The thesis of this chapter is that the reality of life in America today requires a step beyond the traditional creed in which liberty and equality are held in balance. Moreover, individualism needs to be qualified by the recognition of the interdependence of persons in a social order with organic features.

Process philosophers are persuaded that the metaphysical system they espouse will yield insights fruitful for understanding many, if not all, particular topics.[1] "Applicability," according to Alfred North Whitehead, is a test of the validity of a metaphysical scheme. If what one says about what is ultimately real is true, it follows that this grasp of reality at the fundamental level can be used to illuminate specific and/or limited spheres of the experienceable world. This could be, in part, a circular process since, for Whitehead anyway, the metaphysical quest begins with some immediate experience and then seeks for some generality that is explanatory of the data.[2] Any hypotheses thus derived are tested and continually revised by reference to other bodies of experience until an ensemble of general principles is arrived at possessing the virtue of maximal applicability.[3] If this process has been successful, then no basic principles should be operative in any sphere which have not been discovered, else the metaphysical task is not yet done and it never is.[4]

A test case is provided by the social order. Are the principles of process metaphysics useful in interpreting human society? Can the reality of selves in community acting and interacting in the political, cultural, and economic spheres be illuminated by its generalities? If the claims of process philosophy are taken as a guide, what interpretive clues may be derived from its basic insights that one would expect to find exemplified in the social order? What principles of justice and of the good society are implicit in, or at least compatible with, this outlook? Without trying to be exhaustive, a number of suggestions will be made. The following interpretations assume a knowledge of the fundamentals of process philosophy as found in the thought of Alfred North Whitehead, Charles Hartshorne, and others. Stated here are plausible implications for social philosophy of this way of viewing things. Within limits, alternative social philosophies and ethical principles could doubtless be constructed with equal or better grounding in process metaphysics. The only assertion made is that the interpretations offered do not violate those principles, even if they are not necessarily entailed by them.

1. Persons are neither completely independent, autonomous individuals nor merely parts of a unitary organism. Reality contains real individuals, but never as separate, discontinuous entities, but always in mutually determining relations to other persons surrounding them.[5] Individuals are both free agents acting on their own and interdependent members of communities whose actions are constrained by other agents and by the whole society acting as one (through enforced laws, for example). Human societies, then, have organic features while being composed of identifiable individuals who have their own distinctive reality and character.[6]

2. A fundamental characteristic of both individuals and of human societies is that they are constituted by an aim at the good. Whitehead maintained that all life is driven by a threefold urge: "to live, ... to live well, ... and to live better."[7] Hence, the function of reason is to guide this urge toward its fulfillment. If individuals are real and if society has an organic unity and character of its own as something more than the sum of its members, then attention must be given both to the good of each person as a free agent and to the common good that embraces all in their togetherness. Individuals have a good of their own, and they have a shared good with others. Both dimensions are essential and must be taken into account.

3. Three elements enter into theories of the ideal (just and good) society: (a) *The aim at maximizing the good of individuals and of communities.*

(b) *Freedom.* If individuals are real and have a good of their own, they must have sufficient freedom from social restraint to realize their just aims. Moreover, freedom is required in order for each person to maximize the contribution he or she can make to the creation of a communal good to be enjoyed by all. Freedom, then, is not only a right of individuals; it is also a necessity for society as a means to achieve and increase the common good. Individuals are (in part) self-determining agents who seek self-realization. Hence, the rules of society should grant self-determination as extensive as is consistent with a like freedom for other individuals and with the requirements of the common good. Society must be organized in a way to prohibit the exercise of individual freedom in ways that are harmful to other individuals or that damage the common good. But it must also be ordered so as to maximize the potential of each person to contribute creatively to the good of the whole community. The ideal is that each should realize her or his own good in a harmony with others in a cooperative effort to maximize the welfare of all in relationships involving mutuality and reciprocity.

(c) *Equality.* All experiencing subjects have intrinsic value commensurate with their capacity for depth (complexity, intensity, and richness) and breadth (range of inclusiveness) of experiencing. Thus, mosquitos have intrinsic value less than human beings but equal to that of other mosquitos. It follows that all persons as persons have intrinsic value equal to that of any other person. As social beings, individuals should have both equal liberty with others to pursue and enjoy their own self-chosen and merited good within the bounds of justice and also an equal claim with others to share in the common good. Equality is in a special sense a communal norm that arises only in settings in which individuals are bound together by common purposes and share a common destiny in the context of mutually dependent relationships.[8]

The principle of a just and good society, then, can be stated as follows: maximize individual and communal good, maximize individual freedom, and maximize the common equality of all within the constraints each aim places on the others.[9]

Models of Ideal Societies

Three models of an ideal society will be elaborated in this section. The first will be organized around the primary value of individual freedom and the quest for a private good—the Individualist-freedom Model. The second will be organized around the primary value of equality and the quest for a common good to be shared equally—the Communal-equality Model. The third will be framed as a synthesis of the first two in which freedom and equality are balanced and in which attention is given to both individual and communal good—the Individualist-freedom/Communal-equality Model.

The models will be created in two stages. The first stage will state the fundamental underlying principles in their more or less absolute, unqualified form. A refinement of the principles will follow, with the addition of other compatible ideas that do not necessarily inhere in the primordial motifs themselves.

The two models are created initially by combining four different principles,[10] which can be outlined as follows:

Type 1 The Freedom Model	Type 2 The Equality Model
(1) FREEDOM PRINCIPLE Maximum liberty for all. (libertarianism)	(1) EQUALITY PRINCIPLE Maximum equality for all. (egalitarianism)
(2) SOCIOLOGICAL PRINCIPLE Individuals are the unit.[11] The group is the sum total of individuals. (social nominalism)[12]	(2) SOCIOLOGICAL PRINCIPLE The group is the unit. Individuals are organic parts of the whole. (social realism)
(3) VALUE PRINCIPLE The good life is the pursuit and enjoyment of individual good. (individualism)	(3) VALUE PRINCIPLE The good life is the creation and sharing of a common good. (communalism)
(4) POLITY PRINCIPLE Democratic rule. (*Equal* liberty)	(4) POLITY PRINCIPLE Democratic rule. (Equal *liberty*)

The sociological and value principles are independent of the freedom and equality principles.[13] In the modern world, however, both freedom and equality are prominent, and it is the peculiar combination of the first three principles in each case that produces the ideals to be elaborated. Freedom has a natural affinity with social nominalism and individualism. Equality, likewise, fits well with social realism and communalism, although the connection is not a logically necessary or exclusive one. The models developed here will use the other principle in each case as a subordinate ideal. To elaborate, the Freedom Model will use equality as a secondary principle, while the Equality Model will employ freedom in the same fashion. So doing puts each model in a better light than would otherwise be the case.

A cluster of ideas, then, forms the heart of each model. The fundamental motif of Type 1 is freedom. Stated in its unqualified form, the fundamental ideal is: unlimited freedom for all. Freedom refers to the range of unrestricted activity available to a person, the arena in which no coercion or other external restraint exists. But a kind of internal pragmatic logic leads to a modification of this original premise. The uncoordinated quest of all for a self-chosen good would lead at best to a nest of inconveniences or at worst to a "war of all with all" (Hobbes). What one conceives of as happening depends in part on how selfish or egocentric and/or aggressive and violent one believes human beings to be in their natural state. In any case, the pursuit of self-interest (meaning here what the self is interested in) can be carried on best within a framework that allows equal freedom to all and, hence, to the channeling of individual actions within boundaries that do not intrude upon the others' rights to the same pursuits. Mutual respect for and the equal protection of equal rights are to everybody's advantage.

Type 2 in its unqualified form is: complete equality for all. Equality refers to what is or counts the same in one person as in another, whether this pertains to the existence or allocation of status, power, authority, rights, privileges, and opportunities, etc., or to the distribution of income, goods, services, and other socially provided benefits. But in the principle and fact of equality, too, an internal pragmatic logic is at work. While everyone may be equal as persons or regarded as so in some respects, in many, or all, other respects people are unequal. Some can do things others cannot or do some things better than others. People differ in merit and have different needs. Thus, in organized human societies as well as in, to use the traditional phrase, "the state of nature," all sorts of inequalities arise among persons who in some respects may be actually equal or who, according "to the law of nature" should be so regarded. Hence, the pure Equality Model requires a modified ideal in which certain types of equalities are regarded as legitimate and protected, while, in other respects, inequalities are permitted.[14] The affirmation of equal freedom as citizens and equal opportunity to succeed in all phases of society are common to the liberal, democratic philosophies of recent centuries (prominent in Type l). The most idealistic form (emerging only in Type 2) prescribes that persons should contribute according to their abilities and receive according to their needs. This functional recognition of inequality is necessary to maximize common good and to allow equal consideration to all persons as producers and consumers of the common good.[15]

When the polity principle is added, the result—combining pragmatic and idealistic considerations—qualifies the primordial impulse of each type by taking into account the primary value of the other type. In Type 1, equality is added to freedom to produce the ideal of equal freedom for all to seek a private good. The fundamental idea of Type 2 is equality, which when combined with freedom, yields the idea of equality of liberty. This is a consequence both of following out the logic of "equality in all respects for all" and of taking individual freedom into account as an independent and worthy value. Hence, Type 1 assumes that each free person has equal freedom with other persons to seek a private good. Type 2 assumes that equal persons have equal freedom, not to seek a private good but to contribute to and receive from the community as an equal. In other words, both assume that all persons are, in the meanings assigned by each, equally free.[17]

All this leads to the ideal of democracy or rule of the people. In principle this means that all may participate equally in choosing the rules by which they will be governed, or at least in selecting the people who will govern them. In the state and in many other organizations, this means majority or representative rule. In Type 1, this guards against the rule of the strong, as would likely occur if freedom were not restricted constitutionally by distributing power equally (in principle) among all citizens. Moreover, constitutional guarantees of certain rights are necessary to guard against the tyranny of a democratic majority. In Type 2 the ideal of equal freedom guards as well against the rule of the (alleged) "best" or some elite that by virtue of tradition, theory, or simply by taking power presumes to define the common good and to decide how it is to be produced and distributed.[18] Despite these modifications, the threat of the tyranny of the strong is still the corrosive factor in the Freedom Model. Likewise, the threat of the tyranny of "the best" or the elite is the bane of the equality model.[19] Without these qualification of freedom with equality and of equality with freedom, both types would be intolerable.

Underlying the ideal of equal freedom in both types as defined here is a notion of rights that attach to individuals. Each person is a moral personality with an inalienable status and worth (whether inherent or conferred by some transcendent power, for instance, God).[20] Every individual counts and counts equally in the ideal form of both types, since each has rights that must not be violated. Obviously, the Freedom Model tends toward excesses of individualism in which some (who are more gifted, ruthless, or ambitious, or who work harder or whatever) acquire power over others so that equal freedom is threatened. In the Equality Model, individual rights may be smothered for the sake of making all equal or in quest of maximizing the common good. In the latter case the result may be that the freedom of some or of all is threatened by the ruling elite, or even by democratic processes, thus restricting liberty for the sake of the good of the whole.[21] The ideas of individual worth and of equal freedom guard against these excesses and distinguish modern democratic versions of Types 1 and 2 from their counterparts in former times.[22]

The Freedom Model leads to a concept of equal opportunity, while the Equality Model produces the notion of equality of outcomes, as well as of opportunities. At least this is the case initially and in principle. But in the end, neither goal is possible or desirable, the former being more impossible and the latter being more undesirable. Hence, in practice one has to settle for something less than what was originally posited. The question of appropriate definition becomes crucial.

Type 1 is more committed to freedom of opportunity than to equality of opportunity. As a consequence, it is reluctant to go beyond the notion that careers should be open to talent. No irrelevant criteria should be used to keep the most qualified persons from actualizing legal and moral opportunities to secure jobs, income, power, status, authority, respect, and other desirable goods and positions. Meritocracy is the norm. Some are better endowed genetically with gifts and talents, however, and some have the benefit of a head start because of family or class background. Correcting differences in biological endowment is impossible for the current generation. Overcoming the social handicaps that give some unequal advantages requires interference with individual freedom, which violate the norms of the Freedom Model.

Type 2, with its priority of commitment to equality, is more devoted to both equality of opportunity and of result than is Type 1. In fact, in its boldest or purest forms, it is willing to restrict individual freedom for the sake of equality for all in both respects. But absolute equality of opportunity would require both the homogenizing of genetic inheritance (the biological component) and the destruction of the family (a major part of the social component). The first is not now possible and would not be desirable were it possible. The second is possible (if everyone agreed) but is not desirable. The norm of equality of result (the same rewards and provisions for all) not only prevents distribution of benefits according to merit, but also prevents distribution according to need.

Moreover, for functional reasons equalizing opportunities and outcomes might mean that everybody had less of everything (material goods, good music, scientific knowledge and technological advance—everything producible by the best human effort and talent). Unless the brightest and best are set free to maximize their talents in the quest of excellence, that is, given unequal opportunity, less total good will be available to share, whether defined quantitatively or qualitatively or shared equally or unequally. Biological and social inequalities, then, may in practice benefit everybody, despite the attraction of the ideal of equality in all respects. Compromise for the sake of the greater good for all seems inevitable.

The commitment to *equal* freedom creates an internal tension within Type 1. It can be argued on liberal grounds that equal opportunity must be real and effective, not just formal, if it is to be of value. Hence, efforts to equalize the opportunities of the socially disadvantaged can be defended within this framework. Likewise, the commitment to equal *freedom* in Type 2 leads to a different kind of internal stress. The emphasis on equality of outcome as well as efforts to make opportunities effectively equal for all may well come into conflict with individual freedom and merit. Each type has to struggle to resolve the tensions that result from its peculiar way of combining freedom and equality, while giving priority in each case to one or the other.

As already indicated, the principles that make up each model are relatively autonomous, though each has a natural consanguinity with the others. Nonetheless, it is possible to combine each with various versions of the other two principles to form visions of ideal societies different from the ones formulated here. The models presented are those most relevant to contemporary discussions. A brief discussion of each will give further definition and contrast.

Type 1: The Freedom Model

One assumption underlying any theory of society has to do with the relationship between individuals and the groups to which they belong. The Freedom Model presupposes a view that can be called social nominalism. In this way of thinking individuals are regarded as independent and autonomous, the units of which society is composed. Organized societies arise by voluntary agreement or covenant, forming a group for the purposes of achieving ends that are mutually desirable but which cannot be had without cooperative efforts. A state may be formed on this basis. So may any number of other smaller organizations that individuals may create to further their mutual aims. Societies, then, are collections of individuals created for mutual benefit by voluntary covenant.

Individuals have rights that others may not morally violate. Central among these rights is freedom to pursue ends chosen by each individual, without interference from others and without limitation except as their exercise may interfere with the rights and liberty of others. A government may be formed to secure these rights and to protect the free exercise of liberty by each member of the contracting state. The state has the exclusive authority to use coercion to enforce its will. Its role is to prevent individuals from using coercion on each other or to defraud others of the rights assigned them by the contract that created the state initially. The state's role is limited mainly to protecting the society from outside enemies and to policing the internal activities of the society to maximize the exercise of individual freedom. The central authority may also build roads, print money, finance public education, and do other things that individuals cannot do for themselves or through voluntary organizations, or at least not as well. The private ownership of property and a capitalistic form of economic organization fit well with this model.

Type 2: The Equality Model

Type 2 presupposes a theory of social realism in which the group is regarded as the unit, while individuals are organically related to each other and to the whole. In the strongest and purest form, this internal connectedness is regarded as a natural fact—the way things are. In a modified and weaker form, the unity in community is not natural and organic but a voluntary, contractual reality. People may decide to regard the whole as the primary reality and value center and to act as if they were one—all for one and one for all.[23] The individual is subordinated to the whole, and individual good is subordinated to the common good. But when combined with the additional notions of individual worth and equal freedom for all, each person has a claim on the whole equal to the others. This sets up limits within which the individual can be sacrificed or ignored for the sake of the common good. A democratic polity is assumed in which the inevitable tensions between individual rights and communal good are resolved (or compromises worked out) in the public arena with the full participation of all.[24]

The state may be regarded as a natural or given entity into which people are born (as into a family)[25] or as a human creation designed to promote the common good and to protect the equal rights of all.[26] The state's role in Type 2 will be more extensive than in Type 1. It will not only protect the whole from outside threats and guard individual rights, but will also promote by collective means the good of the whole. It may own the basic means of production. Likewise, it will provide standards and mechanisms for the distribution of goods and services, according to norms decided upon—equally, or according to need, or some other formula aimed at an equitable sharing of the common good.[27] If the state does not own the means of production outright, it will control and direct the economic processes in accordance with public aims. The central authority may organize, control, or coordinate cultural and social (educational, etc.) activities as well. Church and state would be separate in a democratic pluralistic society, although an established religion would not be incompatible with the logic of more extreme versions of the model.[28]

The two models may now be summarized and developed further. The following are logical or ideal types based on certain assumptions, although different versions are possible and more-or-less equally compatible with the underlying presuppositions.

Type 1 The Freedom Model	Type 2 The Equality Model
Individual freedom as extensive as is compatible with equal rights and a like freedom for others.	Maximal equality compatible with the functional requirements of maximizing the common good or meeting need.
Individual merit is a primary principle of reward.	Individual merit is a subordinate principle of reward.
Presupposes model of autonomous individuals contracting with each other, engaging in voluntary exchanges and cooperative ventures for mutual advantage.	Presupposes model of organic (or contractual) community of interdependent individuals cooperating with each other for the good of the whole in which each shares.
Democratic rule: all participate in the governing of state and society.	Democratic rule: all participate in the governing of state and society.
Honors equality of opportunity (no formal barriers to careers open to talent).	Honors equality of opportunity in effective fact and equality of result as a persistent tendency.
Meaning and reward come from individual achievement based on merit.	Meaning and reward come from participating in community, contributing to it, and receiving from it.
Freedom is shaped by aim at individual good and constrained by the equal rights and freedom of others.	Freedom of the individual is shaped and constrained by good of the whole and equal claims of all.
Freedom is liberty to pursue individual good in ways non-harmful to others.	Freedom is liberty to pursue common good cooperatively, with others.
Minimal state facilitates individual pursuit of private good.	Extensive state facilitates production and distribution of common good.
Emphasizes differences among people.	Emphasizes similarities among people.

An Ideal Society: A Freedom-Equality Model / 73

Success or failure depends primarily on factors internal to individuals.	Success or failure depends primarily on factors external to individuals.
IDEAL SOCIETY IS THE SUM TOTAL OF AUTONOMOUS INDIVIDUALS WITH EQUAL LIBERTY PURSUING SELF-INTEREST THROUGH VOLUNTARY INTERACTION.	IDEAL SOCIETY IS AN ORGANIC COMMUNITY MADE UP OF MEMBERS WHO, IN A COOPERATIVE EFFORT, PRODUCE A COMMON GOOD TO BE SHARED EQUITABLY.

A third ideal type can now be outlined that combines principles from Types 1 and 2 into a synthesis that differs from either but is closer to both than they are to each other.[29]

Type 3: The Freedom-Equality Model

A preliminary word is necessary, before constructing the final model, to clarify the difference in logical status between freedom and equality. Freedom relates to individuals and comes into play if at least one person exists.[30] Equality relates to what is common to individuals and has no relevance until at least two persons are on the scene. A solitary female shipwrecked on an island would have freedom to do as she pleased,[31] for no one else is around (no other human being) to be equal or unequal with. (Of course, if animals were present, she would be under obligation to be kind and to do no unnecessary harm to them.) But if two persons (male or female) were cast up together, the question of equality or inequality arises. In what respects do they share something in common that justifies equality? Freedom is, of course, also a social concept referring to the range of action open to individuals unconstrained by the coercive power of society as a whole.

To put it differently in terms of the value principle, we may distinguish between the creation and enjoyment of individual good and the creation and enjoyment of a common good. Equality is a regulative concept that applies to both. If individuals are to seek and enjoy a private good, then all should be equally free to do so. If a common good is to be created and enjoyed, individuals should participate in the enterprise equally. Or one could say that two value principles pertain: maximizing individual freedom and maximizing total welfare. Again, equality is a regulative principle. Individuals should be equally free, that is, have a range of freedom or set of liberties that is equally extensive with that of others. In the other case, individuals should contribute and share equally in the creation and enjoyment of the total (and common) social well-being.[32] Hence, while freedom and equality are not logically identical in status, they may for all practical purposes be considered simply as two different value principles. In Type 3 they are to be regarded equally.

Type 3:
The Freedom-Equality Model

(1) FREEDOM-EQUALITY PRINCIPLE
Maximum freedom and equality for all in all respects within the constraints each, along with the quest to maximize the good, puts on the other.

(2) SOCIOLOGICAL PRINCIPLE
Individuals are relatively autonomous in some respects and in some settings but organically connected to social units in other respects and in other settings.

(3) VALUE PRINCIPLE
The good life includes both the enjoyment of individual good and of common good.

(4) POLITY PRINCIPLE
Democratic rule. (Equal liberty)

Unrestricted freedom and complete equality for all in all respects are, of course, not possible or desirable. The freedom of one person limits the freedom of another. Freedom for each is in tension with equality for all. Hence, an optimum arrangement must be sought. Freedom and equality are to be maximized within the constraints each puts on the other. Moreover, the quest to increase the happiness (the good) of all may constrain and be constrained by individual freedom and social equality.

The relationship between individuals and societies is complex.[33] Most theories fail because they oversimplify by leaving out important dimensions required by a wholly adequate view. Seen in one way, a person is both an individual and a social being. Suppose Mary says, "I am an American." Mary is thoroughly and wholly an "I"—a discrete individual not confused with any other person. At the same time, she is thoroughly and wholly "an American"—a participant in that community. Within this framework, Mary is not an individual in some respects and an interdependent member of society in other respects. She is in all respects a particular individual and in all respects a participant in that society indicated by the term "American." Individuality is real, but exists always in community.

Seen in another way, individuals are neither discrete, independent units who create societies by contract or association nor parts of

An Ideal Society: A Freedom-Equality Model / 75

wholes with no transcending dimensions. Rather they are relatively autonomous, relatively interdependent selves. Hence, neither social nominalism nor social realism is solely applicable. Society, then, is neither a mere collection of individuals united only by voluntary contract nor an organism whose members are wholly dependent on the whole in which they exist and function. Individuals are fulfilled and whole only when they function harmoniously in a particular role as a member of a society in which they both contribute to and receive from the total community. A person taken out of his or her society and cast suddenly in the midst of a civilization that is totally alien in language, religion, culture, values, economic and technological organization, and so on, would still be a human being, but one whose potential for achievment and satisfaction would be considerably diminished. Such a person would be unable to participate effectively as a part of a larger whole.[34]

Yet the whole truth is even more complex than this. In some cases, social nominalism is more descriptive of the facts than social realism. Sometimes we do act as independent units, as when we decide which candy bar to buy. Even here, however, no candy bars would be available for purchase apart from the economic processes of production and distribution that take place in the society in which the buyer participates. Perhaps suffering is the point at which the solitariness of individual existence is most real. Moreover, we do our own dying; no one else can do that for us. We live, work, suffer, and die in a social context, as a member of various communities. But there is a particularity and discreteness about individual suffering and dying that raises our individuality, even our solitariness, to an acute point. But, even, here most persons interpret pain and death with socially generated convictions. Communal tradition also creates the religious framework within which individuals believe or disbelieve in God, although it may be true, as Whitehead says, that religion "is what the individual does with his own solitariness."[35]

Sometimes we do contract with each other to form groups for specific purposes, as when we form a volunteer fire department. It is for the common good, as well as for our own, that we do so, but we function as individuals who enter voluntarily into a compact to achieve certain ends which cannot be attained without cooperative effort.

Sometimes we are members of groups which are prior (logically and chronologically) to us and to which we are organically related in both biological and social senses, as when we are born into a family. We do not choose to be born; nor are we offered any alternatives with respect to which set of parents will conceive us, not to mention their social and economic status, race, nationality, religion, and so on. Our "destiny" in this sense is a given. The family name is assigned to us at birth, and the values of our parents begin to shape us at once. While we may choose later whether to make these values our own, before we are able to think or choose, patterns of behavior are already being woven onto the genetic constitution we inherited. Recent studies have shown that genetic endowment plays a considerable role in determining certain basic personality traits, even including whether we are likely to be conformist or rebellious. In these ways, we are indeed, as St Paul says, "members one of another." Various denominations and theologians debate whether becoming a church member is more like being born into a family (the organic, communal model) or getting married (the individualistic, contractual model).[36]

What is the state like? As citizens we are both relatively autonomous and highly interdependent. As producers and consumers of goods and services in the economic order, the same duality holds. The social contract theory with its hypothetical notion of a state of nature inhabited by a collection of discrete individuals who then create the state by an agreement may be useful for some analytical purpose. But it distorts historical fact and present reality if taken as a paradigm of the whole truth. We are born into a given state that has a polity, a history, and a set of values specific to itself. Before we are able to think for ourselves we are immersed in its ethos and are absorbed into its very life in organic ways. Yet we are discrete individuals who can, in some measure, choose whether to accept and perpetuate or to rebel against its traditions and values. Hence, freedom and equality must be viewed in three contexts: (a) the realm of existence, experience, and choice as discrete individuals, (b) our participation in organizations created by voluntary contract, and (c) the dimensions of life in which we are organically related to communal units that are logically and historically prior to us.[37]

The good life is neither exclusively the pursuit of individual good nor solely the creation and sharing of a common good. Rather it is both in a complex, multidimensional combination of private and communal enterprises.[38] We need community and the joy of cooperative effort. But we also need room for pursuing individual projects of our own choice—to do and to take pleasure in what we want for ourselves. We are neither isolated selves nor cells of the social organism, but something of both. The fullest, richest life actualizes all the dimensions of selfhood. Yet the private and the communal are not themselves separate. It is for the common good that individuals realize their own private good. Part of individual good is participating in the common good, in contributing to the well-being of others and in receiving assistance from our neighbors and associates. The highest and absolute good occurs which each person considers the good of others equal to her or his own good. The is the meaning of Jesus' injunction that we should love our neighbors as we love ourselves, not as a discipline of self-sacrifice, but as a means toward achieving self-realization in community with others.

The family provides (potentially) the best example of giving according to ability and receiving according to need. But cooperative enterprises at work and at play as well as in the fulfillment of national purpose offer other possibilities. Unfortunately, the joy of working for a common good is often most deeply felt only in wartime or in some other emergency situation. Overcoming poverty, racism, sexism, disease, and other evils us do not frequently enough unite us in common purpose. It is to our individual and collective detriment that such goals do not.[39]

Equality of opportunity and equality of result each have a legitimate place in the ideal society. The ideal is that every individual with similar gifts who makes the same effort should have equivalent life chances for success. Hence, efforts must be made to overcome the hindrances of family and social background that inevitably cripple some in comparison with others.[40] Yet superior gifts with which people are born, while not deserved, do belong to them, and it is right for them to benefit from their use. A case, full of difficulties and ambiguities, can be made for selected forms of reverse discrimination to favor groups that have been the victim of past injustices. The interdependence of citizens in a highly organized economy provides a basis for social policies that tend toward equality of outcome as far as wealth and income are concerned. But allowance must also be made for reward according to merit and contribution to the sum total of goods and services. Inequalities that benefit all are also justifiable, or at least permissible.

Working out a way to move toward equality in the sharing of goods produced by joint effort while preserving inequalities of reward based on individual merit is difficult indeed. Nevertheless, there is a compelling rationale in fact and ideals for both. One way to achieve both goals would be a socially guaranteed floor on income paid for by progressive taxation high enough to provide a decent living for those who qualify and low enough not to decrease incentive. Inheritance taxes could also help to re-equalize the books over generations.[41] Beyond this the market might be permitted to allocate wealth and income.[42] Functional inequalities of wealth and income necessary for the benefit of all would also be justifiable. "From each according to ability *and* as one chooses" and "to each according to need *and* merit" indicate appropriate elements that in various combinations, in different settings, would have to be implemented with as much wisdom as possible. A more-than-minimal democratic state is necessary and justifiable to carry out these policies.

Priority problems of special difficulty arise when there is a family of first principles. In Type 3, three such principles have been stated: maximizing the good, maximizing individual freedom, and maximizing social equality within the constraints each places on the others. Different orderings of priorities may arise depending on the social circumstances that prevail at a given time and on the preferences of the citizens. In times of great emergency (such as an external threat) or conditions of severe poverty for all, some individual liberties and equal rights may legitimately be temporarily restricted for the sake of survival. Certain fundamental individual rights and liberties are so basic that they should be suspended only under extreme circumstances, if at all. Difficult issues arise in this connection that cannot be pursued here. As peace and normalcy return, the equal meeting of the basic needs of all takes priority although in tension with individual freedom to excel. As prosperity increases, individual liberties and equal rights to share in the common good must be balanced. At higher levels of general well-being within a system in which all are highly esteemed and basic needs are met, equality of results becomes progressively less essential than maintaining the most extensive range of liberties congruent with equal liberties for others. (This assumes, of course, that opportunities for all are as nearly equal as possible and desirable.) Under these circumstances the ideal will be for individuals to pursue their own ends as long as they violate no principles of justice. At every stage the basic principles of the ideal society take precedence over efficiency.[43] Efficiency must always operate within the boundary conditions prescribed by the norms of justice and the goals of a good society. Within this general framework many issues will of necessity be legitimately settled by debate and negotiation through democratic processes.

The model may now be summarized and sketched as follows:

The Freedom-Equality Model

- Allows freedom as extensive and equality as complete as the constraints of each on the other permit within the framework of justice and the quest of maximum happiness for all.[44]
- Presupposes model of individuals who are both autonomous and organically interdependent in various respects.
- Is exemplified by democratic rule based on equal liberty for all.
- Honors effective equality of opportunity and a tendency toward equality of result when each is properly understood and qualified.
- Provides for meaning and rewards both from individual achievement based on merit and from participating in community, contributing to and receiving from it.

- Conceives freedom as shaped by aim at individual good, constrained by equal freedom of others and by the good of all and the equal claims of each on what is produced jointly and held in common.
- Allows the liberty to pursue individual good in some respects and the common good in other respects.
- Establishes a state no more extensive than necessary to facilitate both the individual pursuit of self-chosen interests and the collective pursuit of the common good.
- Recognizes both differences and similarities in people.
- Acknowledges that success or failure depends on factors both internal and external to individuals.

THE IDEAL SOCIETY IS A COMMONWEALTH MADE UP BOTH OF INDIVIDUALS ENGAGED IN PURSUING PRIVATELY DEFINED GOOD THROUGH VOLUNTARY INTERACTIONS AND OF COMMUNITIES (INCLUDING THE INCLUSIVE STATE) THAT PRODUCE AND SHARE A COMMON GOOD TO BE SHARED EQUITABLY.

Contemporary Models

The models described have been created by combining four underlying principles into logical types. The effort has been to keep them pure, that is, introduce only features that the principles logically imply, although this has not been carried through thoroughly. Corollary principles have been introduced, although they have been incorporated in terms that do not compromise or violate the character of the resulting model.[45]

Illustrations of these models can be found in contemporary social philosophy. Robert Nozick[46] and John Rawls[47] have recently provided descriptions of ideal societies (ideal at least in terms of their basic framework and procedures) that reflect the principles of Types 1 and 2, respectively.

Nozick begins with autonomous individuals with inherent rights who engage in voluntary interactions and exchanges in order to maximize private interests. Holdings (income, property, wealth, goods of any kind) are acquired originally by mixing one's labor with the earth to produce goods and property. Such activities are limited only by the constraint that one leaves "enough and as good" (Locke) or provides latecomers with some appropriate minimum and does not otherwise violate the rights of the neighbor. Once justly acquired, all holdings may be used or transferred voluntarily any way the holder chooses. Any violations of just (voluntary) interactions require rectification.

Hence, three principles arise: just acquisition, just transfer, and rectification of unjust acquisition and transfer. A minimal state comes into being to police and guarantee voluntary exchange and to protect from outside enemies. The state may not engage in redistributive efforts that alter the outcome of contracts and interactions freely undertaken by individuals for mutual advantage. Justice is determined solely by procedure: just acquisition and just exchange. Individuals may do what they will with their holdings, including giving it all to the poor. But justice does not require charity on the part of individuals and expressly forbids the state from taking from those who have and redistributing it to those who do not. This is a "historical entitlement" view which is opposed to all "end state" views which distribute according to some pattern to achieve certain outcomes.[48] The employment of "end state" principles prevents "capitalist acts between consenting adults" from producing their own natural outcome.[49] Making results conform to a pattern requires constant interference with the liberty of people to control and dispose of the holdings to which they are justly entitled in any way *they* choose.

John Rawls envisions a group of representative persons gathered behind a "veil of ignorance" in an "original position" (OP) to create the principles of a just society. Since the contractors in the OP are interested in their own welfare but do not know what their position will be in the ensuing society, they have to devise rules that they (and hence everybody) would be willing to live under and regard as just. Since the conditions under which the norms are devised are fair, he calls his view "justice as fairness."

Two principles result from the deliberations in the OP: (a.) Each person is to have liberties as extensive as is compatible with a similar range of freedoms for others. (b.) All social benefits are to be open to fair acquisition by all alike, and are to be shared equally except as an unequal distribution is to the advantage of all, especially the least well off.[50]

Principle (a) has priority over (b) in that liberty is to be restricted only for the sake of liberty and not for a mere increase in material goods or other social benefits. Moreover, the principles of justice take precedence over efficiency and maximizing total welfare. Justice also requires that any permissible inequalities that result must arise under conditions of fair opportunity for all. The state has the responsibility for arranging things so that these principles are implemented, for example, protecting individual rights, seeking to provide opportunities that are equal for all despite given biological and social handicaps, and permitting only those inequalities which benefit everyone, especially the poorest.

In terms of the models previously described, Nozick is a rather pure

An Ideal Society: A Freedom-Equality Model / 81

example of Type 1. Rawls offers a complex position which is best seen as a combination of Types 1 and 2. It would be fair to say either that he represents an example of Type 3 or that he moves back and forth between Types 1 and 2. If they were positioned on a continuum, the result would be something like this:

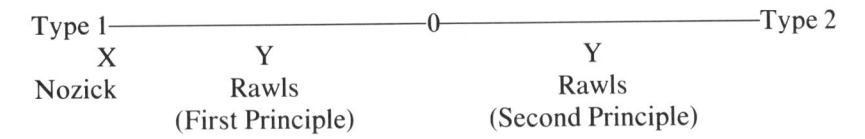

```
Type 1————————————0————————————Type 2
    X              Y                   Y
  Nozick         Rawls                Rawls
             (First Principle)    (Second Principle)
```

Nozick is a social nominalist. Society is a contracted reality created by the voluntary acts of individuals. His only concession to the principle of equality is that he regards individuals as having equal rights to something roughly akin to "life, liberty, and the pursuit of happiness."

Rawls also begins with free and equal representative persons who are concerned to further their own interests and disinterested in the welfare of others.[51] In the OP, however, these contracting parties agree that the talents of all should be regarded as possessed in common and that whatever is produced is to be shared (in principle) equally.[52] Hence, by agreement the community is to be considered the unit. His original premise, then, would appear to be equality for all in all respects or at least in terms of what he calls "social primary values, such as liberty, income, wealth, and self-respect."[53] His first principle is simply an application of the general principle of equality to the issue of liberty. But, since the first principle has lexical priority over the second, liberty takes on the status of a separate principle in addition to equality. Nevertheless, his contractual social realism and his communalism are seen in the fact that people agree to share one another's fate. Moreover, the ideal of fraternity, most closely exemplified in the family, is the affirmed value. No one will want a private or selfish advantage but will seek only those gains which benefit those who are less well off. Again, society is seen as a cooperative venture for mutual advantage.[54]

Already, it is obvious that, in comparison to Nozick's outlook, Rawls's position is complex. He moves back and forth between his libertarian principle and his egalitarian principle. For example, once a social minimum has been provided for everyone with special allowances for illness and other peculiar needs, individuals are free within a market system to seek their own interests. Individuals are also free in general to pursue a rational plan of life in quest of ends defined by themselves, though constrained by justice.[55] Hence, justice has a wide range of procedural rather than substantive meaning. On the other hand, individual merit is not to be rewarded as such, and the quest of individual excellence and private gain is not to be permitted in ways that generate inequalities except as such inequalities benefit everyone.[56] Moreover, these inequalities are not allowed unless all had fair opportunity to begin with. The qualities that enable some to outdo others are the result of inherited genetic superiority plus good family background and social circumstances which engender motivation and hard work. Individuals do not deserve these qualities nor the benefits that flow from them. They are social assets to be used for everyone's advantage. Thus are individualistic (Type 1) and communalistic (Type 2) motifs intermingled and held in a complex dialectic.

Likewise, on many other issues Nozick's position is simple, while that of Rawls is more complicated. Take equal opportunity, for example. Nozick's view is that as long as individuals have come by their assets by natural endowment and by historically just procedures of acquisition and transfer, they are entitled to the benefits that flow from their employment, even it this gives them unequal chances for success as compared to some others. Rawls goes much further. Nozick's views represent what Rawls calls the "system of natural liberty." It simply means that there are no legal or other formal barriers to careers open to talent. But this principle simply allows the strong and the advantaged to leave their less fortunate neighbors behind. Rawls urges that efforts be made to equalize opportunity by giving special help to those who are biologically and socially handicapped. This would amount to "fair equality of opportunity." But since genetic endowment cannot be changed and since families legitimately want to pass their advantages on to their children, some will still have unequal opportunities for advancement. So he proposes "democratic equality," which means that the genetically and socially advantaged may use their unequal chances to the fullest, subject to the proviso that any resulting inequalities are permitted only insofar as everyone, especially the worst off, benefit. Once all have equality of respect and are provided a social minimum, the family need not be abolished in the interest of overcoming the unequal opportunities wealthy and healthy families provide for their children.[57]

Rawls, then, would allow at least the following interferences with market processes and the outcomes of individual actions and interactions: (a) use of social assets to equalize opportunities for all, (b) provision of a social minimum (income floor and special allowances based on need), and (c) limitation of inequalities of wealth, income, etc., to those which benefit all, especially the worst off.

These criticisms by Rawls are based on Nozick's first two principles: just acquisition and just transfer. If we turn to the third principle, which calls for rectification of any violations of the first two, the situation changes—how drastically it is hard to tell. Critics generally agree that the combination of principles one and three provide the most unclarified and problematic aspects of Nozick's theory of justice. Should a large proportion of the continental United States be given back to the Indians, or at least compensation be made to the descendants of those unjustly deprived of their lands? Nozick admits that such issues are very complex and extremely difficult to resolve. He makes a concession with possible consequences that might make him a more radical interventionist than Rawls.[58] Nozick proposes that a possible pragmatic rule of thumb might be that society organize itself to maximize the position of whatever group ends up worst off. The assumption is that the groups on the bottom probably (though not certainly) have been the victims of past injustice. To carry out this program of rectification, a more extensive state may be necessary, though socialism as a punishment for historical sins is going too far![59]

Rawls actually allows a wide range of inequalities. It is not clear just how great inequalities of what kind for whom are permissible in order to enlarge the pie so that everyone is better off than without them. He does suggest that once a social minimum is provided and the basic needs of all are met, an efficient, competitive price system may be allowed to work, producing indeterminate inequalities of income.[60] Inequalities of inheritance are permissible as long as they conform to the difference principle and do not interfere with fair equality of opportunity or equal liberty.

To summarize, Robert Nozick is a consistent example of Type 1. He is clearly a libertarian, though some think he is not a thoroughgoing one.[61] Rawls is best seen as offering a combination of Types 1 and 2. He is, then, a libertarian egalitarian or an egalitarian libertarian. Hence, he could with some justification be called a synthesist. But his outlook is better categorized as a combination, since he moves from one type to the other rather than integrating them into an inclusive synthesis.

Criticism and Evaluation

If Type 3 is taken as the preferred model, the omissions of Nozick become obvious. The exclusive priority he gives to the motif of freedom, his social nominalism, and his conception of the good as created and experienced by independent individuals neglect the corresponding truths of Type 2. He does provide that by voluntary contract individuals can enter into cooperative enterprises. Certainly people may take pleasure in joint accomplishments. Nevertheless, his position is faulty since he does not give any credence to the notion of organic connectedness, the sense of being really in union with others in a deep factual sense, rather than simply making external contracts with them.

Let us grant as well than an ethic of love is quite possible on the basis of Nozick's presuppositions. One can reach out in compassion to one's neighbors to whatever extent one chooses, even to the point of sacrificing one's own interest in their behalf. It would be unfair to accuse Nozick of espousing an ethical view that is inherently selfish, even though it is individualistic. But the basis for an adequate social ethic is lacking. He misses a dimension of social reality arising out of the internal relations that constitute selfhood in a unity in community. Moreover, he has no place for the claims of equality as a part of justice that is rooted in the interdependence and organic unity with others that is factually the case. The Pauline claim that we are "individually members one of another" (Roms. 12:5 RSV) provides an element that is lacking. His extreme libertarianism, nominalism, and individualism need to be incorporated into an synthesis with Type 2 in which egalitarianism, realism, and communalism are given their proper due. It would be superfluous to engage in a criticism of his particular social policy positions, since they are rooted in his underlying presuppositions and consistent with them. His fundamental error lies with his initial assumptions.

Rawls is much more complex.[62] Since he combines principles from Types 1 and 2, his views are more adequate.[63] But his particular way of uniting them leave gaps on both sides. These can be put in the following propositions:

1. *Neglect of Social Realism.* Like Nozick, in his initial set of assumptions, he is a social nominalist. The subjects of his ideal society (insofar as the basic framework of justice is concerned) are free and equal rational subjects whose interest is in themselves and their private ends. But this is only half the truth. While they agree to regard their talents as common assets, presumably, this is because it is to their advantage as individuals to do so.

2. *Neglect of Merit.* Yet despite his social nominalism, he does not allow inequalities on the basis of merit and excellence based on individual achievement. This may be related to the fact that he thinks that people who do well owe most of their success to good breeding and good rearing (that is, to factors external to the individual, a Type 2 theme).[64] At any rate, not to allow inequalities based on merit is an infringement on the principle of individual freedom. Whether one ends up at the top or the bottom of the social pyramid, surely a part of justice is that people ought to get what they deserve. Unless one's own choices and efforts are totally insignificant as a causal factor, then the principle of merit or desert has to be taken into account.[65]

3. *Neglect of Structural Interdependence as a Basis for Equality.* Rawls does create a communal society committed to equality for all with respect to social primary goods, except as inequalities benefit all.

An Ideal Society: A Freedom-Equality Model / 85

But this is a social realism based on agreement, that is, a social contract. It does not recognize the actual interdependencies, organic connectedness, and the structural unity that belongs to social systems, which amount to something more than is created by the sum total of individual choices and acts. These structural features are intrinsic to social systems, and they are something common to all. This fact about social systems itself creates a basis for a tendency toward equality.[66] It indicates that what is actually going on is the creation and enjoyment of a common good. This principle creates an egalitarianism based on social facts. Rawls's system is built on the principle of generalized selfishness. Rules are made that guarantee that everyone gets the best of any worst possible situation.

4. *Neglect of the Enjoyment of the Non-poor as a Possible Basis for Inequality.* Rawls produces a system geared to the advantage of the poor, the weak, the less gifted, the disadvantaged.[67] They can count on outcomes that in principle benefit them, regardless of their contribution. And even when inequalities are allowed for functional reasons, they end up better off than they would have been had the inequalities not been permitted.[68] This is a high-minded ethics geared to meeting the needs and serving the welfare of the worst off in society, an outlook with a strong basis in Judeo-Christian tradition. Despite the fact that it is produced by a kind of defensive and generalized selfishness rather than out of a concern for the other person, this is one of the most commendable features of his theory of justice.

Yet, if this be taken as the whole truth, a countervailing value is left out. Every potential for enjoyment in every person has some claim on resources to bring about its actualization. Still a hierarchy of needs exists so that some claims take priority over others. For example, we must eat before we can enjoy the study of philosophy. Likewise, in a family a reasonable moral rule would be: bread for all before piano lessons for anyone. Some individuals may be willing to endure severe poverty and self-neglect for the sake of living out their commitments. Some families may alter their food budget so that some gifted member may study music. The point is that the hierarchy of needs and desires may be variously arranged and priorities negotiated within broad limits, even though survival requirements are insistent and at some eventual level a necessity rather than a choice.

Nevertheless, the higher enjoyments or needs or wants do have *some* weight. They do constitute countervailing value claims once the basic necessities for survival and minimal fulfillment have been provided for all. At the social level this means that some claims on resources are produced by the needs and desires of the non-poor which must be honored whether the worst off benefit or not. While the general rule of bread for all before piano lessons for any holds for society at large as well as for families, this is not an absolute rule. Must all have indoor plumbing before any tennis courts are built? Does more lighting for a crime-ridden ghetto take absolute precedence over a symphony orchestra? If a small minority possess unusual literary or musical talent whose exercise would benefit an elite group of the sophisticated affluent and not produce novels or music generally enjoyed by the poor, must these talents go undeveloped unless, somehow, the least advantaged are better off? It is a difficult question, but the point is that there may be grounds for inequalities that benefit some but not everyone—based purely and simply on the needs, wants, and potentials for enjoyment of those who possess them.[69] Granted that the poor take priority, but do they take absolute priority always, so that no one can ever rise the slightest bit until all rise equally and together? Must *all* inequalities benefit the disadvantaged?

The effect, then, of moving back and forth between libertarian and egalitarian principles (rather than integrating them into a unified view) is that Rawls leaves gaps that do not adequately honor either. Nevertheless, the fact that he takes into account valid elements from Types 1 and 2 means that his outlook on the whole is far superior to that of Nozick. The latter's views are fundamentally flawed from the beginning and from the ground up by his centering on one set of principles but neglecting (nearly) altogether the balancing counterparts.

Process Philosophy and Social Thought

The final task is to connect the implications of process philosophy for the understanding of justice and society with the presentation of ideal types. Obviously Type 3 is the one that accords with the principles of process philosophy enunciated earlier. It is presented as a superior ideal because it incorporates valid insights from both Types 1 and 2 which each neglects in the other. This illustrates the Whiteheadian notion that when an apparent conflict is encountered, an effort should be made to transform the opposites into contrasts and to incorporate them into some larger and more harmonious frame of reference. Type 1 and Type 2 are set up as more or less polar opposites that contradict each other. Each embodies valid insights but not the whole truth. The most comprehensive and accurate rendering of the social facts requires a larger framework in which each type is both modified by the other and transformed by being set within a more adequate set of assumptions about individuals in relation to the societies to which they belong. In some settings Type 1 has the greater validity, while in others Type 2 is more relevant. Neither encompasses all that is real or just all the time. Type 3 aims at a multidimensional complexity and flexibility that makes some element of it applicable to every situation, although that is a goal too exalted for any to achieve fully. At any rate, the more inclusive vision embodied in Type 3 is closer to adequacy and applicability than its rivals.

Moreover, the synthesis more fully accounts for all our moral intuitions, although in a complex way that is full of tensions. Granted, many people would find their intuitions more in harmony with either Type 1 or 2 than with 3. Yet if there were greater agreement on the facts and on the interpretation of social reality as Type 3 presents them, there would also be more agreement that the ideals of Type 3 are required. Most people believe that what is produced by an individual alone (if that were possible or to the extent that it is the case) belongs to that individual. Most people also believe that what is produced in common should be shared in common, equally if produced that way or more ideally produced in accordance with ability and distributed according to need.[70] At least in families where love is present as the dominant motive, that form of community life is recognized. Most people also have experienced both the joy of joint effort and of individual achievement. No ideal set forth in Type 3 is foreign to experience or to moral intuitions widely shared.

The point on which people disagree most has to do with whether the nominalist, individualist, and freedom ideal or the realist, communalist, and equality ideal applies. Type 3 maintains that each set applies in various ways and in some respects. Which claim is correct? Here Whiteheadian methodology is useful. Theory tries to account for what is immediately experienced. Error may enter in a number of ways. The range of experience may be too narrow and thus lead to generalizations that are not applicable when tested by data arising in other spheres. Dogmas inherited from the past may distort perception of current facts. All sorts of acquired filters may keep us from seeing things as they are. Self-interest may lead to a willing ignorance that produces theories congenial to what we desire but contrary to truth and disinterested moral intuition.

A Whiteheadian orientation would bid us to engage in continuous, critical, rigorous testing of theory by experience in the quest for interpretations most applicable to the widest range of relevant data. Rational adequacy (systematic consistency) and practical applicability (empirical relevance) are hard to come by. Error is extremely difficult to overcome, so tempted are we to enlarge a partial insight into a universal truth. Absolute claims are made for relative interpretations. Careful analysis of experienced data and constant revision of theory are needed to determine which renderings of the facts and which value judgments are most relevant in each instance and to what extent they apply in given cases.

One hunch entertained here is that many Americans have inherited a predisposition toward social nominalism, which blinds them to the systemic interdependence of individuals in today's economy. These individualistic, libertarian notions are encouraged by the rich and powerful who stand to gain by their continuing dominance. Moreover, average citizens frequently entertain hopes of becoming wealthy and so defend conservative ideologies from which they might benefit in the future. Critics of capitalism, on the other hand, all too often neglect the truths and values it embodies and too thoroughly embrace contrary ideas that may be just as limited in validity as those rejected. A case has been made on these pages for a more complex, multidimensional view which seeks to put two sets of partial truths into a synthesis which makes enough but not too much of each claim. What goes on in one setting may tend to validate Type 1, while what happens in another may corroborate Type 2. Sophisticated theories are required so that the applicable insight in particular cases may be recognized without losing sight that other truths may be more relevant in a different context. Doubtless the effort made here is not fully successful. However, any failure to grasp the fullness of truth is not the fault of the Whiteheadian methodology, which urges us to a never ceasing struggle to find a more adequate theory with wider applicability in accord with the whole range of experience.

Equally rational persons with clear perceptions of the facts may differ in their moral theories. Value systems have a certain autonomy grounded in the creative imagination of selves with powers to transcend self-interest and the boundaries of their present conceptions. Hence, even if more agreement on facts and their interpretation did not produce more agreement on values, Type 3 is still set forth as an option along with other ideals in the hope that where agreement is not present, persuasion might produce more than now exists. If even this faith is naive, Type 3 is a preference in whose behalf supporting reasons can be given in harmony with the moral intuitions of some good and wise people.[71]

Finally, the thesis of the entire chapter is that this model is expressive of the metaphysical vision of process philosophy. While not everyone would spell out the implications of this outlook for understanding the social order in this way, the modest claim is that the approach taken here is defensible. This in no way rules out the likelihood that other theories of society and justice might be developed which are equally or more compatible with the thought of Alfred North Whitehead and other exponents of this point of view.

The next two chapters will examine some particular issues in the light of the normative model elaborated here. The first topic to be explored is equality opportunity.

Notes

1. "Speculative Philosophy is the endeavour to frame a coherent, logical, necessary system of general ideas in terms of which every element in our experience can be interpreted" (Alfred North Whitehead, *Process and Reality*, p. 4).
2. Ibid., p. 6.
3. Whitehead describes the search for first principles in terms of an airplane flight. "It starts from the ground of particular observation; it makes a flight in the air of imaginative generalization; and it again lands for renewed observation rendered acute by rational interpretation." Ibid., p. 7.
4. Whitehead repeatedly stresses how tentative, partial, and relative are all attempts to get at the final truth. Ibid., pp. x, 12, 14.
5. The relationship between "individuals" and "societies" in Whitehead's thought is subtle and complex. This is not the place to go into its intricacies. Briefly, according to Whitehead, a human being is a complex "society of societies" with a "dominant occasion" (a "soul"), defined as "an enduring object" with special characteristics of life and continuity through time that is designated a "living person." For my purposes here, I am assuming that a person is an individual center of consciousness and action and, at the same time, a member of various human societies, such as the family, the church, and the state. Perhaps Charles Hartshorne's idea of a person as a "compound individual" constituted by a complex order of subsystems that are also "compound individuals" that, in turn, are themselves finally made up of indivisible or simple individuals (actual occasions) might serve my purposes in this connection. See Hartshorne, "The Compound Individual," *Whitehead's Philosophy: Selected Essays, 1935-1970*, pp. 41-61. For a helpful discussion of the way Whitehead thought of a person as a "society of societies," in the technical sense that he assigned to "individual" and "society," see John B. Cobb, Jr., *A Christian Natural Theology* (Philadelphia: Westminster Press, 1965), pp. 47-91. For Cobb's own views of the relationship of individuals to society, see *Process Theology as Political Theology*, pp. 92-108.
6. For discussions of this aspect of Whiteheadian thought, see John B. Cobb, Jr., and W. Widick Schroeder, eds., *Process Philosophy and Social Thought*. See in particular the following chapters: Cobb, "Explanation and Causation in History and the Social Sciences," pp. 3-10; Cobb, "The Political Implications of Whitehead's Philosophy," pp. 11-28; Franklin I. Gamwell, "A Discussion of John B. Cobb, Jr., 'The Political Implications of Whitehead's Philosophy,' " pp. 29-37; Gamwell, "Happiness and the Public World: Beyond Political Liberalism," pp. 38-54; Schroeder, "Structure and Context in Process Political Theory: A Constructive Formulation," pp. 63-80; and Douglas Sturm, "Process Thought and Political Theory: Implications of a Principle of Internal Relations," pp. 81-102. See especially pp. 18-19, 35-36, 64-66, 90-91, 95-99.
7. Alfred North Whitehead, *The Function of Reason*, p. 8.
8. For brief discussions of freedom and equality in process philosophy, see Cobb, "The Political Implications of Whitehead's Philosophy," pp. 26-28; and Schroeder, "Structure and Context in Process Political Theory: A Constructive Formulation," pp. 66-67.
9. This thesis is spelled out in detail in Kenneth Cauthen, *Process Ethics: A Constructive System*, pp. 195-310. See also the essay by Franklin Gamwell, "Happiness and the Public World."

10. These models are by no means original. Similar contrasts have often been made. See, for example, George Cabot Lodge, *The New American Ideology*, who distinguishes between an "old American ideology" and a "new American ideology"; and William Ryan, *Equality*, who distinguishes between "fair play" and "fair shares."

11. The distinction between the individual and the group as the basic unit involves enormous ontological and epistemological problems. It raises many of the questions in dispute in the social sciences between the "methodological individualists" and the "methodological holists." Certainly the individual and the group have a different status, both in being and in knowledge. The group is not an experiencing subject in the way that an individual is. Terms like "organism" and "organic" are used metaphorically, but the metaphor refers to something in reality that is not reducible to individual agents and their thoughts, attitudes, acts, etc. The common good is not experienced by some superself but by the individuals who make up the group. Yet the good experienced is created and enjoyed by them in their togetherness in a system of interdependent relationships exhibiting structural patterns and dynamic interactions that belong to the group and not to individuals alone. It is not possible or necessary for present purposes to resolve all the problems raised by the distinction between social nominalism and social realism. For the issues in debate in the social sciences between individualism and holism, see *The Encyclopedia of Philosophy*, vol. 4, pp. 53–58.

12. Obviously, I am eliminating extreme versions of each of these sociological principles. Social nominalism taken all the way leads to extreme libertarianism and anarchism (though there may be forms of anarchism that assume a collective self-governing whole). Social realism at the other far end could mean a kind a state totalitarianism in which the good of the whole was everything and particular individuals were nothing.

13. This becomes clear by noting social ideals from the past in which (modern secular ideas of) freedom and equality are not explicit or dominant. The ideal society in Plato's *The Republic* is an organism in which justice refers to the proper functioning of all in their proper places, but the places are not necessarily equal, and individual freedom is limited. In the New Testament the Pauline notion of life in the Body of Christ is based on an organic conception of community in which believers are "individually members one of another" (Roms. 12:5 RSV). Notions of freedom (Gal. 5) and equality (Gal. 3:28) are present, but so are subordination (I Cor. 11:34) and slavery (Philemon). Moreover, it is not evident the extent to which freedom and equality are meant to apply to the secular social order or mainly to the spiritual status of believers before God in faith. In any case, locating the good in the whole to be shared by members can be associated with organic and hierarchical conceptions as well as democratic and egalitarian ones, as Paul's analogy of the body would suggest (I Cor. 12). Historic "catholic" views of the church have certainly been organic and hierarchical, within which neither individual freedom nor equality of status, function, and authority has a prominent place.

Logically one might construct ideal types in which *equal* freedom would be absent from Type 1 and equal *freedom* would be lacking in Type 2. Type 1 would produce a dynamic but unstable society of the free in which the strong dominated and subjected the weak to their own purposes. Type 2 would produce a stable but conservative organic, hierarchical society with a "head" of the "body" which ruled on the basis that each has an equal right to share in the production and consumption of the common good, though not to share equally, and no right to individual pursuits not congruent with common aims. Small societies of Type 2 ruled by love of all for each and each for all might share the common good equally or in accordance with the principle of contribution according to ability and distribution according to need (Acts 4: 32–35).

14. The determination of the ways in which people are or ought to be equal and are either unavoidably or normatively or permissibly unequal constitutes a large part of modern social philosophy. Hobbes, Locke, Rousseau, and Kant provide much of the framework for the traditional discussion, while John Rawls is the center of much of the current philosophical debate.

15. The logic of equality is subtle. It requires that equals be treated equally and unequals unequally. To require the same contribution from unequally gifted persons is to treat them equally in one sense (by the same rule: the same contribution from each). To require contribution according to ability would be treating them equally in another sense (by the same rule: according to ability). The same logic applies to consumers. Treating persons equally (by the rule of need) means giving them different things if needs require that. By this principle giving them all the same things (an equal number of units of the same good) would be treating them unequally. Treating people equally only means treating them by the same rule, but the rule may be, in this case, giving according to need or giving the same units of the same good. Which rule is employed depends on whether "equals" refers to all human beings who each count as one, or whether "equals" are regarded as those who have the same needs and "unequals" as those who have different needs.

16. In the founding documents of the United States, the Declaration of Independence, for example, much is said about equality. Yet what was primarily meant was equal freedom, that is the right to elect one's rulers (political equality) and to have equal opportunity to further one's own individual goals. Certainly, they in no way intended to suggest equality for all in all respects. See Richard W. Crosby, "Equality in America: The Declaration, Tocqueville, and Today," *The New Egalitarianism,* ed. David Lewis Schaefer, pp. 53–65. Or consider John Locke who, in urging that one could acquire private property by mixing one's labor with it, also insisted that in so doing one must leave "as much and as good" for others—an idea of equal freedom and equal opportunity.

17. These are not necessary assumptions, since Type 1 might suppose that while all are free, some legitimately have a wider range of liberties than others (for whatever reason—noble birth, superior racial background, etc.). Likewise, Type 2 might suppose that while all are equal in many or all other respects, some should have a wider range of liberties than others (for whatever reasons—a natural hierarchy of ability that equips some to rule over others without their consent, but for their own good and the common good which all share equally, etc.).

18. One thinks immediately of "the dictatorship of the proletariat" in Marxism and of the role of the hierarchical priesthood in Roman Catholicism. Also, within this framework one can easily understand the protest of democratic socialists against the tyrannical versions found in Soviet and other forms of Marxism.

19. One might argue that the sociological and value principles are the root sources of this model. Yet, the combination of these two apart from the freedom and equality principles might well, as they have in the past, produce organic hierarchical models in which power and authority are concentrated in

some elite that rules by divine hereditary right, divine appointment, some natural aristocracy, etc. When biological metaphors are employed, so that society is an organism, it is easy to think of a "head" that rules over the lesser parts of the body. This is obviously not a democratic outlook.

20. This is the tradition of Locke, Kant, and the deontological school of thought. Or people may be regarded as equal in passion and desire for pleasure and happiness. This is the tradition of Hobbes, Bentham, Mill, and the teleological or utilitarian tradition. In this way of thinking, too, each person counts for one and must be taken into account. This tradition is open to the criticism that it ultimately prefers the maximizing of total good or happiness to the mode of its distribution, so that it may end up being willing to sacrifice the equal claims of all for this end. In any case, the rights tradition is being preferred here. See Amy Gutmann, *Liberal Equality*.

21. Actually, both models may make an appeal to eschatology in justifying present poverty or any kind of inequality for the sake of enlarging the total good. Type 1 never promises equality of outcome, only equality of opportunity, but it may argue that inequalities now and forevermore are necessary for economic growth and promise that the future will yield a larger piece of pie to everybody, though never equal pieces. Type 2 does promise equal outcomes (in some form that may be highly qualified in the end) but may postpone equal sharing until the new age has finally arrived, the present inequalities of opportunity and present restrictions on individual freedom being necessary either to the preservation or enlargement of the common good. See Peter Berger, *Pyramids of Sacrifice*. It is only in the last stage of the promised Marxist utopia that the rule will be "from each according to ability and to each according to need." Hence, Type 1 promises equal opportunity but its ideals may actually result in unequal opportunities, while Type 2 promises equal outcomes but may find it necessary to postpone the realization of the dream until the new age arrives at some indefinite and constantly receding future (like the Second Coming of Christ).

22. A diagram of possibilities:

Totalitarianism of the Right	Democratic Capitalism	Democratic Socialism	Totalitarianism of the Left

23. In other words, the status of the community as real may be regarded as ontological or as created contractually. I will also use the term "organic" to indicate what is here called ontological social realism. Organic suggests a biological model of a unitary organism with parts that are in fact interdependent and mutually sustaining. Social nominalism seems to be the original assumption of modern thought. Persons may agree to create a social unit for mutual benefit, but the primordial fact is real individuals who by contract create the unity. Rousseau speaks of the creation of "a single personality" by the surrender of individual rights to the social unit. John Rawls speaks of a contractual act by which free and equal individuals agree that the talents of all are to be regarded as a common asset to be exercised for the benefit of all. The contractual social realism of the modern world contrasts neatly with the medieval picture of society and of the church as an organic hierarchy in which equal worth and status and equal freedom for all (except in some ultimate theological sense of primordial status before God) were foreign notions. This is ontological social realism. The status of universals was, of course, one of the great points of debate during that period. There were nominalists and realists, and the former which developed later, after the reigning Platonism of earlier

centuries, was a forerunner, philosophically speaking, of the modern world in which social nominalism has prevailed.

24. An internal tension or ambiguity is created in this formulation of the model between an equal right to participate in communal decision-making and to share equally (or proportionately) in the production and distribution of the common good, on the one hand, and freedom to seek an individual good independent of the common good, on the other hand. The former is assumed to be proper for Type 2, while the latter is reserved for Type 3.

25. The givenness of the state into which one is born might also include the hereditary divine right of kings (thought to be the case in former centuries). In any case, if the analogy of the family is taken as paradigmatic, the consequence is that the state may have its own structures and predetermined roles, which may deny equality of rule.

26. The constitution of societies modeled after Type 1 might use this same language, but common good would be defined differently, i. e., as the sum total of individual good, or as needs common to all individuals that require a unified network of activities, such as money or transportation or schooling. But the gravitational pull would be in the direction of doing as little of this as possible, while Type 2 could easily be led into an expansion of activities on behalf of all—considered as a unified whole and not simply as a collection of individuals. Some proponents of Type 1, for example advocate a system of vouchers provided by the state to individual families to be used to purchase education for their children provided by private schools.

27. It is difficult to know what economic and political arrangements are made necessary by the logic of the basic model and which are just compatible with it. Options equally congruent with the operational ideals might be preferred to others on grounds of efficiency or other criteria. A market system could be utilized that was controlled and directed for common rather than private ends. Or a decentralized system of relatively autonomous local activities might be created to be coordinated rather than controlled by the central authority, etc. Obviously, some common networks of transportation, communication, etc., are required, plus some way to maintain security against external threats.

Anarchistic forms of egalitarianism may regard the state as an enemy of the equality of individuals and as inherently tyrannical. Only models that allow a positive role for the state in directing the creation and distribution of the common good are developed here, though this obviously means the elimination of other ideal types that may be worthy of consideration and even, from some points of view, superior. The models that assume a positive role for the state seem most compatible with the principle of social realism, while radical forms of libertarian or anarchistic egalitarianism seem to rest on the principle of social nominalism in combination with the principle of equality.

28. Organic hierarchical versions, unmodified by democratic themes of equal liberty, might easily assume that the "head" of the "body" should be of one mind in religion and in many other areas. In this framework, freedom of thought and a plurality of life-styles are foreign and threatening ideas.

Analysis of several of the issues above suggest that a moderate or extreme version of Type 2 emerges, depending on how much it is modified by the principles of Type 1. In particular, the idea of a contractual social realism rather than an ontological social realism and democratic rule rather than rule by some given hierarchy or some other elite, are characteristic of the moderate versions. The extreme versions are less characteristic of the modern world because of the importance of individualism, nominalism, and freedom. By making equal liberty and a democratic polity an integral part of Type 2 as here presented, the extreme versions have in effect been eliminated.

In particular, Type 2 is already qualified initially by making equal liberty a fundamental premise. This takes both individualism and freedom more seriously than some egalitarian models would. Without them perhaps a purer version of Type 2 would result. Yet this approach has not been followed, since Type 2 would be intolerable and (from my point of view) not very ideal to start with. What this means is that I am as much a libertarian as I am an egalitarian, so that a model which does not make equal liberty a fundamental principle is ruled out of consideration from the start. To be more precise, Type 1 without the premise of *equal* liberty and Type 2 without the premise of equal *liberty* would both be abhorrent.

29. I have constructed a model much like this in content but quite different in form in *Process Ethics*.

30. The contrary argument that freedom is a sociological and political concept has been maintained by numerous thinkers, including F. A. Hayek, T. H. Green, Ludwig von Mises, and F. H. Knight. For libertarians "freedom" refers to the sphere of individual choice and action unimpeded by the coercion of the state. In this sense, it is for them a social concept. See F. A. Hayek, *The Constitution of Liberty,* pp. 12–13, 422, ns. 6 and 7.

31 Would she be free (morally) to do physical harm to her own person or to commit suicide? My inclination is to say that she is morally obligated to honor the intrinsic worth of her own person, but that this obligation is weakened to the point of possible elimination by extraordinary conditions of extreme, pointless, and irremediable suffering. But would not suicide be an offense against God who created her and loves her? My inclination is to say yes, that is the case, but that God would be pained by her taking of her life but would not count it a sin, as it would be if one person murdered another. So high do I honor the principle of individual freedom. Granted suicide would, in one sense, be an act of ingratitude toward God; but since one did not ask for the gift, one is free to reject it as a matter of justice if its reception or perpetuation entailed unavoidable and intolerable suffering, though it might pain the giver whose loving intentions were to give a good gift.

32. Again, to be treated equally does not necessarily mean to be treated identically. Hence, many egalitarian models end up with the notion of "from each according to ability and to each according to need." Unless factual or functional inequalities are taken into account, to treat people identically (without taking into account relevant individual differences) would be to treat them unequally in one sense.

33. I speak now not of the Whiteheadian meaning of these terms, but of the senses in which they pertain to human beings living in communities.

34. I am grateful to Randall Morris for directing me to T. H. Green and L. T. Hobhouse, who elaborated a social ideal that has great affinity with my point of view. Their notion was that rights and duties were to be assigned, not to individuals as such, but to persons as members of communities. Their ideal was framed in terms of a harmony of interests in which the self-realization of each person was coordinated with that of other individuals in the creation of a common good that all shared. The well-being of others is a part of the good which one ought to seek for oneself. While Hobhouse had a sense of the conflict between the good of the individual and the common good, which might necessitate self-sacrifice for the society at large, my impression is that I have a greater sense of the conflicts, ambiguities, complexities, trade-offs, compro-

mises, and tragedies that attend the quest for justice than either he or Green. Their sense of an ideal harmony (in potential and goal,, if not in fact) between individual good and the common good comes from an age and an outlook that could harbor an optimism hardly possible for the contemporary age. Nonetheless, their convictions that individuals are to be seen as members of communities, that the highest ideal is a common good that all create and enjoy, that the individual finds his or her own good in the common good, that both a one-sided individualism and a one-sided collectivism are to be avoided, and so on, are in accord with my vision of the self-realization of individuals in community. See T. H. Green, *Prolegomena to Ethics,* pp. 160–263; *Works of Thomas Hill Green,* ed. R. L. Nettleship, II, 335–465; L. T. Hobhouse, *Liberalism,* pp. 116–37; *The Rational Good,* pp. 166–234; and *The Elements of Social Justice,* pp. 3–138.

35. Alfred North Whitehead, *Religion in the Making* (New York: The Macmillan Co., 1926; Cleveland: The World Publishing Co., 1960), p. 16.

36. Believer's baptism is required by the contractual or covenantal model, while infant baptism more correctly is associated with the organic, communal model.

37. Nozick operates within the framework of 1 and 2, while Rawls begins with 1 and sees society as created by contract, as in 2, but concludes that individuals decide to share one another's fate and to regard all biological and social assets as a common resource for the good of all to be shared equally unless an unequal arrangements helps everyone. At this point Rawls misses the truth of organic social realism by his exclusive preoccupation with the social contract model.

38. March Plattner distinguishes between a traditional view in which income belongs to the earner and a new view which assumes that income belongs to the state and can thus be distributed in accordance with political and moral norms. The latter view he associates with a new egalitarianism that goes beyond the welfare state toward a redistributive state. The two views may well be associated with Types 1 and 2, respectively. Type 3 maintains that there is truth in both views. Income is a joint product of individual effort and a common network of structures that make all workers interdependent. Moreover, the notion that the market distributes income according to some kind of merit (marginal productivity) that has moral validity will not, for many reasons, serve to justify absolute ownership of income. Hence, a redistributionist ethic need not depend on the view that all income belongs to the state, but only that some of it is produced by means common to all. The production of income is both an individual and a social process. That which is the joint product of all or many in a social process may justly be redistributed in accordance with nonmarket norms. See Marc Plattner, "The Welfare State Versus the Redistributive State," pp. 28–48.

39. Two astute observers of the American soul have pointed to the evils of individualism without commitment to common good purposes. See Robert Bellah et al., *Habits of the Heart;* and Daniel Bell, *The Cultural Contradictions of Capitalism.*

40. The extent of the difference made by families is debatable. Christopher Jencks and his associates concluded that only 15 percent of variations in income depends on family background. Frequently enormous differences of income are to be found among brothers in the same family. See Christopher Jencks et al., *Inequality: A Reassessment of the Effect of Family and Schooling in America.*

41. Questions of efficiency and of savings, as well as many other problems,

arise which cannot be argued here. But see Arthur Okun, *Equality and Efficiency;* and Robert Kuttner, *The Economic Illusion: False Choices Between Prosperity and Social Justice.*

42. Questions of political feasibility are ignored in favor of stating an ideal that would be nice if people would buy into it.

43. Efficiency means only that we seek to get the most of what we want for the least cost. But the norm of efficiency cannot come into play until the boundary conditions have been prescribed, that is, the goals desired and the means permitted. See my *The Ethics of Enjoyment,* pp. 64–79.

44. Actually, a third factor enters into the notion of justice and the good society—the ideal of increasing social good. Hence, there are occasions when freedom and equality may be limited for the sake of enlarging the good to be pursued individually or shared communally as well as by each other. This has already become evident in Rawls' and my admitting that inequalities may be permitted if necessary to increase benefits to all. Freedom might similarly be limited under other circumstances. See my *Process Ethics,* pp. 195–310, for an elaboration, illustration, and defense of this view.

45. I have in mind particularly the notions of individual worth and human rights that are not necessarily entailed by the ideas of individual freedom and social equality, though they are compatible and companion concepts. It might the the case, however, that notions of equal freedom and social equality are, in some sense, entailed by the assumption of individual worth and dignity.

46. Robert Nozick, *Anarchy, State, and Utopia.*

47. John Rawls, *A Theory of Justice.*

48. Nozick, *Anarchy, State, and Utopia,* pp. 149–82.

49. Ibid, pp. 153–64.

50. The final and complete statement in Rawls's own words can be found in *A Theory of Justice,* pp. 302-03.

51. I and others have wondered if this does not produce a fatal flaw in the deliberations. The rules that are produced may be prudent in that they are designed to protect one's own interest no matter where one ends up in some actual society. But are they just? Granted that the rules must apply to everyone, so that no legislator in the OP can design rules that will benefit him/her in particular. Nevertheless, the rules are designed to serve a kind of general selfishness so that one ends up with the best deal possible in any bad situation, no matter whether the bad place one lands in is one's own fault. Rawls seems to think that basically we are shaped by heredity and environment so that individual choice plays little role. The result is that he eliminates merit or desert as a rule of justice in and of itself. If his method produces a just set of rules, it is by the coincidence that a kind of generalized selfishness has that consequence. In his defense one could argue that he is providing a way to legislate the "golden rule" of Jesus or his injunction that one should love one's neighbor equally with oneself into the social order. Assuming that one might end up on the bottom, one would want the best outcome in that situation, but willing that for oneself is willing it also for the neighbor who might be in the bad spot instead of you. This is not done for the sake of the neighbor as such, however, but only because one might himself/herself be in that bad spot. Assured that one would be on top and not on the bottom, presumably one would not worry where the neighbor ended up. It is a subtle point.

52. Rawls, *A Theory of Justice,* p. 101.

53. Ibid., pp. 62, 303. These primary values are defined as things that every rational person would want, whatever else they might want as particular individuals.

54. Ibid., pp. 84, 103. Adherents of Type 1 could also view society in this way, but when combined with the preceding points, this statement takes on more egalitarian coloring.

55. Ibid., pp. 90–95.

56. Plattner wonders how far Rawls would go with this. Suppose that originally all have incomes of $5000, but that if some are permitted to earn $25,000, the poorest would be raised to $6000. Suppose further that by allowing some to earn $1,000,000 the poorest will be raised to only $6100. Presumably all these arrangements would be legitimate under Rawls's scheme. Plattner points out that this indicates how important, after all, economic incentives and the increase of wealth are to Rawls. Plattner also asks why not extend the difference principle to sexual favors and to children. Should the sexually attractive and able be allowed their erotic advantages unless the less desirable and unsuccessful men and women are compensated? And should couples who are fertile give up some of their children to the infertile? See Plattner, "The Welfare State Versus the Redistributive State."

57. Rawls, *A Theory of Justice*, pp. 60–108, 511–12.

58. At least one interpreter claims that there are more and better grounds for policies that lead to an egalitarian society in Nozick than in Rawls. See Derek Phillips, *Equality, Justice and Rectification*, pp. 106–8.

59. Nozick, *Anarchy, State, and Utopia*, pp. 230–31.

60. *A Theory of Justice*, p. 277.

61. Some even more thoroughgoing libertarians would insist that Nozick compromises this position by the admission of the legitimacy of a minimal state, but Nozick attempts to justify this move on libertarian grounds. For evaluations and discussions of Nozick's point of view, see Jeffrey Paul, ed., *Reading Nozick*.

62. For an extensive discussion of Rawls, presenting evaluations from many points of view, see *John Rawls' Theory of Justice*, ed. H. Gene Blocker and Elizabeth H. Smith.

63. See my *Process Ethics*, pp. 211–21, for a general discussion and evaluation of Rawls.

64. *A Theory of Justice*, p. 104.

65. How would Rawls answer Daniel Bell who wants to know what we are to say if the worst off or the least fortunate are there by their own choice? See *The New Egalitarianism*, p. 235, note 12.

66. I have argued for this at length in *Process Ethics*, pp. 252–63, 278–310.

67. This comes about, however, because of the possibility that those who are making the rules in the OP may end up on the bottom, not because they are motivated by love for the disadvantaged as such. It comes about for practical and self-interested reasons, not as a consequence of ethical principles espoused by the creators of society.

68. Rawls notes that the rules of society must be such as to evoke the willing cooperation of all. Hence, the rule that all benefits are to be shared equally unless inequalities benefit all would ensure the cooperation of those who are least gifted and least advantaged. Yet numerous critics have pointed out that this is a good deal for the disadvantaged, but it is one-sided. What is to ensure the willing cooperation of the better endowed? See Rawls, *A Theory of Justice*, pp. 15, 100–108; and Nozick, *Anarchy State and Utopia*, pp. 189–97.

69. See *Process Ethics*, pp. 174–79, 238–52, 260–63, 278–81.

70. The problem is that many people regard the creation of what I would call produced jointly or in common as produced by the sum total of individual efforts. I see much economic production in systemic or communal terms, that

is, having organic characteristics rather than as the simple total of individual efforts. Individual efforts have little meaning apart from the system of which they are a part. For example, I view the large salaries of sports celebrities as a joint product of many factors and people in a system. Were it not for TV networks broadcasting over public channels and the interest of people, plus, in many cases, facilities built in part with public funds, etc., not to mention the invention of the games themselves—neither of which is the product of the players—the large salaries would not be possible. Hence, I think it quite just to tax them and redistribute the income produced. It is, of course, possible to view all of this in individualistic or contractual terms, as does Nozick, for example. Given his interpretation of the facts and his view of social reality, I agree with his conclusions. Hence, it would appear that my disagreement with Nozick arises, at least in part, out of a difference in the interpretation of facts and social reality, not a difference in moral intuitions as such. See Nozick, *Anarchy, State and Utopia,* pp. 160–64, and *Process Ethics,* pp. 295–300.

71. This approach to social models as ideal types has all the disadvantages of any kind of high abstraction: it loses contact with all the full, rich complexity of the concrete reality from which the abstracting is undertaken. In particular, this approach abstracts from the concrete reality of actual persons in real life circumstances seeking ways to live and developing ideals as paths toward survival and fulfillment. It ignores the fact that ideals reflect particular perspectives of given people in specific historical settings. Ideals may be a defense of vested interests and take the form of a defensive ideology. Ideals centering on freedom may be characteristic of the strong, the confident, the gifted, and the oppressor. Ideals centering on equality may be characteristic of the weak, the humble, the poor, and the oppressed. Marxism and the whole enterprise of the psychology and sociology of knowledge have much to teach us here. Conservatives are fond of insisting that the demand for greater equality does not grow out of any passion for justice but out of envy of those who are better off. How does my own socio-economic status, my own life history, my own temperament and psychological development, my own existence as a white, male American, and so on. shape if not determine my outlook? Perhaps women see the whole realm of ethics differently from men. (See, for example, Carol Gilligan, *In a Different Voice: Psychological Theory and Women's Development.*) Here I can only acknowledge all these shortcomings and promise to give attention to them elsewhere. Meanwhile, I can only plead that there is some merit and legitimacy in taking the particular approach I have for this occasion. At the very least, I hope that coming at the issue this way might help to clarify underlying philosophical assumptions that give structure and content to moral ideals of justice and the good society.

CHAPTER / FOUR

The Passion for Equal Opportunity

WHAT DOES EQUAL OPPORTUNITY (EO) mean, or what ought it mean, as a normative concept? The issue involves concepts of moral philosophy, social analysis, and determinations of fact. The central problem is to decide what is just and fitting when all pertinent considerations are taken into account.

The concept of EO is a complex idea, not a simple one. Opportunity itself contains three elements: (a) an agent or class of agents—the persons or groups having the opportunity, (b) the goal—that which is sought by the agent, and (c) the prospect of the agent achieving the goal—a chance that lies somewhere between mere possibility and certainty. To say that two persons have an EO means in the strictest sense that, with respect to a particular goal sought by these agents, the same obstacles have been removed, for instance, race or sex. If two women, one black and the other white, seek a job as a TV anchorperson for a news program, their chances are equal if neither race nor sex is a barrier, but equal only in those particular respects. Yet if one is attractive, elegant, and glamorous, while the other is plain, ordinary, and not at all pretty, then their chances in these particulars may be very unequal. Or if the training and experience of one are superior to that of the other, the chances of the better qualified applicant shoot up sharply. Hence, to be precise, it is necessary always to keep in mind that an opportunity is a chance for agent X to achieve goal Y without hindrance Z. To say that opportunity is equal only means that for given agents in relation to particular goals, the same obstacles are not present and/or the identical positive elements are. When all factors are considered, however, their chances might be quite unequal. For opportunity to be equal in the absolute sense would mean that in a given situation, all nonpertaining obstacles (and any and all that mattered) would be the same in every respect, that is, no differences whatsoever would exist to favor some but not others.[1]

Understood in this way, the meaning of EO ordinarily is that certain obstacles not relevant to the goal in question have been removed. Most frequently it is matters such as race, sex, age, ethnic background, religion, and the like that are involved. These we take to be obnoxious impediments, unless one of them happens to be intrinsic to the nature of the opportunity involved. Presumably, we would all agree that a black male actor should be sought to play the role of Martin Luther King, Jr., in a movie, despite the fact that white and female actors would be disadvantaged. Other factors that help or hinder some but not others may also make opportunity unequal, but these unequalizing elements may not be objectionable. Making opportunities absolutely equal for everyone in every situation is not only impossible but also undesirable or even ludicrous in some cases. Does a five-foot, two-inch basketball player have equal opportunity with one who is seven foot two inches? Should he or she? Hence, an acceptable definition of EO will need to specify the obnoxious obstacles that need to be removed as well as indicate the unequalizing factors that are either unavoidable or desirable, or at least acceptable. In light of all this the following definition is offered.

> EO MEANS THAT NO ILLEGITIMATE CRITERIA ARE IMPOSED AND NO INDEFENSIBLE AND AVOIDABLE BACKGROUND CONDITIONS ARE PERMITTED THAT IMPEDE, RESTRICT, OR DENY A PERSON A CHANCE TO COMPETE FOR OR ENJOY SOME GOOD THAT IS AVAILABLE TO OTHERS.

An opportunity is a chance at something, not a guarantee. EO means that everyone has the same chances, at least in certain relevant particulars. The proposal as stated is formal and abstract and in itself settles nothing. Nevertheless, since opportunities can and/or ought never to be (or not always) absolutely (mathematically) equal,[2] the definition as given simply provides a framework for discussion. Moreover, disputes about EO have to do with the very items specified. This can be put systematically under three headings

First Part	Second Part
1. Legitimate criteria imposed that make opportunities unequal	1. Indefensible background conditions that make opportunities unequal, which should be overcome (if possible)

The Passion for Equal Opportunity

2. By the agency or institutions administering the opportunities

3. At the time they are to be actualized.

2. By society (or some subsection of it)

3. In the general life history of individuals prior to the time opportunities are to be actualized.

The proposal simply states the argument in a formal way. All hangs on the content that is put into it. The position that is to be defended here will unfold point by point along with accompanying justifying reasons. The opportunities under consideration have to do with prospects for getting a job, being admitted to a school, or acquiring income, wealth, and other available goods or social benefits. For convenience, job-seeking and educational opportunities will be the main areas under review.

The assumption underlying the proposal is that the kind of EO that can be defended as just and/or fitting is to be distinguished from EO as defined absolutely and mathematically. The latter would mean that every human being has exactly (numerically) the same chances at every opportunity, regardless of the situation or circumstances. At an absolute extreme, to illustrate the point, mathematical EO implies that a Southern Baptist minister in Arkansas has the same chance of becoming the next Pope as members of the College of Cardinals or that a six-month-old child in Florida has the same chance of getting a job driving a taxi in Oregon as a thirty-year-old man who lives next door to the company. The obvious point is that some restrictions on EO are not only inevitable but legitimate, defensible, relevant, and right. And some, such as genetic differences among individuals, may simply be unavoidable and beyond human control. The EO under consideration here is the kind that can be defended as fair or appropriate. The problem, then, is to determine what is illegitimate and indefensible with respect to the chances of a given person at a given opportunity under given circumstances.

Criteria of Legitimacy

Two types of legitimacy come into the picture. The first relates to the intrinsic nature of the particular activity, that is, the opportunity, right, or privilege in question. The second has to do with the social context in which the activity occurs.

Criteria Related to the Activity

The criteria of legitimacy will vary from case to case. Some preliminary examples may help to establish the validity of the proposal. Being blind would be a relevant factor in excluding employment as a bus driver, but being black or female would not. Being one year old is relevant to the denial of voting rights, but being less than six feet tall is not. In both cases the denial of opportunity is based on reasons pertinent to the activity involved. A blind person cannot drive a bus safely. A one-year-old has no understanding of what voting is.

The proposal being made is that opportunities belong to persons as persons. Persons as persons are equal. Any rules or practices governing the exercise of opportunities or their restriction must be relevant to the activity involved. Rules must be devised in order to facilitate the functions and achieve the goals that pertain to a given activity. Actions or characteristics of persons incompatible with these aims are legitimate reasons for denying them the opportunity to participate. Otherwise, when no relevant criteria of exclusion can be invoked, chances should be equal for everybody involved.

In the case of driving a bus and voting, the proposed definition of EO seems clear enough. Anyone who can do what is implied in the activity "driving a bus" should, all other things being equal, have an equal chance with all other persons who have that capacity to the same degree. Activities do differ in their nature, however. In all cases, presumably some threshold measurement can be established by which to judge the ability to perform the function. In some cases, it is fairly easy to determine, within certain limits, who can do it, as well as who can do it better. It is appropriate for reasons of efficiency to give jobs to those applicants who can do them best. In the case of driving a bus, this certainly could be done to a great extent.

In the case of voting, however, it seems best simply to establish certain formal criteria which either apply or do not. The Putney Debates in Cromwell's Army (1647) involved a dispute over whether owning property should be a prerequisite for voting.[3] Today all who can meet the relevant formal criteria, such as age and residence, can vote. Being male, white, and owning property are not pertinent criteria. Here we more properly speak of a socially given right that all who meet the stated conditions can exercise equally. No one today would want to insist that a requirement, such as owning property or being male, is relevant to the act of voting. "Ability to do it" in this case is equivalent to being a citizen of age and mental competence.

Human judgments are involved at some point in every instance of choice, so that disputes are inevitable. Yet certain rational considerations are applicable once one centers on the norm of "ability to

The Passion for Equal Opportunity / 103

perform the function."Reasonable arguments might ensue over what degree or refinement of eyesight is essential for bus drivers, or at what age one should be allowed to vote. Being black or female are irrelevant in both cases to the norm of "ability to perform the function."

Criteria Related to Context

The criteria relating to context presents a more complex situation. All activities take place in a setting with many dimensions. Certain circumstances immediately surround a given situation, but the larger issues pertaining to society as a whole and to history lie in the background. If disputes arise in determining the criteria of relevance related to the activity itself, they are even more inevitable when the wider social context is taken into account. Complex issues of moral philosophy and social analysis come into play. What is relevant to the activity itself is comparatively objective and ascertainable within limits that would command wide, if not universal, agreement. But criteria related to context involve rules of relevance rooted in social understandings, conventions, customs, laws, ideologies, and the like. For example, in the 17th-century disputes over property and voting, conservatives feared that those without property had no permanent or vested interest in the social order and might well vote to eliminate all rights to hold lands. The Levellers in Cromwell's army contended that being a human being and a citizen was all that mattered, regardless of how poor one was. In such instances, judgments among different individuals and groups may vary widely. Disputes of this type are much more difficult to resolve because of the greater degree of subjectivity involved, since philosophical matters are at stake. Different value systems come into play. Not only are the issues quite complicated philosophically, making reasonable disagreement inevitable, but self-interest enters to corrupt ideologies ostensibly based solely on rational considerations and objective analysis of moral principles. Moreover, the general consensus of a society obviously changes over time.

Again consider EO related to getting a job as a bus driver. Suppose the applicant who scores highest on the driving test has just been released from prison after serving time for brutally raping the sister of one of the other drivers, whose friends share his strong hostilities toward the applicant. Are the dissension and conflict likely to result from hiring the former prisoner relevant grounds for passing him by? How can the objective right of a person to find employment be weighed against the subjective feelings of the other workers? One might argue on pragmatic grounds that hiring the former prisoner would negatively affect productivity and otherwise interfere with the function of getting the busses driven. Practically, one might suggest that the applicant seek employment as a bus driver in another city. Or would refusal to hire him constitute a denial of equal opportunity? Should he be hired and then steps be taken to deal with the resulting personal conflicts?

Next suppose that the applicant with the highest score is not the rapist mentioned but a black, and suppose that the drivers are highly prejudiced, so much so that disorder and perhaps violence are likely to follow. One might understand the feelings against the rapist, but do people have a right to feelings of racial prejudice? Do the same pragmatic considerations apply or have the same weight? Should the state simply enforce the right to employment regardless of race, regardless of the amount of force that might be required?

Next suppose that the two candidates with the highest scores are white and the next two applicants in rank are black. The area served by the bus line is 40 percent black, but only 8 percent of the bus drivers are black. It is clear that blacks have been discriminated against in the past. Is it legitimate now to give preference to blacks in order to overcome previous racial injustices? Or should racial discrimination simply be ended, so that henceforth members of all races are treated equally?

Imagine a number of possibilities:

1. Neither of the present two black applicants has ever been refused employment by the bus company on the basis of race, but their grandfathers were.
2. Both of them were refused employment five years ago because of their race.

   Is there any relevant difference between 1 and 2 in terms of whether the two blacks should be given preference now because of their race?
3. There is no evidence that there will be any significant repercussions in either the white or the black community regardless of who is hired.
4. Black leaders have threatened to organize a boycott against the bus company unless blacks are given preference until at least 20 percent of the drivers are black, with the strong possibility that this would create great financial problems for the city that subsidizes bus service.

   Should employment decisions be affected by whether 3 or 4 is the case?
5. An active and effective women's organization argues that only 1 percent of the drivers are women, while half of the riders on the bus and in the city are female. They contend that the two Asian women applicants who made quite acceptable but not the highest scores should be preferred over both black and white males. They too could organize a effective boycott by women.

6. Two American Indians have acceptable scores but are backed by no political organization. They do point out, however, that the land on which the city is built was taken from their tribe without payment or treaty by the early settlers. Hence, they should be given priority over everybody.

Suppose 4, 5, and 6 are the case, but that the two candidates for the two openings with the highest scores are two white males. Who should be hired? Since the two white males are Irish, does it matter that the Irish were discriminated against in this city in the past?

Commentary and Analysis

It is now clear what is meant by saying that all events take place within a context. Decisions about who should get jobs driving a bus pertain not only to being able to do the job but also involve reference (a) to local circumstances immediately surrounding decisions regarding particular individuals and (b) to the more encompassing facts related to a general history of discrimination against blacks and changing social roles of women as groups.

Moreover, if we look at the issues of prejudice and hostility that arise on the immediate scene, we see tension between the demands of justice and the requirements of order. A similar set of issues arises on the larger scene involving the threat of boycotts. Is the threat of disorder ever to be given moral weight, or is it simply a matter of a power struggle, which to that extent makes ethics irrelevant? Usually, conservatives who benefit from the present arrangements opt for order, while the disenfranchised cry for justice, sometimes legitimating even violence if necessary. But how does one adjudicate ethically the conflict between justice and order? The simple answer here must be that the threat of violence or a boycott has moral implications in terms of people being hurt or helped, especially when violence and death may result. Whether one argues on the basis of total consequences (teleologically) or on the basis of competing rights and claims (deontologically), the resolution is not always clear cut. Granted that justice has the priority, one can imagine some situations in which the evil involved in disorder might have more moral weight in the short run than the immediate enactment or achievement of justice.

Perhaps the most troublesome are the issues surrounding the question of whether rectification should be made for past injustices. The extended discussion will proceed in four steps: (a) the case against rectification, (b) the arguments for rectification,[4] (c) the importance of the time frame involved, and (d) the grounds other than redress of grievances on which preference can be given to women, blacks, and others.

The Case Against Rectification

The clearest, simplest, and most easily defended position considers individuals as individuals. Let them compete as autonomous units for jobs based on their abilities alone, totally apart from their race, sex, religion, or any other identity based on group membership.[5] At least four powerful reasons can be offered in behalf of this view.

1. Rectification programs based on group membership offend the consciousness of most Americans, including women and blacks.[6] Fifty-six percent of feminist "leaders" approve of quotas for jobs for women compared to only 18 percent of the general population.[7] A nationwide survey by The Center for Media and Public Affairs, published in September 1985, showed that 77 percent of blacks opposed preferential treatment for minorities in jobs and colleges, although 77 percent of black "leaders" were in favor.[8] Most people in the United States can deal with their own individual behavior and are willing to be held accountable for what they have done in their own lifetimes. This is so because most Americans have simply absorbed a nominalist position (the view that only individuals are real) from their culture. It "just seems right" to them. Factually, it is difficult for us to accept responsibility for what our ancestors did. If my grandparents and the whole generation of white people in their generation discriminated against blacks, that is regrettable, but am I to be held accountable? Our sense of responsibility for what our race in general does or what our ancestors did is diluted in comparison with our sense of what we do here and now.

Hence, it is easy to understand why white workers have resisted, on moral and philosophical grounds, programs that threaten to penalize them in favor of blacks or women. As long as they argue for a strict policy of equal opportunity for individuals as individuals entirely apart from racial or sexual identification, they have a very strong case, notwithstanding the fact that self-interest alone might incline them in that direction.

2. Even if rectification of past injustice is accepted in principle, preferential policies based on race and sex do not meet the moral requirements involved.[9] Aristotle stated a view of corrective justice that would command wide acceptance. Two conditions must be met: (a) Redress must be made by the party causing the injury. (b) The recompense must be proportional to the offense. The clearest case of the rightness of redress occurs when A does wrong to B and then A is made to make appropriate recompense to B. But it is hardly fair if A has offended B and C must make recompense to D. Yet is this not what reverse discrimination does? Preferential polices are based on the assumption that in the past whites have done injustice to blacks that

denied them equal opportunities. Hence, blacks now should be given special treatment to make up for this. If whites *as a group* could be forced to make recompense to blacks *as a group* in some proportionate way, it might make sense, assuming that proportionate reparations could be defined. This is sometimes difficult enough to do when two contemporary individuals are involved, but when groups are involved across the generations, the task seems nearly impossible.

But even if it were possible to resolve the generational problem, if rectification is to be made from one group to another, should not benefits be distributed among all members of that group, not just those lucky enough to qualify for them? What actually happens in practice is one of two things: either the whites and blacks here and now serve as substitutes for white and black individuals then and there, or certain representative individuals in each race are made to serve vicariously for the group as a whole across the generations. The particular whites who are denied jobs to make room for blacks are substitutes for whites in the past or represent the white race making recompense to blacks, whether or not these whites have committed acts of injustice against blacks or have benefited from the offenses other whites committed. Moreover, the blacks who are given jobs may or may not have themselves been injured by past practices, but they stand in as substitutes for blacks in the past or vicariously receive the recompense as representatives of the group. What is the moral and social justification of the theory of substitution or vicarious representation that preferential policies seem necessarily to presuppose? The "Suffering Servant" who, though innocent, bears the iniquities of others is a prominent motif in Jewish and Christian theology (Is. 53). But this is an act of love not required by strict justice, and few volunteer to take on the role.

3. The past is too complicated. How can we possibly determine how much and what kind of rectification is due to whom? What is the time frame to be—a decade, a century? By what criteria is the time period to be decided? Isn't it better simply to focus on the present? We can never untangle the past. Let bygones by bygones: start with a clean slate. Eliminate all references to sex, race, religion, or whatever else is irrelevant to doing the job.

The above illustrations make this point crystal clear. For two places, we have the following applicants: two white Irish males, two black males, two Asian women, and two American Indians (sex not specified). All are qualified, though the two males of Irish background have higher total scores. All belong to groups who have been discriminated against in the past. What kind of formula could reasonably be worked out to determine the past injury score of all these people? Who could be chosen to work out these calculations to determine on the basis of race, sex, or ethnic background which individuals have what degrees of priority? Is the past injury score for these particular individuals, or for the groups to which they belong, or both? If both, in what proportions? These questions show that even if valid grounds based on philosophy, morality, and history exist, the practical problems of implementing preferential programs are overwhelming, if not impossible, to work out. Trying to implement them would create an administrative nightmare subject to all kinds of bureaucratic bungling and abuse. At best, then, the attempt to compensate for past injury can be only crude, blundering efforts—elephant guns that fire away in near darkness at mice.

4. To give preferential treatment to certain individuals on the basis of their sex or race rather than solely to their ability to do the job will simply breed new resentments that will continue to poison the future.[10] White males who are now discriminated against on the basis of race and sex will, with some moral justification, feel that they are now the victims of injustice. The result will be a further politicizing of American life with continuing power struggles and a deterioration of good will between the races and sexes. One might comment that it is good for white males who have long been on top to know what it's like to be unjustly treated. But those just entering the labor market could reply that they did not have the advantage, but their fathers and grandfathers and maybe even their older brothers. Why should they be made the scapegoat?

The Case for Rectification

The case for rectification based on race and sex can be put under three headings:

1. Race and sex are special categories in this society.[11] Discrimination against blacks and women is deep, pervasive, endemic, stubborn, and rooted in the long term past. As long as one is white and male, nationality and ethnic background are not on the same level. Again, class is a powerful factor, but it is not as solid a barrier to opportunity as race and sex. The latter are biologically based and cannot be changed. One can move out of one class into another despite certain initial advantages (or disadvantages) from family background, educational opportunities (or their lack), genetic endowment, and the like. If other things count too, should they count as much? Should not race and sex be the basis for rectification programs related to a type of group membership that is more significant than other groupings of individuals? Statistically, of course, black women suffer both disadvantages. Nevertheless, class membership may mitigate or intensify the bad effects of race and sex identity.

Since social policies of all sorts have to be general and cannot include all the nuances and qualifications that might be relevant in some particular instances, the preponderance of evidence is in favor of preferential programs that are race- and sex-based. Other factors such as genetic inheritance, ethnic, class, and family background, and the vicissitudes of life that create special need do affect one's chances, but relevant differences exist between these influences and past injustices based on race and sex, which count in favor of rectification policies. These other disabilities should be taken into account, but in other ways.

2. The notion that the moral books should be balanced over time has strong support in law, tradition, and human intuition. Either those harmed should be recompensed in some equivalent way or the perpetrator should be made to suffer like damage. "An eye for and eye and a tooth for a tooth"—this biblical phrase contains the principle. In one sense, this principle puts limits on recompense. Only as much redress as the injury deserves is allowed. Aristotle's approval of corrective justice has already been mentioned. But the issues become complicated at once. Granted that rectification of past injustices is appropriate, does it matter in the example given whether the two white applicants were perpetrators of the injustices to the individuals who are to be given the job in preference to them? Suppose they have always, and actively, opposed racial discrimination. But they do want an equal chance for themselves. Are they now to suffer for the sins of others? The standard question is whether two wrongs make a right. Is the fact that there has been a general history of discrimination of whites against blacks in the past morally relevant to the resolution of claims between particular individual whites and blacks here and now? The case for rectification rests on a positive answer to the last question, which must now be developed.

3. Individuals are not simply autonomous units. In some cases at least, they are organically connected to the groups to which they belong.[12] This claim presupposes an answer to a very difficult and controversial problem: What is the relationship between individuals and groups? Are individuals most appropriately thought of as autonomous units, while groups are only collections or covenanted federations of individuals? Or is the group the primary unit, while individuals are best seen as members or participants organically connected to the whole? The argument between individualistic and organic conceptions is at least as old as the Bible. The New Testament is filled with organic notions of selfhood, typified by the Pauline notion of the church as the body of Christ set forth in I Corinthians 12 and summarized in the idea that believers are "individually members one of another" (Roms. 12: 5 RSV). In the Old Testament similar conceptions flourished. Ezekiel, however, heard a word from the Lord which contradicted the proverb that says, "The fathers have eaten sour grapes, and the children's teeth

are set on edge" (Ezek. 18:2 RSV). The new rule is to be strict individualism: the soul that sins shall die, and the soul that is righteous shall live (Ezek. 18).

Which is philosophically true, social nominalism, which asserts that only the individual is fundamentally real, or social realism, which sees society as an organic reality made up of members?[13] In general, a compelling case can be made for the view that individuals are both relatively autonomous and organically connected to corporate realities. This point has been made in previous chapters using the insights of process philosophy as they are confirmed by observation and analysis. But this truth takes on different meanings and proportions depending on the situation under discussion. Some groups and some societies are more organic in character, while others are less so. Families are more like an organic whole than is a crowd of people walking around in the shopping center. With respect to national defense, the country is basically a unit. In war we win or lose together, although particular individuals may do the actual fighting. In terms of individual purchases at the supermarket, we function essentially as individual units. People in general are probably more structurally and organically interdependent in the United States now than they were two centuries ago.[14] The truth is complex, and neither extreme view is totally correct by itself. The full truth has to be determined empirically in particular cases.

Certainly blacks and women have suffered much similar treatment because of their race and sex. To be white and male has been a decided advantage, although women have not been drafted as combat soldiers. Racial and gender solidarity is real in that sense. In considerable measure, group membership has determined destiny as a historical fact over many generations. Being white or male or being black or female is a relevant factor. But we are not totally creatures of our communal heritage or completely determined by our racial membership. The actions of individuals also make a difference in determining the actual course of events, their life trajectories, and their well being. The philosophical truth, then, would appear to be extremely complex and very difficult to state except in quite general terms. Observation leads one to conclude that the position people actually take in each particular case is often dictated more by self-interest or ideological commitment than by careful empirical inquiry and rational analysis. At least personal preference seems to tilt complex truth toward more simple self-serving conclusions.

To move toward some conclusions, it must be said that social nominalism may be partly true as it applies to the question before us, but it is not the whole truth. It is the case that "individually we are members one of another," and that when the parents "eat sour grapes, the children's teeth are set on edge." As difficult as it may be to set out in full empirical detail in every case, the reality of social interconnectedness must be taken into account. In the example given above, the two blacks may never have been refused employment as bus drivers because of their race, but we can plausibly postulate that they have suffered disadvantages in general for that reason. Their two white competitors may themselves not be racist in any personal sense and still have been advantaged in numerous ways by virtue of their color. We could certainly imagine a scenario in which the two blacks came from wealthy families, went to excellent schools, and grew up in neighborhoods shielded from many of the effects of racism. We could also suppose that the whites in question grew up poor and went to inferior schools, etc. Nevertheless, speaking in generalities, it is the case that over the decades whites have been advantaged and blacks have been disadvantaged, despite some individual exceptions. Of course, some whites and some males have been disadvantaged by social and historical circumstances involving injustice (and other factors too) in comparison with other white males, and some rectification seems to be due to them too. Class and ethnic deprivation, where it involves injustice, should count as well as race and sex.

From all this we might reasonably conclude that there is a factual, philosophical, and moral basis for programs of preferential treatment. (a) Individual blacks and whites or males and females presently seeking to actualize an opportunity with high statistical probability have been affected positively or negatively by their group identity. (b) There is enough racial and gender solidarity in general terms to provide a basis for the substitution or vicarious representation that is involved in particular cases, even though the case may be weak and not in itself sufficient. These reasons, however, count for something and can be combined with other justifying arguments yet to be made.

It is less clear what the social policy implications are. What kinds of programs giving preference to which groups under what circumstances to what extent and over how long a period are appropriate? A few tentative generalizations may be hazarded. The more discrimination against certain groups can be empirically documented in particular companies, trades, regions, and institutions, etc., the more such efforts can be justified in those areas. The more programs are voluntarily undertaken and accepted, the more desirable. Time-specified goals are better than quotas immediately enacted. Government may mandate programs for large companies and institutions that have a pronounced public character and in which discrimination has been obvious, blatant, documentable, and recent. These intuitive suggestions are intended to get at the most precise combination possible of moral principles and empirical fact in both diagnosis and prescription. Neither conservative

112 / THE PASSION FOR EQUALITY

total rejection nor liberal unqualified promotion of preferential programs based on compensatory justice will stand up under careful philosophical and empirical analysis. No issue will test social wisdom more than this one. Only approximate success in uniting morality with policy is possible.

The Importance of the Time Factor

It is sometimes said that without preferential treatment, women, blacks, and other previously excluded groups will never catch up.[15] This is not literally true. If a policy of strict neutrality is practiced that gives opportunities to persons as persons based on ability alone, a balance will in time be reached, depending on how many among disadvantaged groups can meet job requirements in a competitive market. But even with preferential treatment, qualified applicants must be found. That raises another set of very large issues to be treated later.

The first issue that needs attention is the moral importance of the time factor involved. Programs of redress will obviously get quicker results, but is this sufficient reason in and of itself to justify them? One might argue that justice deferred is justice denied, that the time for ending injustice is now, that justice is a present demand which requires its enactment in the quickest way possible. These are compelling reasons, however, only if justice is assumed to be wholly or preponderantly on the side of preferential programs. But that is just what is in dispute.

The issue can be made a little clearer by distinguishing three ways to achieve a proper balance (whatever that means) among, let us say, white males, blacks, and women. To simplify the matter, let us assume a total of ten bus drivers in a situation in which half the relevant population (the city, bus riders, whatever) is white and half black and, of course, half male and half female. A mathematical balance would be to reproduce these percentages in the workforce, assuming an equal number of equally, or at least suitably, qualified job applicants in all categories. Assuming a predominance of white males at the moment, three ways could be followed to achieve the desired balance. (a) A sufficient number of white males could be fired at once and replaced with the requisite number of blacks and women (each person, let us say, to represent one race and one sex simultaneously!). Balance would be achieved immediately. (b) A second approach would be to hire only blacks and women as required as openings came up until the goal was reached. This would take longer. (c) A third way would be to adopt a policy neutral to race and sex and hire the most qualified applicants as vacancies arose. Gradually the composition of the

The Passion for Equal Opportunity / 113

workforce would change until it more or less reproduced the makeup of the applicant pool.

These three methods provide a short-term, a mid-range, and a long-term approach to achieving race and gender balance. The first, (a), has the advantage of quick results. But does it provide immediate justice? That depends, because the issues get complicated at once. Technically, one solution would be to have five white males and five black women on the roll. But would white women and black males justifiably object? Suppose, then, that there must be at least two of each sex in each racial group. How would children of racially mixed marriages be accommodated? Which white males would be fired, those with least seniority? If not, why not? Does seniority count? Should they be chosen by lottery or by some sort of merit system, with those dismissed who rated lowest in performance? By some combination of least merit and least seniority? All this gets tedious, but once social engineering is undertaken based on empirical grounds of previous general racial and gender discrimination, must not empirical factors related to the particular pool of present prospective employees be taken into account? The use of rigid quotas immediately implemented poses immense problems of fairness, when all people and all circumstances are factored in.

The second approach, (b), avoids encroachment upon whatever merit may lie in the claims of seniority—having been first in line, contribution to the company, etc. It has the advantage of beginning strong corrective action now out of recognition of previous injustice. Yet it still has all the hazards of approach (a) with respect to using a general formula of race and gender discrimination in the past to make particular corrections in the present. Race and gender take precedence over class position and individual life histories of potential white male employees. This may or may not be just in given instances.

To be specific, do personal and family need count morally as factors supporting preferential treatment, or do only race and gender matter? Suppose two out of six candidates are the poorest and most desperate for a job to support families with special needs are both white males. Suppose their family and class backgrounds gave them little or nothing in the way of a head start, other than being white and male. The use of quotas necessarily uses general categories to apply to specific situations that may or may not exemplify the patterns presupposed by the formula.[16] This is the limitation of all law and legalistic morality. This approach, along with the first, does incorporate the truth implied in social realism, though it does so with a hatchet rather than with a surgeon's knife delicately administered. In many cases, this may be the best that can be done and may, on the whole, be preferable to available alternatives.

The third approach, (c), avoids the problematic features of the first two with respect to present and specific facts, but it ignores the truth of history and the organic connectedness of individuals with sexual and racial identities. It has the effect of pretending that the past connected with group solidarity does not matter as a factor creating unequal opportunities. It delays the achievement of justice for groups that have been unjustly treated as groups. Yet this method does have the formidable advantage of focusing on the primary criteria of relevance—ability to do the job. It is blind to all surrounding features of social context: race, sex, need, class, and everything else not related to capacity to drive a bus safely and well.

Hence, all the complications previously noted that make relevant and just social engineering nearly impossible and terribly inefficient economically are simply jettisoned. Discrimination unrelated to the job itself created all the problems that are now to be dealt with by introducing new discriminations in order to rectify the damage done by the old ones. Yet doing so carries a high risk of arbitrary actions, which may or may not improve the level of justice when all relevant elements in the context are considered. Moreover, with qualified applicants of all categories, the desired balance will be approximately achieved over time.

Grounds Other Than Rectification of Past Injustice as a Basis for Preferential Treatment

Preferential treatment is a larger and more inclusive category than rectification. Possible grounds other than the redress of past injustice for giving priority to some job applicants over others can be put under three headings: those related to the society as a whole, those related to the employer, institution, or agency, and those related to the applicant or person. All have to do with present and future needs, goals, or well-being.

1. *The Society as a Whole.* Society's recognition that its present and future health and well-being require that all remnants of racism and sexism be wiped out as soon as possible is a strong reason in favor of preferential policies, which have the advantage of making rapid changes. Racial and sexual injustice are the source of disorder, conflict, and sometimes violence. All people and groups need a sense that they live in a just society. By these and other lines of reasoning, it can be argued that the good of the whole nation justifies preferential policies.[17] Some who make this point do so despite the admitted fact that the individual rights of some white males may be overrun in the process.

If we consider a public institution like the police force in a city with a high proportion of blacks, there are good reasons why a high proportion of black policemen might be appropriate. Social health requires that all citizens have a sense of participating fully in the community. Given the reality and power of race consciousness in our society, proportionate representation in all areas contributes to the sense of belonging and investment in the well-being of the corporate life. A feeling that justice and fair play prevail now or that steps are being taken in that direction may dissipate some of the resentment of the past. Black citizens paying taxes or black consumers buying products or using services might claim that part of that revenue should provide black employment. A bus company could legitimately use such considerations as a basis for recruiting and hiring blacks preferentially until a better racial mixture among employees is achieved.

But two counterarguments arise at once. (a) Preferential policies involve an injustice to individual white males, so that conflict is set up between a violation of individual rights and collective good. (b) Moreover, preferential policies create unrest and resistance among racial majorities and males, perhaps out of self-interest as much as a sense of moral outrage. But on utilitarian grounds one must consider which policy would produce the better total consequences—preferential programs favoring women and blacks, or equal opportunity for all based on qualifications only. The latter policy works more slowly, but on the whole, one could argue that it is preferable.

2. *The Needs and Goals of Employers and Institutions.* A set of considerations may arise, based on goals and needs internal to particular agencies, that give a basis for preferential treatment to some individuals or groups. These factors arise out of the present but are unrelated to the capacity to do the job or to meet the requirements for whatever is involved. For example, the number of women students in some theological seminaries has risen rapidly in recent years until it has approached or exceeded 50 percent of the total. Most professors are male. Sound educational reasons can be given why the proportion of women on these faculties should be increased, totally apart from any reference to previous injustice. Women students need role models. Women faculty will have a better understanding of the issues, problems, and frustrations experienced by female students and may bring insights, use methods, or discover truth that would enrich the educational process. They will have power where it counts most to balance the bias and self-interest of men, and so on. Overall, these theological schools have a need to increase the number and proportion of women in order to increase their educational effectiveness and for the sake of their total health.

Preferential policies of this sort, while not undertaken to compensate for past injustice, may have the same effect or tendency as rectification programs would. This creates unequal opportunities for some but may not violate the original proposal, which states that EO prevails when no irrelevant criteria are imposed.

3. *The Needs of the Individual.* If we turn to the individual applicant or citizen seeking to actualize an opportunity, still another set of considerations comes into the picture. These have to do with the special situations of particular individuals. Consider the theological seminary that is in the process of increasing the number of women on the faculty. Suppose two applicants are the finalists, more or less equal in qualifications overall. One is independently wealthy; the other is a single parent with no means of support other than the job she seeks and who has a child with expensive, long-term medical problems. Should her presumably greater need for a job give her the edge? Yes, other things being equal. If she has greater need but is less qualified, though meeting minimal requirements, trade-offs arise with no resources in ethical theory to say exactly where the balance lies. A policy of taking personal need into account cannot become a standard policy of institutions or businesses, for many reasons. For one, the administrative problems of investigating all applicants and deciding who has the greatest need would be overwhelming and terribly inefficient. But where feasible, all things considered, it would be appropriate for some employers to do so.[18]

An interesting problem arises here, one related to the difference between policies intended to rectify past injustice and those that give priority to greater need created by the vicissitudes of life, but not involving wrong-doing. Intuitively, greater weight attaches to redress of injury than to doing positive good. The former is a necessary duty, the latter a voluntary act. Hence, where fact and theory determine that it is appropriate, the power of the state is legitimately put behind redress, but is not used to coerce positive acts of well-doing. The latter are more fittingly approached through the cultivation of a sensitive moral consciousness.[19]

Here some clarifications are necessary. Programs to increase and thus to equalize economic opportunities for the disadvantaged, whether by government agencies or by private companies and institutions, have been called "affirmative action." Such efforts are always preferential in some sense in that special attention is given to some persons or groups. This may occur is two forms: (a) programs to recruit and train women, blacks, and other categories of people previously discriminated against, and (b) preferential hiring and promotion of such groups, even though the persons involved may not be the most qualified in a given instance. (a) is the "weak form" of affirmative action, while (b) is the "strong form." Moreover, preferential treatment may be given in either (a) or (b) in order to rectify past injustice or to increase the general welfare.

The weak form of affirmative action does not call for any compromise of the principle that the best qualified are to be admitted to schools and given available jobs. Preferential programs at the point of hiring, admissions to schools, etc., may require only minimal qualifications, and beyond that award opportunities to members of disadvantaged groups either for the sake of compensatory justice (rectification) or in order to increase the well being of society (non-rectification). Hence, programs of the strong form may mean a loss of efficiency for the sake of other social goals, whereas the weak form of affirmative action does not, at least at the point at which people are hired, admitted, etc. Whether the weak form would result in a net gain or loss of efficiency in the long run is uncertain. One could, of course, have a program that gave preference in hiring, admitting, promotion, etc. to the target groups, other things (for example, qualifications) being equal. This arrangement is somewhere between the weak and the strong type. Efficiency would not be compromised, but it would make the programs less effective in achieving results quickly.

In conclusion, four pertinent factors that might justify giving unequal opportunities to some (other than the capacity to perform as well or better than others the function in question) have been introduced: rectification of past injustice, the well-being of society, the goals and requirements of institutions and employers, and the needs of individuals. Each has its peculiar logic and moral relevance.

Indefensible Background Conditions

The second part of the proposal must now be examined. So far the discussion examined the criteria that are relevant or legitimate at the time of application for a job, seeking admission to a school, etc. After a focus on ability to do the job, consideration was given to the social context in which the job takes place. Now the background conditions and social institutions that help or hinder opportunity will be considered—the ingredients that provide the resources necessary to success. Let us assume for the moment that formal equality of opportunity has been established, meaning that there are no legal or other impediments to careers open to talent. No discrimination is practiced against persons because of color, sex, religion, nationality, or anything else irrelevant to the capacity to do the job well.

Four factors usually (or at least potentially) create unequal prospects related to job, education, income, wealth, and the like: (a) native endowment at birth, (b) cultural/family background and rearing, (c) the individual's own choices and efforts, and (d) general social conditions and institutional arrangements which may advantage some and disadvantage others. (The effect of accidents, luck, and the vicissitudes of life histories, that is, circumstances beyond anybody's control, are being ignored at the moment.)

The previous chapters have pointed out that to achieve thoroughgoing EO would require the destruction of the family plus genetic engineering to homogenize biological endowment at birth.[20] Parents naturally want to pass on to their children any advantages of wealth, educational privileges, etc., that they can, while parents with little to offer in this regard will shape their children's prospects negatively, perhaps against their will. Moreover, the family environment shapes the value system and the motivational patterns of individuals. In addition, children receive a biological as well as a social inheritance from their ancestors. In the genetic lottery, some are born with more talent, or at least different talents, than others. The more gifted among us have, in that respect, superior chances compared to the less gifted.

Here it will be assumed that the destruction of the family is too high a price to pay for equalizing opportunity. It will be further assumed that genetic engineering to provide every individual with an identical set of gifts and talents would not be desirable, even were it possible. It can be argued, however, that genetic engineering—assuming it could be done accurately and safely—to produce diverse but equivalent packages of abilities at a high level might be desirable, as would general efforts toward improving the genetic lot of all or preventing serious deterioration of the gene pool, where possible. Policies will be advocated later which will mitigate the effects but not remove the influence of family background and biological inheritance. What the individual does with her/his birth endowment and life opportunities is crucial to how well she/he is prepared to take advantage of opportunities, but that needs no consideration here.

Social policy aimed at securing justice in the form of defensible EO will have at least two dimensions.

1. Efforts will be made to equalize educational and training opportunities. Moreover, equality of outcome of educational achievement will be sought in appropriate but limited ways. Full recognition must be given to the limitations of educational institutions and training programs as such.[21] Complex and deeply interwoven patterns of causation enter into the determination of learning achievement, including family background and training, cultural attitudes toward education and work, as well as individual native ability, motivation, and effort.

Accumulated social wisdom and experience must be the guides in determining what schools, vocational training, and other helps can and cannot do for various groups and settings to maximize the skills of all is done. Special programs for the handicapped are necessary to prepare them for useful lives in jobs they can handle. The aim is to achieve the maximum genetic potential of individuals and to overcome individual handicaps, whether biological or social in origin or the result of unfortunate life events (disease, accidents, etc.). The ideal would be that individuals with the same genetic ability and who made the same personal efforts to succeed should have equal chances at the good things available in a given society. Programs designed to serve this end should be pursued to the extent that social wisdom and budgetary considerations allow, guided by experience and careful cost-benefit analysis.

Three complications enter that must be sorted out. (a) Some studies show that certain cultural values, ways of thinking, and patterns of motivation that enhance or impede the chances for success are characteristic of certain ethnic groups at various times.[22] An attitude of self-reliance seems particularly important for upward movement.[23] Some groups have succeeded despite discrimination against them, while others have not done as well though facing lesser obstacles. Genetic explanations are weakened, if not ruled out, by the fact that the scores of various ethnic groups change dramatically over short periods of time.[24] If attitudes toward work, success, education, and competition not conducive to achievement are passed on to children, their chances may be adversely affected, even though their native abilities are not lacking. The situation is complex, neither easily understood or changed.[25] Where specific differences in culturally induced attitudes are an important factor in a group's success, it follows that what general social policy and educational programs can do in equalizing opportunities is limited. Social policies based on justice have the responsibility only to provide reasonable assistance that tends to equalize opportunities for all who desire them and respond appropriately.

(b) Suppose it could be shown that by providing unequal opportunities for gaining income and wealth to some, everyone would be better off? Self-interest, at least as focused on economic well being, would surely agree to this arrangement. But there may be a trade-off in the minds of the beneficiaries between a sense of dignity and self-esteem, on the one hand, and a larger slice of pie, on the other hand. Perhaps some would prefer the pride of achievement—with what one makes for oneself given an equal chance—rather than more money and other benefits. It would depend, in part, on the nature and size of the trade-off. Speculation on this point is interesting, but an empirical determination of the facts and possibilities would be extremely difficult to come by. A theory of justice would not be involved, since it is a matter of personal preference and not of basic right.[26]

(c) Finally, another general fact about society poses a conflict between equality and excellence. The ideal is equal opportunity for all, but extreme efforts to equalize the chances of all would mean a leveling of all at the lowest common denominator.[27] The worst off, that is, those with the least advantageous situations and possibilities, would always have first claim on resources until all had the same chances, or at least until the genetic potential of the least gifted had been maximized. This means (a) that those who would have excelled if equal (the same kind or quality of) resources had been devoted to all will suffer. And it also means (b) that in general those with extraordinary gifts will not receive the special resources needed to realize them to the fullest, unless they may have private funds to use for that purpose. For example, a potential Einstein or a potential Mozart would not become a world-class scientist or musician unless proper training, which might be expensive, were provided.

In short, a tension arises between equalizing opportunities for all and maximizing opportunities for all. If we hold the view that every gift is worthy of actualization and therefore exerts a moral claim, tensions and conflicts between incommensurable values are unavoidable. Painful trade-offs for which there is no clear moral guidance must be made. One can hope for social consensus, but can expect conflict, testing social wisdom and political decision-making to its limits. Given the trade-off between excellence for some and equality for all, the former must be given its due, although what that means cannot be specified in detail by a theory of justice alone. The principle of "bread for all before piano lessons for any" is valid but cannot be absolutized. Still, some inequality of opportunity is justified for the sake of the pursuit of excellence, whether or not the poor and less gifted benefit.[28]

2. A minimal income should be provided for every individual and/or family, possibly in the form of a negative income tax. It should be high enough to provide the basic necessities of life, but low enough to keep incentive high. (The principle is easy to state but difficult to implement.) It should include special allowances for medical problems and other extraordinary needs. Beyond the compassionate decision of an affluent society that no one be allowed to suffer from fundamental deprivation, a social minimum has several functions in this particular connection. It provides a fall-back because of personal back luck or during hard times because of general economic conditions over which people have no control—illness strikes the family, the local factory closes, foreign competition ruins a domestic industry, regional recession occurs, etc. A minimal income allows the economy to undergo adjustments and shifts without causing the victims inevitable suffering. It provides a guard against the worst results of poverty for those who, for whatever reason—luck, lack of talent, accidents and tragedies, being born into a disadvantaged family, class, race, or region, or pure and simple personal failure, etc.—cannot survive in the competitive world. It helps to make up for whatever societal failures may have

contributed to the lack of opportunity in a complex, interdependent economy. The few lazy parasites who might exploit such programs and who might be content to live with such a low income are insignificant compared to other considerations in determining general social policy.

A guaranteed minimum income is, in part, simply a floor provided for all who need it in recognition of the fact that despite the best efforts, opportunities can be equalized only within very definite and stubborn limits. It is a pragmatic solution to the failure of wisdom or will on the part of society and individuals, as well as a monument to the sheer complexity of the world and the ambiguities of life. Trying to sort out who or what is to blame is futile beyond a point.

Ethical Theory

Before summing up and concluding this lengthy analysis, the ethical theory that has been implicit in the foregoing pages must now be made explicit. Two kinds of judgment have been made: deontological and teleological (or utilitarian). Both types are valid and necessary. In particular, the deontological positions have to do with the protection of individual rights based on the intrinsic worth of persons. The teleological positions rest on judgments about what actions or policies will maximize individual and/or (and especially) collective good. Sometimes deontological and teleological judgments may be in conflict. Maximizing the good may sometimes involve a violation of individual rights.[29] Also involved are factual claims and assumptions about the way democratic polities and largely market economies operate, as well as understandings of cultures, families, human beings, and societies in general.

Summary and Conclusions

An attempt has been made to develop a conception of EO with respect to seeking employment, making money, getting an education, and generally prospering that meets the requirements of a just and good society. Starting with a local situation and ending with the larger background conditions and biological facts that tend to produce inequalities, the pertinent factors were considered under three headings: (a) qualifications peculiar to the activity, function, or opportunity in question, (b) limiting or enhancing factors that may legitimately be imposed when individuals seek to actualize an opportunity, and (c) the background conditions that should and can be changed for the sake of equalizing opportunities for all. The ideal of equal opportunity for all who have the same abilities and who make the same personal efforts is a goal which can be reached with only limited success, since too many other factors come into play. When all things have been considered, the following conclusions pertain:

1. While the family provides a biological and social inheritance that generates unequal opportunities, the genetic endowments of the present generation cannot be changed, and the family is too valuable an institution on other grounds to destroy. (Unavoidable fact plus value judgment)

2. The effects of genetics and family background can and should be partially offset by providing educational opportunities and other assistance that, insofar as is possible, tend to equalize prospects, assuming a given set of abilities and effort. Inculcated family values and attitudes specific to particular ethnic groups that may disadvantage some are not a proper concern of social policy. (Factual claim plus moral judgment based deontologically on concern for individual rights and teleologically on the quest for greatest individual and collective welfare)

3. Formal EO should be maintained; that is, no barriers of race, sex, nationality, religion, or anything else that obstructs "careers open to talent" are permitted. (Moral judgment based on concern for individual rights and individual and collective welfare)

4. A limited case can be made on moral and empirical grounds for carefully designed preferential programs created to rectify injustices done to certain groups in the past, but it is ambiguous, imprecise, and problematic. (Moral judgment based on deontological and teleological grounds but recognizing a conflict between values plus recognition of tension between morality and efficiency)

5. In some cases need is a legitimate basis for differential treatment when other factors are more or less equal or not overriding, but it cannot be the basis of a claim by individuals or groups. Nor is it always practical. It is most relevant in small institutions and informal settings where facts about needs are readily available. (Moral judgment based on deontological and teleological grounds plus factual recognition of tension between meeting needs and striving for efficiency)

6. Grounds may be found for preferential but non-rectificatory programs related to race, sex, etc., based on ends and needs internal to a society, business, or institution in some settings. (Recognition of factors relevant to system functions, plus utilitarian concern for maximizing total good)

7. A minimum income should be provided as a guard against deprivation for those who lose out in the struggle, for whatever reasons. (Social policy recommendation based on factual presuppositions regarding the best way to express charity and do justice, given the factual functioning of complex societies)

The Passion for Equal Opportunity / 123

8. Supposing that a trade-off could be arranged or is unavoidable between unequal opportunities and outcomes for some and greater benefits for all, a societal preference could be expressed democratically without danger of offending justice whether or not the bargain were accepted. (Recognition of tension precipitated by unavoidable social facts and a possible conflict between deontological concerns for individual rights and teleological concern for increasing individual and collective welfare)

9. The unavoidable tension between equality for all and special excellence for some may justify unequal opportunities for those able to take advantage of them, regardless of whether those with less talent or with special handicaps directly benefit or not. (Recognition of inevitable conflict between incommensurable values with no necessary ideal solution)

The same conclusions may be stated in a different way. Imbedded in the discussion are two basic points of reference, at which a legitimate or defensible ideal can be stated. The first comes into play when an individual seeks to actualize an opportunity:

Opportunities are regarded as ideally equal when the only criteria imposed are those relevant to the ability to do the job or otherwise to take advantage of the opportunity in question.

Three reasons, given the proper context, provide a legitimate basis for qualifying this ideal, thus giving unequal advantage to some:

1. Previous injustice done to some persons or groups may in certain limited cases justify preferential treatment to redress injury.
2. Goals and needs internal to the institution, employer, or agency, or the good of society as a whole, may justify preferential treatment.
3. The special need of the applicant may, in some special cases (usually small and local situations), legitimate preferential treatment.

The second ideal point of reference relates to the total set of background conditions that determine what an individual's chances for success are to be:

Ideally, opportunities should be equal for all who are born with the same genetic endowment and who make equivalent efforts.

To actualize this ideal, or to allow legitimate qualifications of it, the following social policies are advocated:

1. Formal EO is to be maintained so that no barriers are permitted to "careers open to talent."
2. Educational and training programs should be designed to equalize the opportunities of all, recognizing budgetary and other limitations posed by the realization of other appropriate goals.
3. Unequal opportunity for some may be justified if there is no way to avoid the trade-off between such inequalities and larger benefits for all, or at least for the least well-off.
4. Moreover, tension arises between equalizing opportunities for all and maximizing opportunities for all, since the latter requires that some be given opportunities others cannot take advantage of. Social wisdom must decide on some appropriate balance between equality and excellence, whether or not all benefit from the resulting excellence.
5. A floor should be put on income for all to take care of those who lose out because of system faults, individual failures, and deprivation due to all kinds of no-fault circumstances and vicissitudes.

These are highly idealistic as well as ambitious goals. In what measure they will be adopted, of course, depends on the values people hold or come to hold and the realities of political power. Another factor is whether the money is available when these aims are put alongside other social goals. Compromises and trade-offs are inevitable. Reality will always fall short of the ideal. These norms can, nonetheless, serve as guides to policy where money and will are present to enact them.

The chapter following will take up a variety of other questions related to equality in the economic order.

Notes

1. For these clarifications I am much indebted to Peter Westen, "The Concept of Equal Opportunity," pp. 837–50. The analysis of opportunity into three elements is his, and I am grateful for his illumination of the subject.

2. For the sake of simplicity, suppose that we begin with job search. In this case, equality of opportunity (EO) may be defined abstractly in a variety of ways, running from one extreme to the other:

  1. EQUAL CHANCE AT EVERY JOB: Imagine a lottery that would be held for every job opening. The most extreme version of the lottery would involve the names of everybody available for work, the employed and the unemployed. When it was time to elect a president of the United States, for example, the names of all available citizens would be entered in a lottery and one name would be randomly chosen. That way everybody would have an absolutely equal chance of becoming president. Theoretically, but not actually, the same kind of drawing could be held for every job opening.

2. EQUAL CHANCE AT A PARTICULAR DESIRED JOB: In this less extreme version of EO, the lottery would contain the names of only those who wished to be considered for a particular job. Names would be randomly chosen from the available pool of applicants.

3. EQUAL CHANCE WITH ALL WHO HAVE SAME SET OF ABILITIES: Here the unconditional lottery is abandoned. No longer are we talking about absolute mathematical equality. This version seeks to match jobs with persons capable of doing them, so that any person with a given set of talents has an equal chance at (a) all jobs requiring those abilities or (b) a particular job for which one applies as any other available person with the same set of capacities. Once jobs are matched with the pool of applicants with equal talent for doing them, then a lottery might be held. This would guarantee that no extraneous factors would enter. Only abilities with respect to the job to be done count. Once these conditions are established, a qualified mathematical equality prevails.

4. EQUAL CHANCE AT REASONABLE EMPLOYMENT IN THE LONG RUN: This is an extended version of 3, which takes into account the total context of job search over an entire career. Since not everyone can have every desired job one is capable of doing, some frustration and temporary disappointment are inevitable for everyone or for most people, even if EO (of type 3) fully prevails in any and every given situation. Moreover, some jobs that equally match job and talent are unequal in other desirable features, such as, pay, location, working conditions, security. Hence, the total context of job search over the long run must be considered. In this framework, EO would prevail if over a lifetime every person who desired a job would have chances that roughly matched everyone else's for finding employment that (a) was congruent with one's abilities and that (b) was roughly equal in other desirable characteristics. Realistically, however, some people are going to have to accept something less than the best whether measured objectively (the empirical conditions) or subjectively (the satisfaction one experiences). EO prevails when over the course of a career every person has chances for employment at all levels of desirability that approximately match those of everyone else with the same set of talents.

While nearly everyone these days claims to be for EO, no one (or at least one hopes that no one) would define the concept in the absolute, unqualified mathematical terms prescribed by definitions 1 and 2. In both cases, jobs are completely disassociated from ability to do them, except by accident of the lottery itself. Reasonable discussion must focus on options 3 and 4. EO defined as an equal chance with others at securing jobs for which one is qualified in practice needs to be supplemented by the idea of an equal chance with others over the long term for a satisfactory lifetime job experience. Since it is impossible to guarantee subjective contentment, the best that can be aimed at is the creation of the objective conditions, which might reasonably be expected to contribute to contentment. Hence 4, unlike 3, includes both a long-term perspective and objective conditions other than congruence between job and talent, which contribute toward subjective contentment.

3. See *The Idea of Equality,* ed. George Abernathy, p. 115.

4. Arguments for and against rectification programs can be found in *Social Justice and Preferential Treatment,* ed. William Blackstone and Robert Heslep.

5. See Nathan Glazer, *Affirmative Discrimination: Ethnic Inequality and Public Policy;* Barry Gross, *Discrimination in Reverse;* and David Lewis Schaefer, ed., *The New Egalitarianism.*

6. See Sidney Verba and Gary R. Orren, *Equality in America: The View from the Top,* pp. 83–88.

7. Ibid., p. 84.

8. *The Chapel Hill (North Carolina) Newspaper,* September 24, 1985, p. 7A.

9. See William Blackstone, "Reverse Discrimination and Compensatory Justice," in Blackstone and Heslop, eds., *Social Justice and Preferential Treatment,* pp. 52–83.

10. Ibid.

11. For a forceful presentation of this claim, see Tom Beauchamp, "The Justification of Reverse Discrimination," in Blackstone and Heslop, eds., *Social Justice and Preferential Treatment,* pp. 84–110.

12. See Kenneth Cauthen, *Process Ethics: A Constructive System,* pp. 158–62, 252–60, 295–305, for a more detailed presentation of this claim.

13. Robert Bellah, Richard Madsen, William M. Sullivan, Ann Swidler, and Steven M. Tipton, *Habits of the Heart: Individualism and Commitment in American Life,* p. 334, make the same distinction using the terms "ontological individualism" and "social realism."

14. For an argument to the effect that we need a new ideology to account for the greater interdependence of people today, see George Cabot Lodge, *The New American Ideology.*

15. This is the import of Tom Beauchamp's argument. What he actually says is that without preferential treatment of women and blacks, discrimination cannot be wiped out in an "acceptable time." But unless we have some criteria by which we can judge how much time is "acceptable," it is hard to know what to make of his argument. His point is that progress has been slow and is very difficult and that without extraordinary measures, even though they may involve some injustice to white males, discrimination will not be overcome. But this seems to be a point about difficulty, not about means. And if it is nearly impossible to get race- and sex-blind policies really implemented because of resistance, what hope does he have that males and whites will not resist and even frustrate and overthrow stronger policies? Reverse discrimination can, of course, be forced if the majority of the people will support such measures, as was the case when majorities in the whole country outnumbered resisters in the South during the 1950s and 1960s. But the Reagan administration has taken a different course on reverse discrimination, backed apparently by national majorities of both blacks and whites. See Beauchamp, "Justification of Reverse Discrimination," p. 85.

16. John Rawls distinguishes between perfect procedural justice (there is an independent criteria of fairness and a sure method of implementing it—dividing a cake equally), imperfect procedural justice (there is a standard but no sure way to guarantee the right outcome—jury trial), and pure procedural justice (there is only a fair procedure so that every outcome is just—honest gambling). Due to moral and administrative difficulties, it is not clear that reverse discrimination can measure up to either of these forms of procedural justice. Race- and sex-blind policies can make a claim at least to being an instance of pure procedural justice. See John Rawls, *A Theory of Justice,* pp. 83–90.

17. Cf. Blackstone, "Reverse Discrimination and Compensatory Judgments," pp. 71–74. Beauchamp's argument in "Justification of Reverse Dis-

crimination" is generally of this nature. Beauchamp admits (in my terminology, not his) that deontological concerns for individual rights of whites might be offended but that the utilitarian concern for the larger good outweighs this by virtue of the requirements of distributive justice. John Rawls maintains, on the other hand, that justice-regarding reasons always take precedence over consequential considerations.

18. Should salaries of seminary professors also be based on need instead of, or along with, merit? There are relevant differences between an initial hiring of a person and the long term association with colleagues where jealousies may develop. Disputes over merit cause enough trouble, avoided frequently by keeping salaries secret. Adding need would complicate the issue tremendously. How is need measured? Some things are obvious—the onset of sickness in a family member requiring expensive treatment, for example. But suppose one teacher chooses to have five children and another one only two. Does the former have greater need or only a different set of priorities (or is just unlucky or ignorant in birth control matters!)? On the whole, I am inclined to think that merit must be the only criterion for salary and advancement, but my commitments to the norm of Christian love make me nervous about it and incline me to a utopian ideal of a community of scholars so dedicated to truth and teaching that no other incentives would be necessary, so that salaries could be equal or based on need. But my recognition of human fallibility and of original sin hold me back. The monastic communities in which the communal ethic prevailed were a select group of people who had abandoned any attachment to material advancement. I do not find this to be the prevailing ethic among Protestant seminary faculty, administrators, and staff.

19. Nevertheless, it can be argued on both philosophical and theological grounds that deontological regard for the worth (intrinsic value) of the neighbor (or in Christian terms, love of neighbor) require both redress of injury and positive, outgoing concern to meet the other's need. See my *Process Ethics,* pp. 37–82, 125–94.

20. See John Rawls, *A Theory of Justice,* pp. 65–90, 100–108, 511–12; and Amy Gutman, *Liberal Equality,* pp. 119–44.

21. As stated in Chapter 3, Christopher Jencks and his associates found that neither schools, cognitive skills, family background, educational attainment, nor occupational status go very far in explaining variations in income. They stressed on-the-job skills and luck as highly important. Moreover, the output of a school "depends largely on a single input, namely the character of the entering children." See *Inequality,* pp. 8, 256, 226–27.

22. See Thomas Sowell, *Race and Economics,* p. 238; and also his *Ethnic America,* pp. 273–96. Lawrence Harrison argues this point on the international scene, claiming that the poverty of Latin American countries is related to culture, attitudes, values, etc.—a "state of mind." See *Underdevelopment Is a State of Mind: The Latin American Case.*

23. "If the history of American ethnic groups shows anything, it is how large a role has been played by attitudes—and particularly attitudes of self-reliance" (Sowell, *Race and Economics,* p. 238).

24. Sowell, *Ethnic America,* pp. 280–82.

25. It is not easy to determine how cultural attitudes are formed and changed. One must assume that in part the explanation lies in the nature, character, and free choice of the groups involved. Yet to assume that the poor themselves are partly responsible for their destiny sometimes evokes the protest that this is "blaming the victim." Yet another strong tradition among us

is that people must "take charge of their own lives" and "become the agents of their own liberation." The relationship between social determinism and responsible freedom is not an easy one to figure out either theoretically or empirically. Surely it is too simple to think that poverty that affects groups in relation to other groups is totally socially determined while individuals within each group are completely responsible for their own situation. Both group and individual destiny are doubtless some kind of complex product of both external (caused from the outside) and internal (caused from the inside) factors. Sometimes we (perversely?) assume that the circumstances we (we and our friends) face justify our behavior and shortcomings, while we hold "them" (the alien and the enemy) responsible for their condition and actions. Hence, if we (we and the groups we like) are bad off, it must be because of "them" or the "system." Conversely, if "they" are not doing well, it is their own fault. Of course, any success we have is due to our own efforts, despite "them." Where truth ends and self-justification begins is hard to tell. Empirically, there is agreement among "leaders" of some groups that black poverty is due to the system: blacks (82%), feminists (83%), Democrats (73%), intellectuals (65%), youth (69%), and labor (52%). "Leaders" of some other groups place less blame on the system: business (40%), farm (26%), and Republicans (37%). See Verba and Orren, *Equality in America,* pp. 73–83.

26. John Rawls, of course, makes the acceptance of this trade-off a basic part of his theory of justice. Inequalities are legitimate only if the worst off are benefited. See *A Theory of Justice,* pp. 60–108. I took the same position in *Process Ethics,* pp. 214–21, although I allowed other grounds for inequality as well. But suppose people decide not to accept this trade-off, should they not be allowed to? What would people decide merely on the issues, when they did not know what their own situations would be? That is Rawls's test, and a good one, but is his conclusion about what choice would be made beyond question?

27. This is the complaint of Daniel Bell and his fellow defenders of meritocracy. "Contemporary populism, in its desire for wholesale egalitarianism, insists in the end on complete leveling. It is not for *fairness* but against *elitism;* its impulse is not justice but *ressentiment.*" See "On Meritocracy and Equality," in Schaeffer, ed., *The New Egalitarianism,* p. 50. Bell opts for what he calls a "just meritocracy," a system in which, given equal opportunity, those who earned their status by their competence are allowed to rise to the top.

28. See my *Process Ethics,* pp. 174–79, 237–40, 280–81.

29. Ibid., pp. 37–82.

CHAPTER / FIVE

The Passion for Economic Equality

The political problem for mankind is to combine three things: economic efficiency, social justice, and individual liberty.
John Maynard Keynes

The time has come . . . to admit that the pursuit of equity and equal economic opportunity demands a fundamental restructuring of the economy.
Lester Thurow

For believers in the American dream of equality, full employment is the best of all policies.
Robert Lekachman

It is possible that the ultimate goods of human life, where to divide is not to take away, may be more easily attained when its instruments and means are less greedily grasped and more freely shared.
R. H. Tawney

The economics of equality can work. . . . The *politics* of equality—that is a little harder.
Robert Kuttner

THE EXISTENCE OF POVERTY in a land as rich as America is a shame and disgrace, nor are the rates of unemployment that routinely occur year after year a credit to a nation devoted to the work ethic. The economic inequality that prevails is an offense to justice as well as to charity. Poverty, unemployment, and inequality are symptoms of ills that call for drastic cures. What stands in the way of the required transformation to create a more egalitarian society are moral and political factors, not any lack of technical knowledge. Were the national commitment present and so expressed through democratic processes, it would be possible—though not easy—to move toward an economic system that meets the requirements of justice without unduly offending against efficiency or individual liberty. It is the task of those who share the passion for equality to work toward the creation of the appropriate values in a politically effective majority so that the egalitarian vision can become incarnate in economic institutions and practices. This achievement would constitute the most authentic fulfillment imaginable of the American dream. Such are the themes that will be explored in the pages to follow.

Let us admit at once the enormous difficulties of combining the elements of the Keynesian trinity: economic efficiency, social justice, and individual liberty. Had we perfect knowledge and a passionate political commitment to the favored ideals, internal tensions inevitably would arise among equality, liberty, and efficiency even in the best of all possible worlds. But we lack complete knowledge of all the best possible economic policies and their consequences in practice, even if we had the will to create a full employment society with no poverty and much less inequality of income and wealth than currently exists.

Hence, a modest agenda will be proposed here that claims only that we now know enough to accomplish more than we are at present, if enough people wanted to badly enough. Certainly hunger and poverty could be removed. Full-employment policies could be adopted. The economic underclass in our cities could be reduced, if not eliminated.[1] Taxation plus other measures in a restructured economy could reduce inequality. How much sacrifice of economic growth, if any, would be involved if the wisest policies were followed is hard to say. How easily inflation could be controlled in the context of full-employment policies is uncertain, although it appears to be manageable. Certainly some liberties (or economic powers) that many individuals presently enjoy would be curtailed, though other persons would find their range of action considerably enhanced. The incomes of the well-off would have to be lowered so that those of the bottom strata could be raised. Equally competent economists equally committed to strong egalitarian goals would inevitably disagree over the most effective means to achieve them. Nevertheless, it is still the thesis of this chapter that the main obstacles to a smoothly working, prosperous, more egalitarian, full-employment society preserving justice-mandated liberties are political and moral, not economic.[2]

It is the burden of this chapter that justice requires more economic equality.[3] Policies should be adopted at every appropriate level of government to achieve that end. Such a claim requires moral justification. To do this, it must be argued plausibly, if not demonstrated conclusively, that more egalitarian policies would not be destructive of the basic rights of the affluent. Some compromises and trade-offs are, of course, unavoidable. Put differently, it must be shown that the Keynesian goals of social justice (here read greater equality), economic efficiency, and individual freedom can be realized simultaneously in some sort of acceptable combination.

The Justification for More Economic Equality

In the American tradition both liberty and equality have been central. But a certain primacy has been granted to liberty. Equality enters first as a qualification of liberty, so that liberties granted to anyone (that is, any adult citizen) must be granted to all. Equal liberty has been the foundational value. Equality also plays a role as a second and independent value: all human beings are created equal and have certain inalienable rights. Primarily, equality has had a personal and political meaning. Every human being is equal to every other as a person and as a citizen. Each has equal claims to "life, liberty, and the pursuit of happiness." This guarantees to all the right to give consent to their governance and to participate as equals in the making of the rules that order the common life. The American tradition has also included a list of civil and other rights that have varied over the last two centuries as social values and judicial decisions have mandated.[4]

In the economic sphere equal liberty has meant equality of opportunity. In principle, all are free, and equally so, to own property, to buy and sell, to work for oneself or another, to employ others, to produce and consume, and in every way to use whatever talents one has in all legal ways to compete for the rewards that society offers. But this has never implied that outcomes were to be made equal. A capitalist system has provided opportunities through the operation of the market to gain unequal shares of wealth and income. Inequality of results is to be expected and has been accepted as normal, unavoidable, just, or even beneficial. Obviously, the reality has often contradicted the ideal of equal opportunity. The denial of equality to blacks, women, Native Americans, and other ethnic groups, as well as to the poor and socially disadvantaged, is written clear and plain.

Governmental actions over two centuries have, of course, had major and minor redistributional effects, both in reducing and in increasing inequalities of wealth and income. In the half-century prior to the Reagan administration, important steps were taken to equalize opportunities and to mitigate the worst consequences of joblessness and destitution. Moreover, the development of a welfare state with a mixed economy has meant that government has taken responsibility for reducing unemployment, controlling inflation, and promoting prosperity in general.[5] Nevertheless, the deliberate attempt to bring about greater equality in the distribution of wealth and income in accordance with some specified pattern of outcomes has never been a matter of explicit policy.[6]

The traditional American norms of equal political liberty and equal economic opportunity have been expressed within a dominating framework of individualism. Individualism has taken many forms and has often been associated with a commitment to the community as a whole.[7] In its extreme form, individualism takes the form of social nominalism. This theory assumes that only individuals are really real and that society is created by voluntary covenant for the achievement of certain common goals. Society is simply a name for the sum total of all individuals. All social processes and patterns can be understood as the aggregate product of individual actions. Within this framework the state's domestic role is basically to make and enforce fair rules of the game and to guarantee equal liberty to all who want to play.

When these assumptions are in force, it follows that the outcome of fair play is not to be interfered with. If some are more successful than others in playing the economic game, so be it. A deliberate policy of redistribution for the sake of reducing inequalities will be interpreted as taking from some to benefit others. Policies designed to redistribute income and wealth as their primary goal are seen as pure and simple theft. To the extent that individuals are separate and independent agents interacting with each other on the basis of voluntary contract and exchange, any efforts by the state to go beyond guaranteeing equality of opportunity to enforce any degree of equality of results are clearly unjust. Egalitarian measures involve the use of coercive power by the state, which is destructive of individual liberty. A society out of charity may decide by democratic means to give aid to the poor and helpless, although justice as such does not require it. Of course, individuals motivated by love are free to equalize matters by any kinds of voluntary or cooperative actions they care to undertake.

Modern individualism has been connected to the self-interest of burgeoning commercial classes who wished to be free from the restrictions placed on trade, profit, and social mobility in previous eras.[8] In fact, one of the consequences of the rise of capitalism with its market economy was the disruption of the organic ties that had bound the various classes to the land and to each other.[9] The spirit of these emerging economic forces was aided and abetted, or perhaps mutually and reciprocally generated, by the virtues sponsored by the spread of Protestantism, especially in its Calvinist form.[10] New social philosophies found in John Locke, Adam Smith, and others provided the ideological foundations of the new era. In short, a host of social and intellectual forces were conspiring and mutually reinforcing each other to produce the distinctive features of the modern age. Democracy, capitalism, and Protestantism are the most prominent institutional expressions of these creative and dominating influences. All three flourished in America. Emphasis on equal individual freedom on the part of the rising economic classes was but a natural expression of their self-interest. These motivations were rationalized by ideologies that provided the happy thought that in their strivings the hope of success and the comfort of moral virtue coincided.

Any proposal designed to justify state action to guarantee greater equality of wealth and income must be based on sociological assumptions different from those that have prevailed in the past and that dominate many contemporary libertarian philosophies.[11] Equally important is the question whether the required constellation of political forces can be mustered, armed with a cogent intellectual vision that is sufficiently motivating, to bring about the necessary changes. The democratic left at the moment is in such disarray, both ideologically and politically, that sanguine hopes cannot be easily entertained. Still, the future may tell a different story. The task at hand is to make the moral and economic case for a more egalitarian society.

The modern American economy is an enormously complex, highly organized, interdependent system. Interdependence implies more than coordination (as seen on an assembly line, for example) and suggests an interconnectedness among mutually sustaining parts. These organic tendencies characterize the relationship among its internal components and its relationship to the world economy as well. Coordination is illustrated by what is involved in getting a head of lettuce from California to a dinner table in North Carolina. When one considers all the associated products, technologies, and people that surround the growing, selling, transportation, and purchase of lettuce, the imagination is staggered. Fertilizers, tractors, trucks, gasoline, the chemical industry, and all the work of all the producers, laborers, truck drivers, store clerks, executives, managers, etc., are only some of the cogs in the complicated network of interlocking events that provides lettuce from a farm on one coast to a family on the other.

Interdependence, then, requires but involves more than the coordinated ordering of a string of events in proper sequence to produce the desired outcome. Adjusting prices send signals through the market and thus do a marvelous job with this. More important for ethics is that mutual dependence among causally interconnected events, persons, organizations, and processes bind persons together in an integrated system of activities. This can be demonstrated in four ways.

1. Occupational groups constitute a division of labor in a framework of reciprocal dependency. Farmers provide food for factory workers,

who build the tractors that plow the fields that grow the cattle, grain, and vegetables. Truck drivers transport oranges to cities and fertilizer to farms. A multitude of professionals provide essential services from medical care to insurance to producers and transporters of goods. Farmers, truck drivers, factory workers, and physicians perform work that others depend on in a network of mutually sustaining activities. This is an elementary lesson in economics, but its implications for an equalitarian social philosophy are profound.

2. Equally simple but important is the fact that developments in one region, industry, or economic sector send ripples of major and minor proportions through the system. It would be too much to say that everything affects everything else. The system is much too extensive for that. Much can be absorbed locally or segmentally without nationwide repercussions. The failure of the orange crop in Florida due to a freeze probably will not depress salaries for college professors in North Dakota. But large-scale unemployment in heavy industry, such as steel or automobiles, does have multiple negative effects on a massive scale. Likewise, impacts from outside—for example, OPEC and the oil shocks, competition from Japan and elsewhere, purchase of grain by the USSR—affect the domestic economy regionally, segmentally, and nationally. The point is that we are connected by many mutually determining chains of action and reaction in complicated networks of causation—reciprocal, unilateral, and otherwise.

3. Interdependency also suggests the connectedness and reciprocity among a multitude of economic processes.[12] While the Phillips curve may not describe a universal and unavoidable law, some inverse relationship does seem to hold between unemployment and inflation. Policies designed to cure unemployment may benefit some persons and groups while at the same time stimulating inflation, which helps and harms a different combination of persons. It is difficult to find mechanisms that benefit all and hurt none. In the short run, at least, a zero-sum factor appears to be unavoidable in any proposed solution. Trade-offs abound all over: one's loss is another's gain.[13] Likewise, some compromises between efficiency and equality may be unavoidable. It is probably too pessimistic to think, as many economists imply, that all equality gains come at the cost of efficiency. But it is also clear that some egalitarian policies do carry with them efficiency losses. Many efficiency-equality bargains can doubtless be made, some of which increase both at the same time.[14] The point is that mutual dependences and processes of reciprocal influence, if not causation, exist among various economic phenomena. Moreover, cures of one ill may bring on another. In the process different groups of people have their incomes raised or lowered in patterns that vary with the alternative policies.

4. The economic order is a system, a complex organization of

The Passion for Economic Equality / 135

organizations large and small, interconnected and mutually affecting each other. More and more the work of the world is done by organizations, agencies, and institutions—hospitals, farms, large corporations, small businesses, schools, governments, and on and on through a long list. Individuals function in the economy largely as members of these organizations. Participation in one or many of them provides income, meaning, satisfaction, and security.[15] Not to belong, not to have a place, not to have a paying job in some organization is for most Americans a source of major distress and catastrophe, except as the society provides resources to stave off total destitution. Our welfare is bound up with the prosperity of the organizations in which we work. The whole system of organizations is bound together in causal chains of mutuality and reciprocity that not only affect our income but also are an important source of meaning, purpose, and fulfillment.

The point of all this is that the economy has holistic features that cannot be reduced to the sum total of all individual transactions. "Organism" says too much, but organic characteristics abound. The economic order is a system with mutually sustaining parts. While not everything may be influentially connected to everything else, many things that happen in one sector ripple through every other. Many processes are interwoven into a network of mutual causation and reciprocity. A multitude of factors and forces interact in mutually determining ways. The internal dynamics of the economic order exhibit law-abiding tendencies, although it is currently impossible to combine precise relevant data with reliable theory to make accurate predictions in all cases.

Involved in this complex system are human beings whose lives and destinies are dependent on its health and vitality but whose own actions, taken singly, cannot control its ups and downs. Individuals (even when, to use the economists' jargon, responding as rational utility maximizers) are at the mercy of forces that may leave them unemployed and devastated. Luck—just being in the right place at the right time—along with hard work and skill determine success or failure. The truth is that we are all in it together. We are bound up in a common system of operations with internal structural features that are more than the sum of its individual parts and specific processes. Unpredictable contingencies on the world scene, the invention of new technologies, the power, prejudice, and selfish design of groups and classes whose interests are not ours, pure happenstance, and numerous other factors beyond the control of any individual, region, or economic sector all create a web of interdependence and commonality.[16]

The polemical side of the argument is that social nominalism is a theory totally unfit to serve as a presupposition for understanding the reality of today's economy and for developing a theory of justice. The positive apologetic is that society has organic features that require at least a moderate theory of social realism. Social realism views the total system as having a reality, a unity, a structure, an ensemble of mutually determining dynamics that cannot be reduced to the aggregate of all individual actors and actions. Individuals are independent and autonomous in some respects, and interdependent and socially conditioned or determined in other respects. To paraphrase the words of Paul the Apostle, "For as in one [physical] body we have many members, and all the members do not have the same function, so we though many are one body as an economic system, and individually members one of another" (Roms. 12:4–5). There is a common good to which we contribute and from which we receive as members of a common system.

The moral argument is that this commonality creates a ground for some measure of equality of outcome as well as equality of opportunity. The intuitive presupposition is that good created in common should be enjoyed in common. More specifically, what is produced cooperatively by equal contributions should be shared equally. If three persons jointly and equally bring into being three units of Good X, then each of them has a claim to one unit of Good X—all else being equal. Many factors have been set forth on these pages as a basis for qualifying the equal distribution of goods: merit, efficiency (or the larger good), the quest for excellence, previous agreements, the good of the larger community, need, and rectification of past injustice. No claim is or will be made that wealth and income should be distributed equally to all. A more modest and defensible contention is that moral justification exists, based on an adequate theory of justice interpreted within a proper understanding of the social facts, for more equality than now obtains.

In particular, justice—not simply compassion and charity—requires a flexible limit at the top and a minimum but generous floor at the bottom of the wealth and income scale. Ethical theorists despair at the inability to give precise weighting to all the moral factors that determine just distributions, just as economists despair at being able to measure some economic determinants and to make precise predictions about the consequences of alternative economic policies. The proposition being defended is that ethical theory and economic fact create a presumption in favor of some measure of equality of outcome and put the burden of proof on those who would propose the contrary.

In the economic order, then, what is created in common should be enjoyed in common.[17] What is so produced, or to the extent that it is equally produced, all else being equal, should be shared equally. Granted, what counts as "in common" is not subject to precise

The Passion for Economic Equality / 137

calculation. Granted, many other factors are relevant in determining what a just distribution is. Granted, in complex situations exact measurement of all the relevant factors is difficult. Granted, differences exist in the intuitive and theoretical moral judgments of people about what should count for how much and which trade-offs are morally superior. Nevertheless, the case for the positive claim that justice in today's world requires not only fair and effective equality of opportunity but some measure of equality of result is too strong to ignore. Moreover, the case for the contrary is so weak that it fades into insignificance.

A provocative and much-discussed example offered by Robert Nozick to establish the validity of his own libertarian views may actually be more instructive in refuting the social nominalism on which his theory of justice rests.[18] Imagine, he says, any just distribution that suits you—D_1. Now suppose that Larry Bird (a contemporary player rather than his outdated reference to Wilt Chamberlain) makes an arrangement by which each person pays a surcharge of 25 cents on each ticket, to be paid directly to him. The fans are perfectly willing to do this in order to see him play. The result will be a disturbance of D_1 and the creation of a new distribution—D_2. In triumph, proleptically celebrating his supposedly irrefutable point, Nozick asks to have stated the principle of justice by which one could justify some third party (the state in this case) interfering coercively to restore the original situation. Presumably, there is none. Redistribution schemes rob some persons in order to give to others. Since justice is done when the right procedure is followed—individuals who rightfully possess holdings engaging in voluntary transactions with others—any outcome is just no matter what inequalities are created.

Given Nozick's assumptions, his conclusions are irrefutable. But by abstracting these particular exchanges from the total concrete setting in which they occur, his analysis conveniently omits the interdependence of persons within a complex system of economic activities. Let us grant that Nozick can no doubt account for everything that occurs to his satisfaction within the terms of his social nominalism. Nonetheless, given a more holistic understanding of society, economic transactions are viewed as social-historical processes organically connected within a system. From this perspective, which is certainly as plausible as Nozick's, his analysis lacks cogency. Indeed, it fails completely.

The transactions that enrich the talented Mr. Bird take place within a complex social and historical context involving as necessary presuppositions many persons, events, and processes. Note that he did not invent the technologies that make possible the manufacture of the basketball. Nor is he to be given credit for the game of basketball itself, its popularity, or the TV technologies and industry that give him the widespread coverage that makes him famous. The arenas in which he plays, or some of them anyway, were probably constructed in part with public funds. The fact that individuals are willing to give up their quarters to see Bird play does not mean that he is not dependent on their interest in the game, which preceded him and will last after he is too old to perform his marvelous feats. The list could go on and on. The point is that these particular arrangements that fill the pockets of Larry Bird with cash emerge out of a rich stream of historical events and occur in a complicated matrix of contemporary happenings. The transfer of funds from fans to Bird requires for its reality and meaning a connectedness both with the relevant past and essential present facts. All of these happenings, necessary to the transactions at hand, are interconnected in organic ways in a total system that is more than the sum of its parts.[19] Viewed in its full concreteness, the arrangements between Bird and his fans might well lead to the association of redistributive taxation with justice without the shock of incongruence.

Conservatives and libertarians sometimes maintain that redistributionist theories ignore how goods come into being and act as if they just appeared, like manna from heaven. Precisely the opposite is being done here. It is a consideration of how, by whom, and in which historical and social contexts things are produced that leads to the egalitarianism being proposed. Those who think that economic processes can be reduced to the aggregate of individual transactions, contributions, exchanges, etc., based on voluntary contracts and acts, each separate from all the others, commit what Alfred North Whitehead called "the fallacy of misplaced concretion."[20] This error occurs when, ignoring the fullness, richness, complexity, and depth of the total being and event in question, an abstraction is taken for the concrete reality. It leaves out the temporal and spatial connectedness of realities and events, i. e., the essential surrounding context in which particular things occur and which create and shape what is immediately present. There are, says Whitehead, no "brute facts" unconnected from neighboring events and past occurrences.[21]

Economic analysis that abstracts a set of happenings and relationships called "the market" can easily be seduced into the same fallacy.[22] According to numerous critics, contemporary neo-classical economics disastrously ignores the total social and historical framework in which market processes occur.[23] This school of economics assumes for its purposes a world of many buyers and sellers operating as rational utility maximizers with perfect information. All actors function in a perfectly competitive setting in which labor and capital are perfectly mobile. In this setting adjusting prices clear all markets. With this imaginary world in mind, deductive reasoning produces elaborate mathematical models in the presumption that real world deviations do not undermine its fundamental validity.[24]

Such abstractions about the market leave out much that is essential to the fullness of reality. People, for example, are viewed as rational utility maximizers; that is, they are efficient agents who always seek to gain the most they can—usually (but not exclusively if the theory is to work) money or what it can buy. Consequently, no matter what they actually do, they are presumed to have chosen the course of action that promised the greatest satisfaction.[25] If a person takes a job paying less than another available one, then there must be some "psychic income" that makes up and surpasses the utility deficit associated with the lower salary. Hence, the proposition is either irrefutable, because it is either tautological, or empirically sometimes false, since people have many— and frequently conflicting—motivations, even self-sacrificing ones.[26] The political realities by which power is unequally distributed among economic actors and which may give unfair advantage to some play a role only insofar as they produce inputs into the present system in terms of the factors that the model itself uses. The same is true of the values of individuals, groups, and classes that shape motivation. It is not that economists are (necessarily or unusually) ignorant of or oblivious of these matters, for they often are acknowledged in the textbooks.[27] Yet whatever else may be regarded as real beyond purely economic phenomena is translated, in economic science proper, into terms and formulas that fit and express market processes as pictured in the hypothetical model.

These abstractions have undoubted value for certain purposes. Economic models necessarily simplify situations for the sake of focusing on factors essential to theory-building. The danger is that the unwary may assume that market theory presents a more complete picture of reality than is actually the case. The analyses of mainline economic science must be taken for what they are—highly abstract, partially true, but potentially misleading descriptions of the real social world.

It is not enough merely to distinguish between "positive" and "normative" economics. The way "positive" economics is done involves value presupposition, which in turn creates a bias favorable toward some rather than other ways of organizing the economy.[28] It may be assumed too quickly in much contemporary economic theory that what is optimally efficient in its abstract models may also be best for the real world. Hence, a discipline with aspirations to be scientific may become an ideological instrument, whether this is consciously intended or not.[29] More specifically, the message is that a competitive economy will somehow, if not interfered with, produce the best outcome, given the real resources and preferences of the agents involved. "Best" may strictly mean only "most efficient." But subtly and surreptitiously the term takes on moral associations. For example, the "marginal productivity" theory of income distribution functions as a description, but may easily slide over into the judgment that such outcomes are right or just. Actually, they may or may not be. But for that reason, no one should take the distribution of wealth and income as determined by the operation of the market as just without examining the presuppositions that are at work in such a claim.[30]

To return to the main theme, the productive capacities of the economic system are the product of many persons, groups, and classes over a long period of time. Hence, to isolate present operations and individual transactions as the sole object of moral consideration is pure folly. This heritage from the past creates a common treasury upon which all now living have claims—greater than zero, but not translatable directly into absolute equality. A similar pull toward at least minimal equality is established by the common claim of all to the basic natural resources of the earth.[31] Of course, rights of ownership historically established must be given primary weight, despite the fact that theft, violence, and plunder as well as legitimate claims of possession pervade the past. But no ethical theory is adequate that does not, at the foundational level, see a primordial tug toward equal sharing of the fruits of the earth, whose original potential is the creation of no human agency (Ps. 24: 1).[32] A notion of stewardship of the earth for the sake of the fulfillment of all is called for rather than a notion of absolute ownership by particular persons or groups.

Moreover, individuals and firms are subject to many contingencies, created by the actions of others within an interdependent system, over which they have little or not control. To hold them completely responsible for the consequences ignores vital considerations. Luck itself often is a social creation. A farmer who owns rural land that becomes valuable because the city moves out toward it is the beneficiary of actions and processes that he had little to do with creating. Is it unjust if through taxation the whole community—which helped generate his wealth—shares in part in his good fortune? Hundreds of thousands may become unemployed because of new technologies, foreign competition, changing tastes, and a multitude of other contingencies that have system-wide repercussions. Is it justice or merely merciful compassion that demands assistance for those caught up in transitions systemically generated? Our destinies are bound up together. We are, to use the organic imagery of Paul the Apostle, "individually members one of another (Roms 12:5 RSV)." Justice requires that we take responsibility for each other through corporate action.

A theory of justice appropriate to an economic order with holistic qualities fundamental to its functioning will incorporate a view of individuals both as independent selves and as interdependent members of a community of communities.[33] The ideal in each of these settings—from the family to the global society, with the local region and the nation in between—is self-realization in community.[34] Mutuality and reciprocity in the creation and sharing of a common good must complement the quest for individual good. Each contributes to and receives from the whole. Initially and abstractly, the norm is for equality in responsibility and reward, although circumstances introduce numerous qualifications. The meaning of equality must be defined in ways relevant and peculiar to each setting in which persons cooperatively generate and share a common treasury of goods and services. In the family a basic, though not necessarily the sole, rule may be from each according to ability and to each according to need. Such an ideal presupposes a high commitment of each member to the welfare of others and works best where love is the dominating motive. Such conditions cannot be assumed in the larger society, yet even there the ideal has relevance as a transcending point of reference to serve as a lure toward higher attainments.

In the nation justifiable inequalities will derive from the weight that must be assigned to individual liberty. Opportunities must be provided for the pursuit of excellence. Merit achieved through the exercise of individual freedom must be rewarded. Inequalities that result from choice may be completely justified.[35] Legitimate inequalities may also result from the role assigned to efficiency. The provision of incentives is necessary to evoke contributions, to prevent the shirking of duty, and thereby to enlarge the good from which all will benefit. The biblical rule that those (able-bodied but lazy—author's qualification) who do not work, do not eat has its place (II Thess. 3:10). This proviso is justifiable when appropriately invoked both for the sake of efficiency and of morality.

The moral calculus is complex.[36] The overall principle—identical with the norm of self-realization in community—is that individual freedom, social equality, and private and public good are to be maximized within the constraints each places on the others. Obviously, it is easier to say what the principles of justice are than to apply them in complicated situations. The case is being made here, on the basis of justice, for greater equality of income and wealth than now prevails. How much and what kinds of equality are appropriate and produced by what mechanisms remain to be specified. The best that can be hoped for is some general approximation of justice, given all the factors and weightings and trade-offs that inevitably arise. All conceptions of justice suffer from these same limitations. The one espoused here at least has the merit of matching its basic ethical assumptions to the social facts. This virtue is not shared by theories of justice which, consciously or in innocence, presuppose some variant of social nominalism as its sociological partner.

The moral arguments set forth above do not lead to precise formulas and equations to explain how much economic equality justice mandates. Unfortunately, some vagueness is inevitable when dealing with such complex realities. Intuition as well as pragmatic judgments must of necessity strive for rough approximations to the moral norm in the absence of exact indicators. Disagreements are unavoidable, even among those who are persuaded by the theory of justice elaborated on these pages. The main point is that moral considerations create a tug, a dynamic lure, in the direction of more equality than now prevails. Pragmatically, this pull leads minimally to the following goal: in a society as prosperous as ours, no one must be allowed to fall beneath a certain level of decency with respect to basic needs of health, security, and meaningful participation in the society. Two more specific propositions related to this aim are: (a) Full employment policies must be adopted, and (b) a minimal level of income (and/or material well-being) should be guaranteed for all. In addition, special provision must be made for the sick, the elderly, and the disabled. Some egalitarians will want to press for more, but surely no one who takes the lure toward greater economic equality as a mandate of justice can be content with less.[37]

Economic Realities and Economic Remedies

All truths are half truths.
           Alfred North Whitehead
Accept complexity.
           Marshall Shulman
Seek simplicity—and mistrust it.
           Alfred North Whitehead
There are no facts, only interpretations.
           Friedrich Nietzsche

It will be useful to turn from philosophical discussion to an empirical rendering of the currents facts regarding poverty and inequality.

Some Facts and Figures

In the United States, the poverty level for one individual in 1984 was $5,278, and for a family of four, $10,609.[38] (This definition of poverty is based on an analysis by the federal government of what a minimally decent life costs.) By that definition, 14.4 percent of the population was below the poverty level—11.5 percent of the white population and 33.8 percent of the black.[39] When the market value of food, housing and medical benefits received is factored in, the number of persons living below the poverty line in 1984 was reduced from 33.7 million to 22.6

million,[40] which lowered the percentage from 14.4 percent to around 10 percent, or 7,277,000 families.)[41] This was a modest improvement from the 1959 rate of 8,320,000 families, or 39.5 million persons, who were below the poverty level.[42] Table 5.1 shows the actual income of households in dollars.

Table 5.1   Money Income of Households, 1984 (in dollars)

Under 5,000	5,000– 9,999	10,000– 14,999	15,000– 19,999	20,000– 24,999	25,000– 34,999	35,000– 49,000	50,000 and up
7.9%	13.2%	12.2%	11.4%	10.4%	16.9%	15.3%	12.8%

Median income, all households: $22,415
white households: 23,647
black households: 13,471
Spanish households: 16,992

Source: Statistical Abstract of the United States, 1986, p. 445.

As Table 5.2 shows, little change in the distribution of income has occurred in the last third of a century. A significant change did occur, however, between the beginning of the Great Depression and the end of World War II. The share of income going to the bottom fifth rose from 3.9 percent in 1929 to 5.5 percent in 1970.[43] Meanwhile, the portion going to the top fifth declined from 51.4 percent to 41.6 percent during approximately the same period.[44] Perhaps even more striking is that between 1929 and 1984 the percentage going to the top 5 percent slipped from 30.0 to 16.0. To complete or at least to balance the picture, it should be noted that while these overall figures have not changed much recently, within that framework mobility in observable.[45] Numerous individuals and families have risen out of poverty into higher income ranks. For example, the black middle class has expanded considerably in recent decades.

Table 5.2   Distribution of Income to Families (in percentages)

Population	1984	1980	1970	1960	1950	1929
Lowest fifth	4.7%	5.1%	5.5%	4.9%	4.5%	3.9%
Second fifth	11.0	11.6	12.0	12.0	12.0	8.6
Middle fifth	17.0	17.5	17.4	17.6	17.4	13.8
Fourth fifth	24.4	24.3	23.5	23.6	23.5	19.3
Highest fifth	42.9	41.6	41.6	42.0	43.6	54.4
Top 5 percent	16.0					30.0

Source: 1984, Stastical Abstract of the United States 1986, p. 452. 1929, Roy J. Ruffin and Paul R. Gregory, Principles of Economics, p. 657. Other years, William J. Baunmol and Alan S.Binder, Economics: Principles and Policy, p. 707.

The distribution of wealth is far more unequal than the spread of income. Studies give varying results, but all show a high concentration at the rich end of the spectrum. According to one source, in 1972 the top 1 percent owned 24.1 percent of the wealth, while the top one half of 1 percent (0.5%) possessed 18.9 percent. In 1929, however, the top 1 percent had 36.3 percent of all wealth, considerably higher than in 1972.[46] According to a study by the Congressional Joint Economic Committee released in July 1986, the top one half of 1 percent—the wealthiest 420,000 households—in 1983 controlled 27 percent of the country's wealth. This was a gain of 2 percent since 1963, when the top one half of 1 percent held a little more than 25 percent.[47]

How are we to interpret these figures? After all, it is never the fact of inequality as such that matters, but the extent of inequalities that prevail resulting from what causes and judged by what criteria. Even granted that some inequalities are unavoidable, that some are necessary, and that some are justified,[48] no one can say with assurance just what the distribution of money and property in the United States should be. No direct line can be drawn from the qualitative judgments associated with moral theory to the quantitative measurements of the distribution of income and wealth. As Aristotle noted centuries ago, the methods of each discipline must fit the subject matter under investigation. Intuitions and informed judgments must create the link between moral theory and empirical fact. On such a vast scale only the roughest of approximations is possible. Hence, all that can be done here is to set forth a set of claims, along with supporing reasons. The result is offered to the arena of public debate where disputes can be settled theoretically by persuasion, if at all, and politically by the exercise of power expressed through electoral processes.

Some Proposals

It is the passionate claim of this chapter that the social facts respecting the interdependence of economic actors in the United States call for a more equal distribution of wealth and income than presently prevails. The arena in which justice lies is somewhere between the present pattern and the straight line featured in the Lorenz curves found in economics textbooks.[49] The primary concern is to eliminate poverty. A secondary goal is to reduce inequalities generally in the direction of a more even spread across the whole population. Beyond that the market can be left to distribute wealth and income by its own processes, assuming that fair and effective equality of opportunity prevails throughout. This is probably about as well as one can do in approximating moral norms and in accommodating social facts.

Economists are fond of telling us that poverty is a relative term and that it can be defined in various ways. They are, of course, right. An *absolute* concept would establish the minimum that an individual or family needs in order to meet basic needs of food, housing, clothing, medical care, and so on. The government set that figure for 1984 at $5,278 for one person and at $10,609 for a family of four. That is probably about as good a measure as one can find for the purpose. We need not be bothered by the recognition that even this so-called "absolute" measure is itself quite relative when compared to the desperately poor of Africa and Asia, to nearly everybody in medieval Europe, or to Americans of two centuries ago. A *relative* concept compares the poorest portion of the population with all the rest. Average citizens as well as philosophers have frequently set this measure at one-half the median income of all families in the nation. For 1984 the median income was $22,415. One-half of this is $11,208, only a few hundred dollars higher than the poverty level officially set by the United States government. Hence, steps should be taken to see to it that every family of four has a package of income and/or goods and services that does not fall below about $11,000, adjusted for smaller families and individuals.

But other complications enter. Just what is to be taken into account in determining how poor people are? Those who are in control of definitions and statistics have great power. They can determine what "the facts" are and define the limits of the possible. Reality often recedes behind interpretations that manipulate empirical data for ideological purposes. Yet there is no escape from the problem. Social scientists are to be commended and encouraged in their attempts to provide understanding. One study, for example, demonstrated the undoubted advantages for some purposes of using a criterion of "earnings capacity" rather than current money income as a measure of economic status.[50] Suppose family A (F-A) has a money income of $8,000 and family B (F-B) of $13,000. In current income terms, F-A is below the poverty line, while F-B is above. Yet the fact may be that in F-B both wife and husband work outside the home, while in F-A only one spouse does, although their domestic situations are similar. Both working spouses make $8,000. F-A, it appears, is no worse off in terms of total well-being, although they have less money. They just put a value on housework and having a parent at home, which F-B does not. The capacity to earn money may be the same in both families. They just make different choices. This only illustrates the many complications regarding definitions and facts that pose tough value questions.[51]

An important part of a total scheme to overcome poverty and reduce economic inequalities is a full-employment policy.[52] A job for individuals and for breadwinners in families is a fundamental way in which persons participate in the society with a sense of belonging. Gainful employment is not only a source of income but a provider of meaning, self-esteem, and security. The overwhelming majority of people want to earn their own way, to be self-supporting, to have the sense of independence and success that comes with a decent income. A complex, interdependent society dedicated to the welfare of its citizens will take responsibility for providing a job at reasonable pay for all who want and need to work.

The mechanisms by which this end is realized are, as such, secondary to the achievement itself as long as efficiency and effectiveness prevail. If the market operating on its own can provide jobs that pay enough for all who need and want to work to stay above the poverty line, then so be it.[53] But if this does not happen—and it has not recently and is not likely to any time soon—other steps are necessary. The overall unemployment rate in June 1986 was 7.1 percent. While economists like to argue the definition of "full-employment," surely this rate is unnecessarily high.[54] If reducing this rate by as much as is reasonable requires government to aid or jointly plan with private enterprise or even to subsidize wages or employers, then so be it. But if all else fails, the government must become an employer of last resort. The pay scale should be equal to prevailing wages for given skills. Jobs should be provided that benefit society. For example, the infrastructure of the country needs rebuilding—highways, bridges, sewers, harbors, mass transit, railroads, water supply, and so on through a long list.[55] Government-sponsored employment could conceivably involve competition with private businesses in some areas if public enterprises do not provide sufficient work for all. Once the goal is adopted, economists, business people, and planners with the necessary expertise and experience can devise the mechanisms.

One barrier to government sponsored employment is the cost, though one might reasonably expect that such programs would pay for themselves by generating additional revenue in a prosperous society.[56] Another threat that arises from full-employment policies is inflation. Perhaps within limits, this is a necessary price worth paying. An incomes policy may be required. Other efforts to hold inflation within reasonable bounds will certainly be necessary if current economic theory is to be believed. Again, the final question is what do we want most and what costs we are willing to pay in comparison with other alternatives. The final resolution must be worked out politically. The economics can be handled if creative imagination is allowed to work out a set of policies once the priorities have been socially set through democratic processes.

Conservatives usually want a work requirement as a condition of providing money to the able-bodied with no inhibiting family responsibilities. Such a policy is acceptable if the conditions and the administration of it are humane. The principle of requiring work from the healthy is sound, though carrying it out becomes complicated and involves administrative costs. However, if good jobs are available at decent pay, why shouldn't those who can be required to work if they expect help from society? Most people want to earn their way and only need the opportunity. In fact, a primary goal should be to provide as much income as possible through employment programs—public and private, including job training and other aids—so that the number requiring cash assistance from the government is reduced to the absolute minimum. Always there will be parents with small children, the disabled, the sick, and so on, who are not free or able to work. Those who are able but not willing to work should not be supported by public means.

A cruel dilemma arises. A refusal to assist able-bodied persons who choose not to work involves the risk that family members who are dependent on them—children or disabled adults—will suffer. To illustrate the complexity, some worry that if mothers with pre-school children are exempted from work, they might be tempted to have another child when the youngest approaches school age. One suggestion is that mothers with small children take turns providing each other day care, thus making them eligible for work outside the home. The debate gets mean on occasion when it appears that some had rather risk starving a few people, including mothers and their young children, rather than take a chance that a few lazy dead-beats might get a hand-out without working. A preference is being expressed here for taking the risks in the opposite direction. At the same time, to employ the biblical injunction, it is also being urged that those who are able but unwilling to work do not eat at public expense (II Thess. 3:10-11).[57]

If a full-employment policy were in effect and effective, conceivably some modification of the present welfare system might be sufficient. Where work requirements are in effect, a carefully crafted supplemental program of aid—of money and/or goods and services—directed at the needs of the unemployable, the underemployed, the old, the young, and the sick and disabled may serve about as well as any alternative. Policies should be adopted, however, which are designed to keep husbands and wives together rather than to tempt fathers to abandon their families.

If we modify the present welfare system so that the desired goals are achieved, numerous problems will still exist. If work requirements are to be enforced and generous benefits provided to meet specific needs, a core of administrators is necessary to carry out the program. They would also be needed as well to prevent (reduce?) abuse and fraud, which would be more tempting since the rewards would be greater. But this would involve complicated regulations and an expensive bureaucracy with all the demeaning intrusions into the lives of the poor and all the possible bad judgments and injustices that result when fallible and corruptible people must enforce a bundle of rules. Not only would the specifications be cumbersome and ill-fitted to meet all the varying circumstances of individual cases, but also the problem of ascertaining the relevant facts is formidable. Gathering them would require an invasion into the private lives of individuals and families that would inevitably produce resentment and hostility, as well as encouraging lying and cheating.

In light of all these difficulties, numerous economists prefer a Negative Income Tax (NIT). This would supplant the many types of welfare now in effect, while making allowances for those with special medical or other needs. A national health insurance program to cover all for catastrophic illnesses, chronic medical conditions, and so on, as well as some reasonable level of basic medical care is an essential part of the total package.

Two figures are needed to institute an NIT—a minimum level of support and a tax rate. Suppose the former is set for a family of four at $11,000 and the latter at 50 percent. Table 5.3 will show how the NIT works.

Table 5.3 A Negative Income Tax

Earnings (in dollars)	NIT Received	Total Income
0	$11,000	$11,000
$ 5,000	8,500	13,500
10,000	6,000	16,000
15,000	3,500	18,500
20,000	1,000	21,000
22,000	0	22,000

The NIT has two obvious advantages. (a) It would reduce the administrative costs involved in the present welfare system. The Internal Revenue Service could be used to carry out the program. (b) It would preserve work incentives. Low income families could keep half of what they earn. The basic drawback is that if the basic minimum is set high (to benefit the poor) and the tax rate low (to preserve work incentives), persons of moderate income above the guaranteed level receive some benefits. This makes the program very expensive. In the example above, families with incomes of up to $22,000 will get some kind of grant. If the NIT is set at one-half median family income and the tax rate at 50 percent, half the families in the country will receive at least a small amount of aid. It is impossible to have high benefits, strong work incentives, and low cost. Put differently, efficiency is gained either at the price of low benefits to the poor or high costs to taxpayers. In short, the liabilities of the NIT are so formidable that other options ought to be kept open.[58]

Obviously, some tough decisions are required. Welfare reform is a messy, complicated business in which competing values come into conflict. Compromise is inevitable. The trade-offs are exasperating. Some corruption and abuse of any system are unavoidable. It all comes down to a question of what the primary goals are to be and what trade-offs are acceptable in order to get the most of the best and the least of the worst that alternative policies can offer. Priorities must be set, the costs must be accepted, and the necessary compromises made. The case is being made here for finding ways to make it possible for all cooperating citizens to have benefits equal to one-half the median family income. Administratively efficient programs should be sought. Work incentives need to be preserved. Individual needs and special circumstances should be taken into account. Chiselers should be punished. Those responsible only for themselves should perhaps be allowed, in certain limited ways, to live outside the system, if they choose to do so.[59] Parents and spouses, however, should be coerced—as gently as possible but as effectively as the situation requires—to act responsibly in relation to their children and the partner of the opposite sex with whom they conceived their babies. Males, married or unmarried, should assume responsibility for the children they beget, and the system should be provide incentives that encourage this. When all that is desired cannot be had, it is necessary to choose what is most important, accept the least bad compromise, and do the best that can be done.

The Underclass

A problem of special difficulty is posed by the existence of an underclass. No one doubts its existence, but disputes about its definition, size, composition, and character abound. In particular, controversies rage about underlying causes and effective remedies. The underclass includes the hard-core poor and also others who are defined primarily by deviant behavior and who may not live in poverty. Disproportionately black and concentrated in cities, this peculiar segment of the lower class challenges social will and wisdom, perhaps beyond their capacity. Several (perhaps as many as 9 or 10) million people—white and black, rural and urban—exist at the margins of society, unable or unwilling to function in accordance with majority patterns of work and success. The urban group contains aggressively violent street criminals, hustlers operating in the underground economy, the passive poor who depend on welfare, and the traumatized who roam around aimlessly, often under the influence of alcohol or other drugs.[61] Poverty, crime, drugs, gangs, prostitution, joblessness, high infant mortality rates, and general disorder are daily facts of life in the ghetto.

A high drop-out rate from high school is common. Nationally an estimated 45 percent of Hispanics and 35 percent of blacks quit school before graduating. In New York City the rate is more than 50 percent for both groups. In one Chicago neighborhood 89 percent drop out. The unemployment rate for black teenagers has hovered around 40 percent, but in July, 1982, it was 49.7 percent.

Poverty in the underclass is frequently connected with family life in which babies are born to the unmarried—a shocking number of whom are adolescent girls. In 1950 17 percent of black babies were born out of wedlock. Now the rate is 60 percent, and in some places in Chicago and New York it is 75 percent. An Urban Institute study (1981) showed that more than half of all Aid to Families with Dependent Children (AFDC) went to women who had been or were teen-age mothers. Another study (1979) revealed that in New York City, about 75 percent of all children born out of wedlock during the previous eighteen years were still on AFDC.

Increasingly, poverty is connected with females. In 1979 just over half the total number of poor people lived in single-parent families headed by women or were women living alone or with non-relatives. More than 40 percent of black families are headed by a single woman, as compared to 12 percent of white families.

Here they all are, living on the boundaries—too complex a group in behavior, outlook, habits, and moral code to describe in any simple way. The street criminals and the hustlers are generally not poor, while most of the rest are. Some desperately want a job and can't find one. Others assiduously avoid honest work, preferring to hustle, steal, or stay on welfare. Yet whether rural or urban, white or black, frequently they are hostile and passive, have poor work habits and low self-confidence, and suffer from alcohol or other forms of drug addiction. They tend to be unskilled and of low educational attainment. No one of these elements in the profile is by any means limited to these marginalized people, but a peculiar and diverse ensemble of circumstances and characteristics is concentrated among them.

If we turn to diagnosis and prescription, ideology leaps into prominence. From the political right we learn that a pathology of culture and character is responsible.[62] The poor have mainly themselves to blame. Other conservatives, however, stress economic causes, often blamed on antibusiness policies in government.[63] Moreover, welfare programs, well-intended of course, have created a corrupting dependency, making it even more difficult for the poor to work their way out.[64] The poor actually need the spur of poverty to goad them toward success. From the left we learn that the existence of an underclass is largely the fault of society, making it nothing less than cruel to "blame the victim."[65] The problem is not that government programs have done too much but that they have done too little or not enough of the right things.[66]

Prescriptions follow diagnosis. Economic conservatives would have us dismantle the welfare state, reduce benefits, and get the free enterprise system going so that prosperity can trickle down to those who are willing to work hard enough. This might include the creation of enterprise zones in the inner city by tax inducements to provide both entrepreneurial and employment possibilities. Or they advocate mainly self-help from within.[67] Others on the right who see the problem in terms of deficient values and attitudes within the underclass—a pathology of character and culture—are pessimistic about cures.[68] Beyond charitable relief of the very young, the aged, and the sick, some would have us do little more than contain the malady as much as possible. Liberals would have the government make jobs and training available and give money, goods, and services to the poor to make up income deficits. Some liberals, however, also stress the need for self-help among the poor, including changes in outlook and behavior as well as efforts to overcome poverty.

Compounding and often confounding the situation is the dispute over whether race or class is the more important factor. Some black scholars speak of "the declining significance of race" and urge that primarily it is general economic conditions or the lack of education and skills that keep the poorest blacks from moving up.[69] Let us grant that racism still stands in the way of many blacks and that the black underclass suffers today from the long history of deprivation and oppression to which their color subjected them. Nevertheless, it is important to distinguish poor blacks of the underclass from middle class blacks who, with education and effort, can make and have made rapid progress. Those left in the ghettos lack the skills, the work habits, the character, the self-reliance—and the opportunities. Hence, economic factors take on increasing importance as the fact of race subsides.

Black conservatives join their white counterparts in placing their hope in free enterprise unencumbered by illusions that government welfare programs are the answer for either blacks or whites. They raise a number of questions. Have not many ethnic groups succeeded despite discrimination? Does not the fact that the new immigrants—the Vietnamese, Koreans, Cambodians. West Indians—have often outperformed blacks recently tell us that ethnic culture, individual character, and family values are the more reliable clues to upward mobility?[70]

Cutting across all these analyses is a controversy over whether economic or behavioral factors are primary. Some liberal and conservative diagnosticians assume that the problem is economic, while disagreeing over the causes and cures of poverty. If there is a cultural pathology, some—whether conservative or liberal—who advocate a large scale or "wholesale" solution think it surely must have been created by social and economic factors.[71] Against this is the behavioral point of view that assumes that attitudes, values, and choices of ethnic groups, families, and individuals are fundamental. Economic realities provide the basic clue neither to the source nor the remedy of the ills of the underclass. Instead, the phenomena represents a cultural malady that either cannot be cured or requires a transformation in values and behavior that must come from within and not as a mere consequence of economic change. Hence, society should do little in addition to providing minimal assistance for the helpless and handicapped.[72] This is the "Laissez-faire Option."[73]

If we are to make any headway in either understanding or improving the situation of the underclass, it is necessary to "accept complexity" (Marshall Shulman's phrase) and recognize with A. N. Whitehead that "all truths are half-truths." Liberals and conservatives—regardless of the extent to which they are economic determinists, cultural behaviorists, or some of both—frequently talk past each other. One wonders sometimes if the antagonists care more about defending cherished ideologies than searching out the truth, which is likely to be complicated. For the left to admit that individuals and groups have responsibility for themselves and their actions might weaken or undercut the rationale for government to provide assistance. For the cultural behaviorists on the right to admit any social causation of a persisting underclass might justify doing something that they oppose, at least philosophically, on other grounds. Both liberals and conservatives, who propose opposite remedies, often seem more sure of the efficacy of their solutions than the evidence justifies. In normative economic philosophy, faith overcomes many mountains of empirical uncertainty. Observing this defensiveness and ideological arrogance, one is tempted to say, "a plague on all your houses!" Surely the competing views are frequently right in some or much of what they affirm, and wrong in a lot of what they deny in the claims of the other side.

Doubtless the underclass does give evidence of a "tangle of pathology" (Kenneth Clark) or a "culture of poverty" (Oscar Lewis) in some sense, although the issue is highly controversial and emotionally volatile. Care must be taken that white and black middle-class values are not inappropriately used to judge lower-class ethnic and racial groups (whether white or black) in invidious fashion. Some ways of living, however, may not be psychologically healthy, morally defensible, or economically productive. To acknowledge this is not necessarily just "blaming the victim" (William Ryan). It may be to recognize

The Passion for Economic Equality / 153

that people are what they have become, whether by biological inheritance, ethnic traditions, social circumstances or individual choice. Some attitudes, habits, styles of life, and outlooks are not conducive to economic success, however they came about, whether by social causation or free responsive reaction to circumstances. Neither does a recognition that racial or class culture plays a role in shaping individual character mean that social conditions are not fundamental as well. While some individuals may be beyond hope, whether the reasons are biological, cultural, or personal, surely most are able to make progress with proper opportunity and assistance. Within limits nearly all people have some options. Families and individuals can and must decide how they will appropriate their past and deal with their present.

Social conditions, including a long history of racial oppression in the case of blacks, have doubtless played a role in creating a prevailing ethnic culture and a set of unhealthy values, attitudes, and behaviors that are reproduced through families over the generations. Government programs may have helped to create a dependency on welfare that is not conducive to self-reliance and patterns of self-help and hard work. Economic policies dictated by the interests of the powerful and the well off have often neglected the poor and disadvantaged. This has occurred perhaps more inadvertently as a consequence of the non-poor majority pursuing their own interests rather than out of any deliberate malice toward the less well off.

Economic facts, ethnic culture, family values, and individual choices mingle and reinforce each other in a history made up of many mutually conditioning forces. Certain environmental circumstances increase the likelihood of some human responses rather than others. At what point does a conditioning factor become a cause? Are there causes of human choices or just shaping influences? It is not easy to tell.

The whole truth in all its dimensions is very hard to get at. No simple generalizations cover all cases. Individuals respond differently to similar circumstances. Environmental conditions that destroy one family challenge another toward heroic efforts to preserve dignity and integrity, as well as to overcome adversity. Some escape the downward pull of the ghetto ethos, while others succumb to it. What makes the difference? Apparently it is the presence of real opportunity—and sometimes just plain luck—plus some internal human factors, whether innate, taught, or chosen, that enable some to succeed while others don't. Society and individuals, biological inheritance and social conditioning, circumstances and choices, family/ethnic culture and personal character—each and all play a part in producing patterns of behavior and consequences in ways that defy exact analysis.

Two large migrations helped to account for the black underclass in large urban areas.[74] Since 1910, 6.5 million blacks have moved from the rural and small-town South to the cities, especially in the North. A good deal of this movement occurred during the 1950s and 1960s. Mississippi lost 25 percent of its black population in the 1950s. Many of these blacks brought with them the handicap of long years of poverty, poor education, and lack of job skills. Their family life was often disordered and had its own peculiar patterns, practices, and values. A culture of dependency, deprivation, and low self-esteem had been created by white prejudice and discrimination.

The 1960s and 1970s saw the movement of many middle- and working-class blacks out of the ghetto. In the 1970s, 100,000 black Chicagoans moved to the suburbs; 224,000 blacks did the same in Washington, D. C., and 124,000 more in Atlanta. This left the poorest and least resourceful families in the inner city at a time when jobs for the unskilled were becoming less available. A shift from a goods producing to a service economy was taking place. Heavy industry was declining or moving away from locations where the poor were concentrated. A welfare culture developed in which numerous families were trapped. These appear to be some of the reasons a large urban underclass developed that threatens to become permanent unless something drastic is done.

If the factors that led to an underclass are complex, then so must the solution be multidimensional. Jobs must be provided along with necessary training. A revised welfare program, perhaps an NIT, is necessary to provide money and services for the desperate. Work requirements for the able-bodied must be strict, but only if good jobs at decent pay are available. Enterprise zones created by special inducements to business and that encourage inner city capitalism might help. Some of the young probably need to be removed physically from their debilitating surroundings for a period. A new Work Projects Administration (WPA) or Civilian Conservation Corp (CCC) built on the model of New Deal experiments days may be worth a try.

But economic self-help and positive changes in attitude and behavior from within are also required. Individuals, churches, families, schools, and community organizations must be mobilized. Just making jobs available is not enough. Some won't take them or are ill-equipped by virtue of character and habits to keep them or do well. Discipline, motivation, self-esteem, self-reliance, and good work habits must be developed. Perhaps, above all, hope must be instilled in the redeemable. A transformation of values is necessary. The indiscriminate production of babies by adolescent girls and by older women on welfare with no supportive male partner must be discouraged by effective positive and negative reinforcements that may appear harsh. Some crime-prone and violent persons may be beyond redemption and must be simply removed as permanently as is required. The system of

The Passion for Economic Equality / 155

socially provided support must be generous and humanely administered, but cheaters who try to beat the system must be dealt with severely. On and on the list might go. Both the stick and the carrot have a place in social strategy.

In short, a new way of life has to be created. It will not be easy, and it cannot be done in a short time. Government at all levels must intervene effectively, taking the dangerous risk of making decisions about "the needs of strangers."[75] It is not the prerogative of the middle and upper classes of whatever race to dictate ways of life for the poor of any color. Different racial and ethnic cultures have their own validity and positive features. But surely some things are destructive no matter who practices them. In fear and trembling, some judgments about better and worse must be made by society, especially if relief of poverty is being paid for by tax money. The hazardous but necessary task of imposing standards and encouraging healthy values and behaviors must be undertaken with as much wisdom, humility, and compassion as possible. Always a self-critical spirit must prevail, one that learns and profits from mistakes.

Society as a whole must act through political mechanisms, but so must intermediary institutions and individuals on a voluntary basis. Community action is needed within the underclass on a self-help basis. No easy, simple cures are possible within a short time. It took many years and a whole complex of circumstances to produce the ills of the underclass, and it will take a long time and a complex set of remedies to overcome its ills.

The transformations that are required are so drastic, the lack of social wisdom so profound, the frustrations and trade-offs involved so acute, the long-term commitment at every level required so thoroughgoing, the ideological defensiveness and conflict so great, and the political realities such that the probability of effective action to overcome the ills suffered by the underclass is probably close to zero. What is more likely is bits and pieces, a series of puny efforts and partial remedies, partly depending on which political party is in power.

Let it be said that corruption, degeneracy, disrupted family life, and cheating are not limited to the underclass nor universal even there. Nor are integrity, ambition, or moral health absent. Drugs and divorce are everywhere. The family is in trouble in every segment of society. Irresponsible sexual behavior occurs in all classes. Expensive call girls serve the lusts of wealthy lechers. Children are born to the unmarried and to teen-age girls in every race and class. Crime in the executive suite is not unheard of. Corporations cheat each other, the government, and the public and then are given a mild slap on the wrist. Industries pollute the environment and then profess innocence. Watergate did not occur in the ghetto. Middle-class people and the rich do scandalous things to make a buck and then cheat on their income tax in disturbing numbers. No class, group, race, or income level has any room for self-righteousness, arrogance, and self-congratulation for its superior virtues. Let those races, classes, individuals, and ideological fanatics without sin cast the first stone (John 8:7, Matt: 7:1–5). Given their inherited abilities, opportunities, and circumstances, most people in the underclass have probably done pretty well.

Taxes

Additional taxes will be required to overcome poverty and reduce inequalities. Acquiring these revenues will not only take more from the wealthy, but will also require something from those with moderate incomes. The incentive problem is real but manageable. Let it be granted that transfer payments to the poor are carried to them in "a leaky bucket."[76] Nevertheless, one suspects that frequently ideology outruns established fact in urging that the poor must be kept near starvation to get work out of them, while the rich must be allowed to get much richer so they can save and invest and to keep them from substituting leisure for labor.[77] The empirical evidence on the effect on incentives of an NIT is in dispute, but certainly what is so far known does not conclusively undermine it as an option.[78]

It is possible that for the affluent, *before* tax income serves to some extent as a motivating factor, with money used "to keep score," that is, to measure success.[79] Conservatives argue that steep progressive taxes reduce work effort and make luxury and leisure less expensive.[80] Certainly the raw desire for money and the power it brings should not be underestimated. The more stubborn resistance to a generous NIT with good work incentives may understandably come from those just above the median income level who are called on to support those just below the middle as well as the desperately poor. Obviously the more willing the compliance on the part of those who pay the bills, the better, but their cooperation will not be easily gained. Without a shift of social values among large numbers of people and/or militant political efforts on the bottom 51 percent of the population, the proposals set forth here have no chance at all of being enacted. The only claim made here is that the nation could afford to do so if it wanted to—and without wrecking the economy.

The year 1986 saw a rather thorough rewriting of the federal income tax laws. Only time can tell what the results will be as far as equity and equality are concerned. It can be said, however, that the system prior to 1986, taking federal, state, and local taxes into account, was "either moderately progressive or slightly regressive, depending on the incidence assumptions for the major taxes."[81] State and local taxes are either slightly U-shaped or regressive. Federal taxes are, however, progressive though only mildly so.[82]

Total taxes for large segments of the population have probably been largely proportional. Hence, they have little effect on the distribution of income. For 1980 the before-tax and after-tax distributions are virtually the same.[83] Transfer payments, however, are highly progressive and have a "major effect."[84] Transfer payments exceeded taxes in the lower 30 percent of the population, while taxes exceeded transfer payments in the top 60 percent, while the fourth decile showed about an even balance between taxes and transfers.[85]

From the point of view of equity and equality, the situation worsened from 1966 to 1985 as a result of changes in the federal tax laws.[86] Depending on the incidence assumptions made, the total tax levy became either less progressive or more regressive. During the period the tax burden declined sharply for those at the top, increased for those at the lower end of the scale, and remained about the same for those in the middle.[87] As a result, the "distribution of income *after* taxes and transfers was more unequal in 1985 than in 1966."[88] The federal tax cuts under President Ronald Reagan contributed to this change of fortune for the rich and the poor. The happy outcome for the wealthy was due mainly to the reduction in corporation and individual income taxes and the drop in property taxes. Those at the lower end of the scale suffered primarily because of the rise in payroll tax rates.[89] The distribution of income from market activity became more unequal during this period.[90] Fortunately for the less well off, transfer payments increased dramatically at the same time.

Analysts agree that the poor are considerably worse off than they were before Reaganomics.[90] One study maintained that the disposable income of the poorest 20 percent of families fell by 9.4 percent between 1979 and 1984, partly as a result of recession but mainly because of the Reagan program.[92] The Congressional Budget Office reported that the Reagan tax and budget changes of 1983 to 1985 decreased the disposable incomes of households earning less than $10,000 by $17 billion and gave $55 billion in tax benefits to those with incomes of over $80,000.[93]

A few more facts and figures and this section will conclude this chapter. Many of the complaints against government transfer programs are baseless. The suspicion that hordes of healthy, shiftless no-goods are soaking up public funds without lifting a finger is without foundation. Of $227 billion in transfer funds provided to individuals in 1980, apparently only $6.6 billion—a mere 3 percent—went to able-bodied persons. The overwhelming amount of money goes to people who are poor and/or cannot find work, or cannot work because they are too old, too young, too disabled, or are female heads of households with young children.[94]

Moreover, many people overlook, or are just ignorant of, how many benefits actually go to middle-class or even affluent families. Large increases in social benefits recently have gone to the middle class:

158 / THE PASSION FOR EQUALITY

Unemployment Insurance, Workers' Compensation, Social Security, and Medicare, and the like.[95] Social Security and Medicare are the largest programs ($153 billion in 1980, $260 billion in 1985), and all incomes classes participate. People with higher incomes take disproportionate advantage of many publicly supported enterprises—colleges, cultural programs, free medical services, commuter transportation, and the like.[96] On the other side are "tax expenditures" and tax loopholes that especially bless those who already have. The interest deduction for home mortgages amounts to about ten times what is spent directly on the poor for public housing. That may or may not be the way it should be, but the point is that the well off can afford to buy houses and thus benefit from the deduction. The richer the taxpayer, the greater the reward. Those in the higher income brackets save more on taxes for the same dollar deductions for dependents, medical expenses, and interest on mortgages, for example. The 1984 budget contained $388.4 billion in "tax expenditures." According to some reformers, at least $100 billion of this could be recovered for the public treasury by closing certain loopholes lacking justification.[97] A prime villain is the special treatment given to capital gains by taxing them at a lower rate than earned income. Tax exempt bonds benefit those who can afford to buy them. Granted, one person's loophole is another's just and deserved tax break. Nevertheless the sum total of all such possibilities for reducing taxes that those with high incomes can avail themselves of makes the federal tax structure at worst mostly proportional, and at best only slightly progressive. And this despite the fact that the rates have been graduated.

The purpose of this section is to counter the impression—sometimes the suspicion, and now and then the charge—that welfare recipients "have it good" by living off the workers, while the non-poor are being robbed of their hard-earned money to support the undeserving. The complexity of the situation is such that enough evidence can be found for such claims to convince those who are eager to believe it that this is the whole truth or nearly so.

That taxpayers in this country "don't have it so bad" after all, comparatively speaking, is confirmed by looking at policies in other places in the world. Among the major industrial nations the United States government takes a percentage of the Gross Domestic Product that, with the exception of Japan, is smaller than most.[98] For the period 1974 to 1976, the US figure was 27.5 percent, while for Sweden it was 47.0 percent, for West Germany 38.3 percent, for France 37.2 percent, for Britain 36.0 percent, and for Japan 22.1 percent. Yet from 1973 to 1979, the growth rate of France and West Germany was as good or better than that of the United States, that of Sweden only slightly behind, while only Britain lagged. Moreover, unemployment was generally lower—6.7 percent for the US, 1.9 percent for Sweden, 3.5 percent for West German, and 4.6 percent for Britain.[99] The United States offers fewer and/or lower social benefits and services. It is the only Western democracy not to have a national insurance plan. And with the possible exception of France, the US has the most unequal distribution of income.[100]

It may well be that better systems of taxation exist than now prevail. Neither death nor taxes is welcomed, but some ways of extracting revenue from the populace are doubtless more equitable and efficient—maybe even less objectionable—than others. The best system is, of course, the one that takes more from you and less from me! The essential point here is that more equality is desirable on moral grounds. Taxation is one method by which that can be achieved. Just how it is done is secondary to its being done, as long as the most fair and efficient way is found. Creative imagination may yet invent better means to good ends.

Quoting statistics and playing comparative economics is always a hazardous game. The situation domestically and internally is too complex and too susceptible to contrary renderings to justify dogmatism on anybody's part. Friedrich Nietzsche was almost right when he said, "There are no facts, only interpretations." Yet the figures quoted here have some point. A study of the facts certainly provides no invulnerable rock of security for those who profess to *know* that if we would only lower taxes on the rich, dismantle the welfare state, and let the market reign free, all would be better, even for the poor who would benefit as the blessings of *laissez-faire* eventually trickle down. They certainly do not contradict the claim that higher taxes, the alleviation of poverty, lower rates of unemployment, and less inequality can all be combined with prosperity and efficiency.[101]

It should just be noted that the bloated military budget contains one source of indeterminate billions that could be used to lift the poor without endangering national security. While some defense contractors and their employees would suffer temporarily, the consequences of shifting some of these massive funds into non-military uses would benefit the whole country in numerous ways.[102]

Here the argument for more economic equality must rest. A few reflections in a concluding chapter will bring the entire study to a close.

Notes

1. See Ken Auletta, *The Underclass,* for a description and analysis.
2. See Lester Thurow, *The Zero-Sum Society,* for an analysis and prescription that I find appealing.

3. For another appeal for more equality, see Herbert Gans, *More Equality*. A half-century old classic is R. H. Tawney, *Equality*.

4. I am for the moment ignoring the fact that the actual situation is much more complicated than this paragraph summary indicates. The reality of American life has frequently and sometimes fundamentally deviated from the professed ideal. Opportunities may be equal in principle for all, but in fact the actual and effective power of individuals to take advantage of possibilities that are available in a formal and legal sense vary widely (are unequal), for all sorts of reasons. Moreover, various groups at one time or another have, in ways both legal and extralegal, been deliberately denied both political equality and liberty to compete as equals for social and economic rewards. Slavery, the denial of the ballot to women, and prejudice against persons because of race, sex, religion, nationality, and the like are obvious examples. See J. R. Pole, *The Pursuit of Equality in America*.

5. For a penetrating account of contemporary American capitalism in the context of the political and cultural contexts in which it functions, see Daniel Bell, *The Cultural Contradictions of Capitalism*.

6. See Sidney Verba and Gary R. Orren, *Equality in America: The View from the Top;* and Herbert McClosky and John Zaller, *The American Ethos*.

7. See Robert N. Bellah, Richard Madsen, William M. Sullivan, Ann Swidler, and Steven M. Tipton, *Habits of the Heart: Individualism and Commitment in American Life*.

8. See Joyce Oldham Appleby, *Economic Thought and Ideology in Seventeenth-Century England*.

9. See Karl Polanyi, *The Great Transformation*.

10. These are the familiar themes discussed in Max Weber, *Protestantism and the Spirit of Capitalism;* and R. H. Tawney, *Religion and the Rise of Capitalism*.

11. For example, see F. A. Hayek, *Law, Legislation and Liberty;* Milton Friedman, *Capitalism and Freedom;* and Robert Nozick, *Anarchy, State, and Utopia*.

12. See Robert Heilbroner and Lester Thurow, *Five Economic Challenges*, for a brief review of the interconnected problems that the American economy has recently faced.

13. See Thurow, *The Zero-Sum Society*.

14. This is the thesis of Robert Kuttner, *The Economic Illusion: False Choices Between Prosperity and Social Justice*.

15. See Gar Alperovitz and Jeff Faux, *Rebuilding America*, pp. 113–21.

16. This account of the economic order has much in common with a school of thought that has been called "Post-Keynesian Institutionalism" (PKI), which is "holistic, systemic, and evolutionary," has an "appreciation for the centrality of power and conflict," recognizes the "importance of nonrational human behavior," sees that "everything is connected with everything else," and requires a "historical view of the market economy." The terminology includes "historical time, dynamic behavior, and continuous change." See Charles K. Wilber and Kenneth P. Jameson, *An Inquiry into the Poverty of Economics,* pp. 154, 155, 156. See pp. 145–66 for a summary of its basic theoretical assumptions. The economy is studied as a system with a peculiar history all its own and that has specific patterns of behavior and performance that have developed over time. PKI has its roots in the thought not only of John Maynard Keynes, but also of Thorstein Veblen, the founder of American Institutionalism.

17. I have made the case for this in considerable detail in my *Process Ethics: A Constructive System*. See esp. pp. 252–63, 278–310.

18. Nozick, *Anarchy, State, and Utopia,* pp. 150–64.

19. Elsewhere I have argued that the social philosophy presupposed here is part of a major paradigm shift in many areas of thought. See Kenneth Cauthen, "Imaging the Future: New Visions and New Responsibilities," and "Process Theology and Eco-Justice."

20. Alfred North Whitehead, *Science and the Modern World* (New York: The Macmillan Co., 1925; New York: Mentor Books, 1948), pp. 52, 59.

21. Alfred North Whitehead, *Process and Reality,* p. 21. As indicated already, the point of view I am developing is heavily dependent on the philosophy of organism espoused by Whitehead. See also his *Adventures of Ideas*. For an illuminating series of essays developing the implications of Whiteheadian metaphysics for social ethics, see John B. Cobb, Jr., and W. Widick Schroeder, eds., *Process Philosophy and Social Thought*. The chapters by Cobb, Schroeder, Douglas Sturm, John Spencer, and Franklin Gamwell are particularly helpful for the points at hand.

22. While not put in these terms, John Kenneth Galbraith and the radical economists makes similar criticisms. In particular, they charge that mainline economics is ahistorical and naive about power. For a brief discussion, see William J. Baumol and Alan S. Blinder, *Economics: Principles and Policy,* pp. 864–74.

23. Many of these points are made in Lester Thurow, *Dangerous Currents*. See also Robert Kuttner, "The Poverty of Economics." Cf. Wilber and Jameson, *An Inquiry into The Poverty of Economics,* pp. 62–91, 145–66.

24. Wassily Leontief surveyed articles appearing in *The American Economic Review* from March 1977 to December 1981. He found that 54 percent of the articles consisted of mathematical models using no empirical data at all. See Kuttner, "The Poverty of Economics," p. 78.

25. Obviously a great deal hangs on the question of what satisfaction means. If it refers to maximizing money or what it eventually buys (goods and services) for self, it is falsifiable if it can be shown that people sometimes pursue other goals. If it means fulfillment of total life aim in some larger, personal sense (such as psychic or spiritual self-realization), then it may be in some sense true. But, that being the case, it would seem to be too comprehensive and vague for its specialized use in economic thought or, worst of all, a contentless tautology. Suppose one's supreme motive in life were gaining power over other people, and money were wanted for that purpose, how would that fit into economic thinking? If this person were a businessman, he might well seek to maximize his profits, so the model would properly predict his behavior. But it certainly would not, by itself, tell us the whole truth about him and the world. And that is the main point I want to make, along with the suggestion that constant use of the assumption without all the necessary qualifications may seduce people into believing it is truer than it is, or even that it is an adequate theory about human nature.

26. If sacrifice of self-interest is assumed to maximize utility, then a paradox is involved that introduces more confusion than clarity. For the proposition that people are rational utility maximizers to be a universal truth, utility has to be defined in such general terms as to become a contentless tautology, true but noninforming about the real world. It is simply an analytical statement like "All brothers are males." It amounts to no more than "People do what they do." If it is an empirical claim, then it has to be defined in more limited and

precise terms (money and/or what it can buy for oneself) and so becomes falsifiable on the basis of evidence, clearly only partly true, and certainly not universal. Nevertheless, it may have a wide range of usefulness. It may be generally assumed that if A can buy B cheaper at store C than at D, he or she will likely do so—all else being equal. However, suppose A believes that C is guilty of unfair labor practices, while D is not. A might well pay more and buy at D. If one says, "Yes, but A clearly got more satisfaction, more utility, by buying at D," then we are back to the contentless tautology and left with the empirical question of what ensemble of particulars makes up the total package of motivations which specific people have. E, for example, might approve of C's labor practices and not only buy product B from store C but also buy F, which is cheaper at D—*ceteris paribus*.

27. In addition to Baumol and Blinder, *Economics,* see Roy J. Ruffin and Paul R. Gregory, *Principles of Economics,* and Edwin Mansfield, *Economics.*

28. "Despite the laborious techniques and scientific pretensions, most brands of economics are covertly ideological. . . . Neoclassical economics, with its reliance on the efficiency of markets, is a lavishly embroidered brief for laissez-faire" (Kuttner, "The Poverty of Economics," p. 83).

29. Cf. Robert Lekachman, who points out that prevailing economic theory creates a "scientific" bias in favor of "efficiency, growth, and free choice." See "The Conservative Drift in Modern Economics," in Lewis A. Coser and Irving Howe, eds., *The New Conservatives,* pp. 165–80, esp. p. 173.

30. Irving Kristol worries about this and expresses concern over the fact that F. A. Hayek refuses to describe the outcome of market processes as just. See "When Virtue Loses All Her Loveliness," *The Public Interest* (Fall 1970): 3–14. For Hayek's views, see F. A. Hayek, *The Constitution of Liberty,* pp. 93–99. For recent discussions of the market in relation to morality, see Roger Skurski, ed., *New Directions in Economic Justice;* and Gerald Dworkin, Gordon Bermant, and Peter G. Brown, eds., *Markets and Morals.* J. B. Clark (1902) took marginal productivity theory to be a theory of desert, though most economists today do not equate market outcomes and justice. Paul Samuelson, however, notes with astonishment that not everyone recognizes the arbitrariness involved in the way the market produces varying outcomes and incomes. See Amartya Sen, *On Economic Inequality,* p. 101 (n 33).

31. This claim, of course, involves a host of assumptions and presuppositions. But the denial of its validity also involves assumptions and presuppositions no more self-evident and no less arbitrary than those at work here. Psalm 24:1 suggests but does not exhaust the background from which I approach such issues. Life is a gift to us from some non-human Source, which I assume to be an all-inclusive Loving Purpose that seeks the fulfillment of all persons. The sun, the earth, and all the resources that make life possible and which can potentially enhance its enjoyment come to us with strings attached, that is, are the gifts of God to be used to carry out the intentions of God. Hence, mining the ore of the earth and making steel establishes a formidable but not absolute claim by the laborers to the products of their labors.

32. See my *Process Ethics,* pp. 284–89, 306–7.

33. For two economists who stress the importance of community, see Alperovitz and Faux, *Rebuilding America.*

34. This perspective has been developed in detail in my *Process Ethics,* pp. 125–263.

35. Julian Le Grand argues that the degree of fairness depends on the extent to which inequalities are the result of individual choices. See *The Strategy of*

Equality: Redistribution and the Social Services, pp. 143–47. That is a good principle, but much more needs to be said, as I have in considerable detail in this book.

36. My position respecting how some of these complexities should be factored into the moral equation has been developed in previous chapters, as well as in *Process Ethics.*

37. For a program similar to the one proposed here containing both a full-employment and a guaranteed annual income provision, see Wilber and Jameson, *An Inquiry into the Poverty of Economics,* pp. 230–63.

38. *Statistical Abstract of the United States, 1986,* pp. 430, 461.

39. Ibid., pp. 430, 461.

40. Ibid., p. 461.

41. Ibid., p. 459.

42. Ibid., p. 458.

43. Cf. Kuttner, "The Poverty of Economics," p. 260.

44. Mansfield, *Economics,* p. 675.

45. This is a point George Gilder insists on. See *Wealth and Poverty,* pp. 10–13.

46. *Statistical Abstract of the United States, 1980,* p. 471. Cf. Ruffin and Gregory, *Principles of Economics,* p. 661. Kuttner's figures make the concentration of wealth at the top look even worse: the top 1 percent of people have 35–40 percent; the top 10 percent have 65–70 percent, while the top 20 percent are in possession of 80 percent of all net wealth. On the other hand, the bottom 50 percent own only 1 percent of the wealth of the country. Here too, however, the share controlled by the very rich has declined. The top one-half of 1 percent in 1922 owned 41 percent. This dropped to 19 percent by 1953, rose to 21.9 percent by 1972, dropped again in the mid-70s but is apparently rising again now. (In contrast, in Sweden, the top 1 percent have 15 percent of the wealth, dropping from 50 percent in 1920.) See Kuttner, *The Economic Illusion,* pp. 259–60.

47. Reported by The Associated Press. See *Rochester (NY) Times-Union,* July 25, 1986, p. 1-A, or *The Chapel Hill (NC) Newspaper,* Friday, July 25, 1986, p. 2-A. This report originally put the wealth owned by the top one-half of 1 percent at 35 percent. A report on National Public Radio (August 21) indicated that a mistake had been made and that the figure should have been 27 percent.

48. Chapter I spelled this out in detail.

49. See, for example, Baumol and Blinder, *Economics,* p. 708; Mansfield, *Economics,* pp. 674–77; and Ruffin and Gregory, *Principles of Economics,* pp. 655–67.

50. Irwin Garfinkel and Robert H. Haveman, *Earnings Capacity, Poverty and Inequality.*

51. Suppose Joe, who is single, quits his $50,000 job at El Richo Co. so that he can devote himself to writing poetry. The change provides him with great personal satisfaction but with an income from the sale of his not-so-good writing of only $4000. Is he among the deserving poor who should receive from the government a grant of $1228 to bring him up to the poverty line, or should he be judged by his "earnings capacity"? What principle can we use that will apply to Joe and to F-A and F-B? And to all the rest of us who take jobs earning less than we might if we sought the highest-paying job for which we were eligible? What does "earnings capacity" imply for policy purposes in this regard? How do we relate having an "earnings capacity" to our maximum

utilization of it or to availability of jobs so that we can use our talents, and so on?

52. This is, of course, a standard position for the Democratic left. See, for example, Robert Lekachman, *Economists at Bay* pp. 70–79; Thurow, *The Zero-Sum Society,* pp. 191–214; Kuttner, *The Economic Illusion,* 136–86; Michael Harrington, "The Welfare State and Its Neoconservative Critics," in Coser and Howe, eds., *The New Conservatives,* pp. 29–63; and Alperovitz and Faux, *Rebuilding America,* pp. 113–54. For Michael Harrington, see also *Decade of Decision* and *The New American Poverty,* pp. 230–55.

53. Conservatives tend to think that the unemployment problem would go away if people were only sufficiently eager to work and would work at cheap enough wages. Doubtless, much truth is to be found in this insight. For example, I would be willing to hire someone, which I normally don't do, to cut my lawn during the present hot spell, say for 25 cents an hour. When it is 100° outside, as it was yesterday, I would even pay three times that much! It is also true that most any house will sell, say real estate agents, if the price is low enough. So why should there ever be a problem with getting a job or selling a house or getting one's lawn mowed? (I know that wages are set competitively, so that no one would likely mow my lawn for 25 cents or 75 cents an hour if they could earn more elsewhere or at least close by. The question is whether people should be compelled by pangs of hunger to work at *whatever* level of wages is set by the free market.)

Karl Polanyi quotes Ludwig von Mises as saying if workers "did not act as trade unionists, but reduced their demands and changed their locations and occupations according to the requirements of the labor market, they could eventually find work." Polanyi's response is apt: "It is not for the commodity to decide where it should be offered for sale, to what purpose it should be used, at what price it should be allowed to change hands, and in what manner it should be consumed or destroyed." Karl Polanyi, *The Great Tranformation,* p. 176.

Let us hope that we have come a long way from William Townsend who, in his *Dissertation on the Poor Laws* (1776), said, "Hunger will tame the fiercest animals, it will teach decency and civility, obedience and subjection, to the most perverse. In general it is only hunger which can spur and goad the poor to labor." See ibid., pp. 115, 103–29, 170–71. It must be admitted that compared to the authors Polanyi mentions, today's libertarians mostly sound more humane. But how much further along than this is George Gilder, who urges that the poor need the spur of poverty in order to succeed? See Kuttner, *The Economic Illusion,* pp. 1, 281(n 1).

54. See Baumol and Blinder, *Economics,* pp. 88–96; and Mansfield, *Economics,* pp. 151–63.

55. See Alperovitz and Faux, *Rebuilding America,* p. 125.

56. One prominent economist who thinks so is Lester Thurow. See *The Zero-Sum Society,* pp. 202–6. Cf. Alperovitz and Faux, *Rebuilding America,* pp. 121–26.

57. Granted, it is not always easy to distinguish between unwilling and unable, but the principle is sound. All these matters are full of difficulties both in terms of policies and in terms of implementation.

58. For example, one study showed that when economic status was defined by "earnings capacity," AFDC was much more effective in targeting the needy poor than a NIT, though the NIT was quite efficient when a current income

criterion was used. See Garfinkel and Haveman, *Earnings Capacity,* pp. 61–69.

59. Obviously, difficult questions arise here too. Should the Amish be allowed to exempt themselves from the Social Security program? How far should parents be permitted to go in choosing to exempt themselves and their children from the rules of society in order to march to another drummer, say in choosing a medical treatment that is unorthodox?

60. I am particularly indebted to Ken Auletta, *The Underclass,* for the analysis that follows. The book is especially valuable in two respects: the recognition of complexity and the empirical data it contains, including personal interviews with real persons who live in the underclass. I also learned much from two articles by Nicholas Lemann, "The Origins of the Underclass," appearing in June and July of 1986.

61. Auletta, *The Underclass,* pp. 43–44.

62. Edward C. Banfield, *The Unheavenly City: The Nature and Function of Our Urban Crisis* (Boston: Little, Brown, 1968). "The lower-class forms of all problems are at bottom a single problem: the existence of an outlook and style of life which is radically present-oriented and which therefore attaches no value to work, sacrifice, self-improvement, or service to family, friends, or community." See Banfield, *The Unheavenly City Revisited,* p. 235. He also says, "As long as the city contains a sizable lower class, nothing basic can be done about its most serious problems" (ibid., p. 234).

63. Cf. Jack Kemp, a conservative congressman, "I used to think that people create their own environment and that blaming the 'environment' was not much of an excuse. I now realize that crime and social problems, to a larger extent than I thought, result from economic problems." Quoted in Auletta, *The Underclass,* p. 280.

64. See Gilder, *Wealth and Poverty;* and Charles Murray, *Losing Ground: Social Policy 1950–1980.*

65. William Ryan, *Blaming the Victim.*

66. Michael Harrington, "The Welfare State and its Neoconservative Critics," pp. 29–63, and *The New American Poverty,* pp. 24–38. The new poverty of the '80s of which Harrington speaks is the result in part of international competition and new technologies.

67. As does Glenn Loury, a black conservative who teaches at Harvard. See "Redefining the American Dilemma," *Time Magazine,* November 11, 1985, pp. 33, 36.

68. Banfield lists a number of things that are "feasible" (that would help a little) but finds most of them to be "unacceptable" (not politically possible). See *The Unheavenly City Revisited,* pp. 260–78.

69. William J. Wilson, *The Declining Significance of Race.*

70. Walter E. Williams, *The State Against Blacks;* and Thomas Sowell, *Race and Economics, Ethnic America,* and *The Economics and Politics of Race.*

71. "The Wholesale Option" is what Auletta calls those prescriptions which attempt to deal with the underclass by large-scale economic remedies, believing that both the cause and the cure lie here. See *The Underclass,* pp. 267–88.

72. Edward Banfield and Thomas Sowell illustrate this position. See the works previously mentioned by each.

73. This is what Auletta calls those proposals which say that basically society cannot do much to solve the problem. See *The Underclass,* pp. 289–97.

74. This is a point stressed by Lemann, "The Origins of the Underclass."

75. See Michael Ignatieff, *The Needs of Strangers*. The author points out that in a large, complex, interdependent society, the problem of determining and meeting the needs of those distant from us raises some very complicated issues.

76. This well-known phrase of Arthur Okun has made its way into much of the current literature of the issue. See his *Equality and Efficiency: The Big Trade-off*, pp. 88–120.

77. I would put George Gilder in this camp.

78. Cf., for example, Mansfield, *Economics,* p. 688, with Baumol and Blinder, *Economics,* p. 719. See also Philip K. Robins, Robert G. Spiegelman, Samuel Weiner, and Joseph G. Bell, *A Guaranteed Annual Income: Evidence From a Social Experiment*. This study concluded that while the recipients worked somewhat less, they had happier homes. Some studies show little drop in work effort on primary earners who received money grants. See Joseph A. Pechman and P. Michael Timpane, eds., *Work Incentives and Income Guarantees: The New Jersey Negative Income Tax Experiment*. See also studies reported by Alperovitz and Faux, *Rebuilding America,* pp. 117–18, 291 (n 11), which show no important adverse effects of transfer programs on work effort. For an opposite view, see Gilder, *Wealth and Poverty,* pp. 118–20. Cf. Auletta, *The Underclass,* pp. 268–78.

79. Just this very morning (June 27, 1986) on public radio, a very wealthy investment banker was interviewed. He said that he worked 100 hours per week for the love of it, money no longer being important and used only to keep score. While one sparrow does not a summer make, surely he is not alone in his attitudes and commitments.

80. Cf. Gilder, *Wealth and Poverty,* p. 173.

81. Joseph A. Pechman, *Who Paid the Taxes, 1966–1985?* p. 10. The subject of tax incidence is highly controversial. Two important studies a decade ago came to rather different conclusions. Joseph Pechman and Benjamin Okner concluded that in the 70s the total tax system was basically proportional. Only those at the very bottom and those at the very top of the income ladder disturb the uniformity more or less exhibited otherwise. Edgar K. Browning and William R. Johnson concluded that the system is highly progressive. Their main disagreement was over how sales taxes were to be counted. See Joseph Pechman and Benjamin Okner, *Who Bears the Tax Burden?* and Edgar K. Browning and William R. Johnson, *The Distribution of the Tax Burden*. I am a theologian and philosopher who struggles with questions like the existence of God. I will not venture into the tangled thicket of tax incidence theory. However, as a biblical realist and skeptical observer of the human condition, I am inclined to ask: is it significant that these two studies were published respectively by the Brookings Institution and the American Enterprise Institute? Does ideology ever play a role in these matters?

82. Pechman, *Who paid the Taxes, 1966–1985?* pp. 70–71.

83. Ibid., pp. 51–52.

84. Ibid., p. 5.

85. Ibid., pp. 60–61.

86. For an account of struggles over taxes instigated by the affluent in the late '70s, see Robert Kuttner, *Revolt of the Haves: Tax Rebellions and Hard Times*.

87. Pechman, *Who Paid the Taxes, 1966–1985?* pp. 8, 71.

88. Ibid., p. 10.

89. Ibid., p. 75.

90. Ibid., pp. 9–10. Lester Thurow agrees. See *The Zero-Sum Society,* pp. 155–56.

91. See Frances Fox Piven and Richard A. Cloward, *The New Class War: Reagan's Attack on the Welfare State and its Consequences;* and Robert Lekachman, *Greed Is Not Enough: Reagonomics,* for analyses highly critical of the Reagan program. These two books representing the political left should be compared with Gilder's *Wealth and Poverty* and Murray's *Losing Ground* to learn the views of the political right on contemporary issues regarding the poor.

92. The study was made by Frank Levy and Richard C. Michel of the Urban Institute. See Kuttner, *The Economic Illusion,* p. 58.

93. Ibid., pp. 57–58.

94. Alperovitz and Faux, *Rebuilding America,* pp. 116–18.

95. For an informative series of articles on taxation and welfare, see *The Public Interest,* Spring 1986.

96. Kuttner, *The Economic Illusion,* pp. 38–41.

97. Joseph Pechman is one of these reformers. See *Setting National Priorities: The 1984 Budget;* referred to in Alperovitz and Faux, *Rebuilding America,* pp. 123, 292 (n 20).

98. Gilder admits this but nevertheless claims that the United States imposes a relatively larger burden on the rich and less on the rest than do many of these countries. His point is that they raise more of their revenues by regressive taxes, such as social security, excise, and value-added taxes than does this country. He also claims that the higher rates start on lower income levels here than some other places. See *Wealth and Poverty,* pp. 182–86.

99. See Kuttner, *The Economic Illusion,* pp. 46–49, 284–85, 291.

100. Alperovitz and Faux, *Rebuilding America,* pp. 12, 283 (n 8).

101. The thesis of Robert Kuttner in *The Economic Illusion* is that efficiency can be combined with greater equality without giving up economic growth or falling into other ruinous patterns.

102. Let me grant that this is a highly controversial area. It would take another book to make my case. Here I will merely assert that the propositions made in this paragraph are reasonable, given some alternative background assumptions that are at least as plausible as those on which present defense budgets are based. More must be said in the next chapter about the tragedies and ironies of history that arise in this regard.

CHAPTER / SIX

The High-Minded Passion: Some Unconcluding Personal Reflections

> The entire history of social improvement has been a series of transitions, by which one custom or institution after another, from being a supposed primary necessity of social existence, has passed into the ranks of a universally stigmatized injustice and tyranny. So it has been with the distinctions of slaves and freeman, nobles and serfs, patricians and plebians; and so it will be, and in part already is, with the aristocracies of colour, race, and sex.
> — John Stuart Mill

> I am optimistic about possibilities, pessimistic about probabilities.
> — Lewis Mumford

YEARS AGO A BLACK STUDENT was refused admission to the University of Mississippi, I am told, because he was alleged to be "crazy."[1] If true, that story has an air about it of the comically tragic. In those days before integration, a black man who applied to that bastion of white supremacy indeed must, in some peculiar non-psychiatric sense, have been a little off-base if he expected his application to be taken seriously. What, then, is one to say about an author who argues at great length that justice requires considerably more economic equality at a time when Ronald Reagan has twice been elected president of the country? Is not such a person "crazy"? One can hardly deny the appropriateness of that description if any illusions are entertained that the ideals endorsed in this book might actually become the guiding norm of national policy anytime soon.

Nevertheless, it may not be altogether unreasonable to suppose that there is kind of sanity about such "craziness," even though a democratic majority cannot at present be assembled to vote in its favor. Surely the black student who sought to study at that thoroughly segregated university was in possession of a healthier mentality at some deeper level of rationality than those who imagined him so out of contact with reality that he could only be dismissed as a lunatic. The economic egalitarian must be consoled with such reflections in an era when Ronald Reagan has an approval rating of 63 percent among the American populace.

Those who are inspired by a passion for more equal distribution of wealth and income as the mandate of justice are apparently faced with two unhappy alternatives. On the one hand, they can fly on wings of imagination into a hopeless utopianism, dreaming of what is not likely to be. On the other hand, the lovers of equality can work day by day wherever opportunities arise for bits and pieces of progress—tiny incremental gains—that make some but not much difference in the real world.[2] But while such pessimism might be plausible at the moment, surely it is not so well founded when the long view is entertained. Once those who thought that slavery would be eliminated, that women would someday vote, that segregation would crumble—all those starry-eyed idealists—were thought to be "crazy."

John Stuart Mill's historical observation has some merit. History does reveal as part of its story a series of transitions by which what was defended as essential to society has fallen into universal disfavor. Racial attitudes are still far from what love and justice require. Yet who would dare to offer a defense of slavery in the land where once cotton was king? It is incredible that only 130 years ago learned preachers quoted St. Paul and Aristotle in their apology for the right of one person to own another—*if* the owner were European and the owned were African! How shocking it is today to think that rational persons with pretensions of being morally serious could propose that an edict of God or of nature gave benediction to such an outrage. The equality of women with men is far from being acknowledged by the defenders of tradition. Women still meet resistance in many areas of endeavor outside the home. Yet long after slavery was "gone with the wind," females could not by their own ballots even give consent to their governance. But who today would invoke the Deity and the Law of Nature to forbid women to vote, as did many Americans of both sexes less than a century ago?

Such reflections about the past give some basis for hoping that in time the defenses of such great economic inequalities as now prevail may also fall prey to the gradual encroachment of higher ideals. Richard McKeon comments that the history of the idea of equality reveals a twofold long-run tendency: "increase in the number of those who are considered 'equal' and the diversification of what is sought as 'equal.' "[3] Perhaps the goal of greater economic equality is an idea whose time will yet come in America as an illustration of the second half of McKeon's trend.

Few and far between are those among our contemporaries who would simply submit to the proposition of Governor John Winthrop that "God has ordained that some must be rich, some poor." Those who are blessed with high income or considerable wealth need no more than self-interest to energize their enthusiasm for the *status quo*. But when legitimation of present arrangements is sought, more than likely some alleged economic law or social fact is invoked to justify on pragmatic grounds—if not to give moral sanction to—the unequal division of this world's goods among the high and low quintiles into which economists separate the nation's households. The rationalizations of privilege range from simple, home-spun snobbery to sophisticated accounts of the necessary mechanisms by which the free enterprise system produces and distributes wealth and income.

Once my college roommate and I were discussing the low wages of young women who worked in what were then called "dime stores." His father joined in with the definitive word. "If they were paid more," he philosophized, "they would not have sense enough to spend it and would be no better off in the long run." Less arrogant and more an amusing reflection on the social uses of the poor were the ruminations I used to hear among neighborhood farmers sitting under the tall oak trees to shade themselves from the Georgia sun. They laughed as they wondered who would do the hard, dirty work the world requires for its maintenance if "everybody were a millionaire." These country economists consoled themselves with the certainty that even if everyone could be rich for a day, it would not be long before human folly and ingenuity would conspire to reproduce the present unequal distribution. This would, of course, leave enough poor people sufficiently in need of work to ensure that the unpleasant tasks got done. Perhaps their wisdom would have pacified Senator Russell Long who, in public debate, expressed concern about who would launder his shirts if things got all that good for everybody.[4]

More elaborate are the dissertations on the requirements of production and economic growth in a capitalist society, which just happen to be compatible with, if not inseparable from, the concentration of wealth in a small minority. The engine of material progress is driven by the desire for more money. The well off will be motivated to produce by the hope of increasing their incomes by hard work. The rich will be inspired by the prospect of new wealth to invest in money-making ventures which incidentally produce goods and jobs and so help everybody. By contrast, the working poor, it seems, are not necessarily led to sweat and work hard merely by high wages. A little recession now and then may tame the demands of workers for higher wages and keep them docile and manageable. The poorest actually need, according to some, the near threat of starvation to goad them on. Hence, poverty for them may be a good thing, although among the affluent the loss of even a little income to taxation dampens their desire to labor—or so it is argued.

Frequently an associated argument is that the system also works to distribute widely as well as to produce generously. Yet inequalities of varying degrees are also to be expected, given the workings of the market. Equality of opportunity will produce inequality of result. Unrestrained capitalism will enlarge the economic pie so that all may have more, even if the rich may have much more than the poor. In any case, whatever equality may result is a happy by-product of capitalist processes, but is in no way an imperative of justice. If the procedures have been fair—competitive enterprises entered into voluntarily, untainted by fraud—whatever inequalities come about will hear no outcry from morality. Moreover, any interference with the free enterprise system for the sake of reducing inequalities is certain to be ruinous to efficiency and thus inimical to growth—the supreme imperative.

The question whether market outcomes are just is a matter of controversy among libertarians and conservatives. But, in any case, they are sure that to modify the workings of free enterprise for the sake of reducing inequalities is unjust. Any intervention for that purpose by the heavy hand of government would require coercive interference with liberty—a plain and egregious corruption of justice. Hence, whether the free market produces just outcomes or merely a neutral set of facts in which some end up better off than others, the end results must not be tampered with. F. A. Hayek denies any necessary congruence between justice and the distributive processes of capitalism but expresses a personal preference for greater equality among persons. Unfortunately, the only way to get it is to infringe on individual freedom by forceful measures—a move that is strictly forbidden.[5] That great concentrations of wealth in private hands or that market processes themselves may have coercive dimensions destructive of the liberties of the nonpowerful never seems to occur to some of the valiant guardians of liberty. But as R. H. Tawney said, "Freedom for the pike is death to the minnow."[6]

If the argument that economic inequalities are at least congenial with, if not necessary to, economic growth and the general welfare or are incurable by just means is not enough, then other moves are possible. If some fail in the economic race, then it is surely their fault. The unsuccessful are lacking in either ability or effort. Perhaps they are where they are by their own choice. Or they do not have the right attitudes, habits, motivations, or personal character. The fact that social structures and contingencies beyond individual control may in some cases play a role—even a predominant one—either escapes notice or justifies no systemic change. All would be well, or as well as things can be, if the free market were allowed to work its way toward efficient increase of the general welfare.

Finally, the motives of egalitarians are suspect! It is not, some say, the objective situation of the poor that gives energy to demands for equality on the part of the unsuccessful but envy. Other complain that disgruntled intellectuals craving power and jealous because they lack it may join in to give ideological support. The cry of injustice is only a rationalization of a shameful lust for what the rich and powerful have. The losers are unable or unwilling to accept their fate with equanimity. Instead, out of spite they would deny to their betters what they cannot or do not have. One does not know whether to laugh or cry at those who proffer such charges, apparently in total innocence of their own possible smugness, arrogance, pride, and self-righteousness.

In short, the inequalities that prevail call for no redress. At best, they may be justifiable. At worst, they are the neutral outcome of fair processes when equality of opportunity has existed and honest, voluntary interactions have transpired. Compassion and charity may dictate that society assist the deserving poor or those who are unable to work because of illness, disability, or age. A "safety net" should be preserved to prevent the worst consequences of deprivation. All this has been put in terms most often found in libertarian and conservative ideologies. Such views have been given new life recently and thus deserve attention. The social welfare legislation of the last fifty years has, of course, gone beyond what this segment of opinion would approve and is fact under severe attack.

Surely in the face of all this barrage the egalitarian should retreat in silence. Some truth is to be found in the foregoing antiegalitarian arguments, but not the whole truth or even the most important truth in some cases. Many inequalities can be accounted for without reference to injustice. No claim is made here for an absolute equalization of wealth and incomes. Instead, the question is whether justice requires inequalities that are more, less, or roughly identical with those that now exist. Between the division of all wealth and income into equal shares and the present distribution lies the elusive area toward which the mandates of justice, not to mention love, would direct us.

The basic argument has been that a new paradigm is needed that matches ethical theory with social fact. The holistic features of the present economic order involve interdependencies that make social nominalism an inappropriate theoretical base on which to rest a theory of justice. A communitarian ideology is needed that recognizes that we are members of one economic body and, to quote St. Paul, "individually members one of another (Roms. 12:5 RSV). Even when all the principles and norms that modify the equalitarian bent of this outlook are taken into account, a pull can be felt toward lessening the inequalities that now prevail.

A move toward greater equality of wealth and income would contribute toward the fulfilling of the American promise rooted in the proclamation that all are created equal and have certain inalienable rights. The quality of "life," the effective expression of "liberty," and the money-dependent aspects of "the pursuit of happiness" would be greatly enhanced by lifting the poorest from their squalor and reducing the gaps between the relatively deprived and the overprivileged.

America has been, to its everlasting credit, the "sweet land of liberty." Its moral greatness would be increased if it moved toward being the "sweet land of equality" in ways not yet part of the national creed. The fact that equality of opportunity (equal liberty) has been the historic norm should not invalidate the appeal that some measure of equality of result is fitting for this day and time. Equality of opportunity may have been the appropriate ideal for the past, but that fact does not necessarily mean that it should be the standard for evermore. The social situation of the last quarter of the 20th century is different from the circumstances that prevailed in 1776. "New occasions teach new duties, time makes ancient good uncouth."[7]

A partial case for greater economic equality, both of opportunity and of result, can be argued from the premise of *equal* liberty—a central theme of the traditional liberal philosophy. Liberty that is real and effective—and not simply formal and legal—requires some measure of equality. To exercise liberty in ways that matter, citizens must have sufficiently equal power to function cooperatively and some relatively comparable ability to take advantage of opportunities in a competitive society. Otherwise the strong, the rich, and the advantaged can simply make and preserve gains that unfairly leave the underprivileged, the weak, and the poor behind. Such an outcome violates the professed norm of equal liberty.

Ideals must have some congruency with social facts. Therefore an additional argument has been made here: the organic features of the present-day economic system with its webs of interdependency call into play the principle that what is produced jointly should be shared in common (equally when all relevant factors are equal, which they never are). It is impossible to work out such calculations precisely. Nevertheless, the principles that must be taken into consideration have been argued at length throughout this book.The minimal consequences of this principle, I have argued, based on theory pragmatically interpreted is that a minimal level of goods and services should be provided for all in the context of a full-employment policy.

The new paradigm implied in these pages results from the matching of contemporary social facts with ideals rooted in America's past, which proclaim a commonwealth of moral and political equals grounded in the common humanity of all. The consequence is that the idea of the equality of the politically *free* needs to be conjoined to the notion of the liberty of the economically *equal* (when all other relevant factors are equal in both cases). To the idea of equality of opportunity (properly qualified) should be united the idea of equality of outcome (properly qualified).

These guiding ideals do not represent the majority opinion at the moment.[8] Therein lies the problem. Policies out of harmony with prevailing beliefs and values won't work. Generally speaking, people will not voluntarily cooperate well with systems whose operating assumptions are contrary to what they truly think is false or unjust, unless perhaps they do not see any available alternatives. Self-interest is also fundamental, of course. But most people prefer that the pursuit of self-interest not be in basic conflict with their sincere and deeply held moral principles. Yet we are easily seduced into believing that what benefits us corresponds with the general welfare: "What's good for General Motors is good for the country."

The American psyche is filled with many and sometimes conflicting notions. A populist feeling is prevalent among the poor and lower middle classes that the cards are stacked in favor of the rich and powerful, along with individualist dreams of acquiring private wealth that could not be taxed away. The sense of the unfair advantage held by the rich and powerful coexists with the hope of becoming one of them. Even many of the poor embrace the ideological premises of the well-off. Though they may never be very successful, they would not want the government to have the power to redistribute their wealth if they had any. Blacks as a total population are more conservative than their "leaders." Poll-takers have found that more Americans favor particular forms of social legislation that have redistributive effects favorable to the middle and lower classes than indicate ideological preference for the political outlook that such programs presuppose. "Give us some of the benefits; just don't call it socialism."

But perhaps more important pragmatically is the fact that America has been so successful in raising standards of living for large majorities. A high percentage of people can look back over the last few generations and see a curve of rising prosperity for their families. Hence, as increasing numbers are benefited by the system and continue to have hopes of improving their lot, they tend to become less inclined toward measures that would substantially lift those at the bottom. Ironically, egalitarianism might have more of a chance if there were more poor people to whose votes appeal could be made!

This is not the place to discuss why socialism never gained the hold in America that it did in Europe. Perhaps it is no more complicated than that a new land truly offered opportunities to all in the context of a dominating individualistic ideology. People who feel themselves free and equal and who have hopes of improving their condition, especially if they are confident that their children will be better off than they, are not likely to be attracted even to milder versions of socialism, much less Marxism.

Hence, the fundamental issue has to do with beliefs and values. Ideologies—pictures of how the world works and of how it ought to work—are produced by the creative imagination of persons in particular historical situations. They provide an understanding of reality as people experience it. But, equally important, they contain a value system—norms and goals. Beliefs cannot be reduced to a rationalization of economic self-interest, nor are they pure creations of minds in touch with a realm of autonomous essences that define the true, the good, and the beautiful.

Ideas and values have some relative autonomy, even though embedded in the real world of interests, class conflicts, and stubborn facts. Ideologies emerge in a complex interaction between persons searching for meaning and fulfillment in specific settings that themselves have a history. Ideals must be in some kind of congruence with facts, though ideas and values have a relative independence of their own. Utopias created by imagination can become a motivating lure toward making the dream come true. Hope arises in the tension between what is and what could be, could *really* be on earth as it is in heaven. Illusion and finally despair appear when the dream contradicts not only the present but any possible future as well.

Alfred North Whitehead quoted Gibbons approvingly in noting that the fall of the Roman Empire came about because of "barbarism and Christianity." He generalized from that judgment to speak of two dynamic factors in history: sheer unconscious force and the power of ideals. A modern equivalent, he noted, was "steam and democracy."[9] We can generalize that the first factor includes the whole realm of facts—technologies, the means of production in the Marxist sense, whatever it is that makes up the givenness of human nature with its biologically based drives and impulses, plus the heavy impact of the past and the inertia of what is, and so on. The second embraces the realm of ideals created by reason as it functions to guide the inherent "urge to live, to live well, and to live better."[10]

Such norms and goals when coupled with beliefs about the "facts"— the world as it really is—order the lives of people and have the power to inspire change. Perhaps, as John Maynard Keynes said in a famous, oft-quoted passage, the world is finally ruled by what people believe. Said he, "I am sure that the power of vested interests is vastly exaggerated compared with the gradual encroachment of ideas."[11]

Of course, the world is actually ruled at any given moment by the ideas of those who are in power. This is the case whether or not those ideas correspond with either truth or justice. The point is that a political majority—whether motivated by self-interest or just ideals—supporting the kind of egalitarianism espoused here does not presently exist. The powerful who actually rule are themselves governed by a set of ideas and values. Not infrequently the ideologies entertained are held to correspond with both truth and justice. But whether their claims are warranted or merely rationalizations of interest, their ideas and values determine the immediate course of events. Voting majorities at present are persuaded by ideas and values other than those announced and defended in this book.

Hence, the impassioned egalitarian must find hope in the "gradual encroachment" of the proposed idea—in this case the notion that greater economic equality is the mandate of justice most in tune with contemporary facts. Only when a new paradigm, a new ideology, comes to dominance in the culture will it be time to talk politics. At present the required coalition of forces to constitute an electoral majority is not present. Without a transformation of values in the egalitarian direction specified and defended here, the economic inequalities that have marked the past and present will never pass "into the ranks of a universally stigmatized injustice and tyranny" (Mill). For the emergence of these new ideals in a sufficient number to become politically effective, those of us who are moved by a passion for equality must both wait and work—in militant hope. With Whitehead, we must rely ultimately on the gradual but relentless power of persuasion. But maybe we who hold such notions are just "crazy."

This book began with the question whether equality is the supreme ideal of the high-minded or merely the expression of envy and jealousy. Perhaps we must conclude that it is some of both. What is clear is that equality is an endlessly fascinating idea. It has been shown to be inexhaustibly complex. It takes on different meanings in different circumstances. Some of its imperatives or possibilities conflict with others. It is an ideal whose realization frequently and unavoidably involves compromises and trade-offs. Some difficult choices must be made with respect to whose equality in what regard is to be preferred in relation to that of other claims that may have equal weight.

Its own internal complexities are enough to baffle even the most ardent egalitarian who wants as much equality for everyone in as many respects as is possible and desirable. But beyond that, equality is only one of many ideals that must be honored in a comprehensive rendering of justice. Liberty is prominent among the rival claimants. The achieving of a greater good for all may sometimes require some compromise of greater equality for all. Suffice it is say that equality will always challenge us with its many and diverse aspects. Equality is like a diamond with numerous facets that can be viewed only a few at a time, always displaying a specific beauty when turned toward the light at a particular angle. But for some sides of the diamond to dazzle us with their brilliance, other dimensions must remain hidden from the eye.

Equality is a lure toward a greater good and toward a higher justice that must function contextually. Its imperatives can only be discerned in the moment in a given circumstance with its own peculiar history. Even there its demands will not be clear or universally agreed upon, even by its most passionate devotees. But it will never let us go. It will challenge, motivate, and exasperate, but it will always be there, requiring us to wrestle with its meaning and mandate. With it we can never rest easy in any *status quo*. Without it we can never be guided toward justice and the good life. In that lies its utter and never ending fascination.

Notes

1. I make no judgment about the merit of his application other than to say that in that time and place, the mere fact of his being black was enough to merit the label in some senses of that word. The story is true as parable if not in fact, plausible if not literally the case, in that it might have happened.

2. Any minor gains should not be despised. If the federal tax revision of 1986 eliminates 6 million poor people from paying income tax, as newspaper reports claim, and if some shelters and loopholes for the affluent are closed, that is indeed a cause for rejoicing.

3. Richard McKeon, "Justice and Equality," *Nomos VI: Justice,* Carl J. Friedrich and John W. Chapman, eds., p. 45.

4. Robert Lekachman, *Economists at Bay,* p. 43.

5. F. A. Hayek, *The Constitution of Liberty,* pp. 87–88.

6. R. H. Tawney, *Equality,* p. 128.

7. James Russell Lowell, used in the hymn "Once to Every Man and Nation."

8. See Sidney Verba and Gary R. Orren, *Equality in America;* and Jennifer Hochschild, *What's Fair? American Beliefs About Distributive Justice* (Cambridge: Harvard University Press, 1981).

9. Alfred North Whitehead, *Adventures of Ideas,* chapter 1.

10. Alfred North Whitehead, *The Function of Reason,* p. 8.

11. J. M. Keynes, *The General Theory of Employment, Interest and Money* (London: Macmillan & Co., 1936), p. 383.

Bibliography

Abernathy, George L., ed. *The Idea of Equality: An Anthology.* Richmond: John Knox Press, 1959.
Ackerman, Bruce. *Social Justice in the Liberal State.* New Haven: Yale University Press, 1980.
Alperovitz, Gar, and Faux, Jeff. *Rebuilding America.* New York: Pantheon Books, 1984.
Appleby, Joyce Oldham. *Economic Thought and Ideology in Seventeenth-Century England.* Princeton: Princeton University Press, 1978.
Aristotle. *Politics.* London and Totowa, N.J.: Everyman's Library, 1959.
Auletta, Ken. *The Underclass.* New York: Random House, 1982.
Bailyn, Bernard. *The Ideological Origins of the American Revolution.* Cambridge: Harvard University Press, 1967.
Banfield, Edward C. *The Unheavenly City Revisited.* Boston: Little, Brown, 1974.
Baumol, William J., and Blinder, Alan S. *Economics: Principles and Policy.* 3rd Edition. San Diego: Harcourt Brace Jovanovich, 1985.
Bedau, Hugh A., ed. *Justice and Equality.* Englewood Cliffs: Prentice-Hall, 1971.
Beitzinger, A. J. *A History of American Political Thought.* New York: Dodd, Mead, 1972.
Bell, Daniel. *The Cultural Contradictions of Capitalism.* New York: Basic Books, 1976.
Bellah, Robert N.; Madsen, Richard; Sullivan, William M.; Swidler, Ann; and Tipton, Steven M. *Habits of the Heart: Individualism and Commitment in American Life.* Berkeley: University of California Press, 1985.
Bellamy, Edward. *Looking Backward: 2000–1887.* New York: Houghton, Mifflin, 1888; reprinted Cleveland: The World Publishing Co., 1946.
Benne, Robert. *The Ethics of Democratic Capitalism.* Philadelphia: Fortress Press, 1981.
Bennett, John. *The Radical Imperative.* Philadelphia: Westminster Press, 1975.
Berger, Peter. *Pyramids of Sacrifice.* New York: Basic Books, 1974.
Blackstone, William T., and Heslep, Robert, eds. *Social Justice and Preferential Treatment.* Athens: University of Georgia Press, 1977.
Blocker, H. Gene, and Smith, Elizabeth, eds. *John Rawls' Theory of Social Justice.* Athens: Ohio University Press, 1980.
Brandt, R. B., ed. *Social Justice.* Englewood Cliffs: Prentice-Hall, 1962.
Browning, Edgar K., and Johnson, William R. *The Distribution of the Tax Burden.* Washington: American Enterprise Institute, 1979.
Bryce, James. *The American Commonwealth.* Vol. II. (1888) New York: Capricorn Books, 1959.

Bryson, Lyman, et al., eds. *Aspects of Human Equality*. New York: Harper & Brothers, 1956.
Buchanan, Allen. *Ethics, Efficiency and the Market*. Totowa, NJ: Rowman & Allanheld, 1985.
Buhle, Mari Jo, and Buhle, Paul, eds. *The Concise History of Woman Suffrage*. Urbana: University of Illinois Press, 1978.
Butler, Nicholas Murray. *True and False Democracy*. New York: The Macmillan Co., 1907.
———. *Liberty-Equality-Fraternity*. New York: Charles Scribner's Sons, 1942.
Carlyle, Thomas. *Chartism*. (1839) Boston: Charles C. Little and James Brown, 1840.
Cauthen, Kenneth. *Science, Secularization and God*. Nashville: Abingdon Press, 1969.
———. *The Ethics of Enjoyment*. Atlanta: John Knox Press, 1975.
———. *Process Ethics: A Constructive System*. New York: Edwin Mellen Press, 1984.
———. "Imaging the Future: New Visions and New Responsibilities." *Zygon* (September, 1985):321–39.
———. "Process Theology and Eco-Justice." In *For Creation's Sake*, ed. Dieter T. Hessel. Philadelphia: The Geneva Press, 1985. Pp. 84–95.
Cobb, John B., Jr. *Process Theology as Political Theology*. Philadelphia: 1982.
Cobb, John, Jr., and Schroeder, W. Widick, eds. *Process Philosophy and Social Thought*. Chicago: Center for the Scientific Study of Religion, 1981.
Coser, Lewis A., and Howe, Irving, eds. *The New Conservatives: A Critique from the Left*. New York: Quadrangle/The New York Times Book Co., 1974.
Croly, Herbert. *The Promise of American Life*. New York: The Macmillan Co., 1909; reprinted Cambridge: Harvard University Press, 1965.
Dworkin, Gerald; Bermant, Gordon; and Brown, Peter G., eds. *Markets and Morals*. Washington: Hemisphere Puhlishing Co.,1977.
Edsall, Thomas B. *The New Politics of Inequality*. New York: W. W. Norton, 1984.
Elliot. E. N., ed. *Cotton Is King and Pro-Slavery Arguments*. Augusta, Ga., 1860.
The Encyclopedia of Philosophy. Vol. IV. New York: The Macmillan Co. Pp. 53–58.
Fairchilds, Cissie C. *Poverty and Charity in Aix-En Province, 1640–1789*. Baltimore: Johns Hopkins University Press, 1976.
Fitzhugh, George. *Slavery Justified*. Fredericksburg, Va., 1850.
———. *Sociology for the South*. Richmond, Va., 1854.
———. *Cannibals All*. Richmond, Va., 1857.
Flexner, Eleanor. *Century of Struggle: The Woman's Rights Movement in the United States*. Cambridge: Harvard University Press, 1975.
Frankena, William. *Ethics*. 2nd ed. Englewood Cliffs: Prentice-Hall, 1973.
Friedman, Milton. *Capitalism and Freedom*. Chicago: University of Chicago Press, 1962.
Friedrich, Carl J., and Chapman, John W, eds. *Nomos VI: Justice*. New York: Atherton Press, 1963.
Galson, William A. *Justice and the Human Good*. Chicago: University of Chicago Press, 1980.
Gans, Herbert. *More Equality*. New York: Pantheon Books, 1973.
Garfinkel, Irwin, and Haveman, Robert H. *Earnings Capacity, Poverty and Inequality*. New York: Academic Press, 1977.

Gilder, George. *Wealth and Poverty*. New York: Basic Books, 1981.
Gilligan, Carol. *In a Different Voice: Psychological Development and Women's Development*. Cambridge: Harvard University Press, 1982.
Glazer, Nathan. *Affirmative Discrimination: Ethnic Inequaity and Public Policy*. New York: Basic Books, 1978.
Green, Thomas Hill. *Prolegomena to Ethics*. Oxford: The Clarendon Press, 1883.
———. *Works of T. H. Green*, ed. R. L. Nettleship. Vol. 2. London: Longmans, Green, 1886.
Gross, Barry R. *Discrimination in Reverse*. New York: New York University Press, 1978.
Gutman, Amy. *Liberal Equality*. New York: Cambridge University Press, 1980.
Hadley, Arthur Twining. *The Conflict Between Liberty and Equality*. Boston: Houghton Mifflin Co., 1925.
Haksar, Vinit. *Equality, Liberty and Perfectionism*. Oxford: Oxford University Press, 1979.
Harrington, Michael. *Decade of Decision*. New York: Simon & Schuster, 1980.
———. *The New American Poverty*. New York: Holt, Rinehart & Winston, 1984.
Harrison, Lawrence. *Underdevelopment is a State of Mind: The Latin American Case*. Washington: University Press of America, 1985.
Hartshorne, Charles. *Whitehead's Philosophy: Selected Essays, 1935–1970*. Lincoln: University of Nebraska Press, 1972.
Hayek, F. A. *The Constitution of Liberty*. Chicago: University of Chicago Press, 1960.
———. Law, Legislation and Liberty. Vol. 2. Chicago: University of Chicago Press, 1976.
Heilbroner, Robert L., and Thurow, Lester. *Five Economic Challenges*. Englewood Cliffs: Prentice-Hall, 1981.
Heimart, Alan. *Religion and the American Mind*. Cambridge: Harvard University Press, 1966.
Heimert, Alan, and Miller, Perry. *The Great Awakening: Documents Illustrating the Crisis and Its Consequences*. Indianapolis: The Bobbs-Merrill Co., 1967.
Himmelfarb, Gertrude. *The Idea of Poverty*. New York: Alfred A. Knopf, 1984.
Hirschman, Albert. *Exit, Voice and Loyalty*. Cambridge: Harvard University Press, 1970.
Hobhouse, L. T. *Liberalism*. New York: Henry Holt, 1911.
———. *The Rational Good*. New York: Henry Holt, 1921.
———. *The Elements of Social Justice*. New York: Henry Holt, 1922.
Hofstadter, Richard. *The Age of Reform*. New York: Alfred A. Knopf, 1955.
———. *Social Darwinism in American Thought*. Boston: Beacon Press, 1955.
Hole, Judith, and Levine, Ellen. *Rebirth of Feminism*. New York: Quadrangle Books, 1971.
Hopkins, Charles Howard. *The Rise of the Social Gospel in America, 1865–1914*. New Haven: Yale University Press, 1940.
Ignatieff, Michael. *The Needs of Strangers*. New York: Viking Press, 1984.
Jencks, Christopher; Smith, Marshall; Ackland, Henry; Bane, Mary Jo; Cohen, David; Gintis, Herbert; Heyns, Barbara; and Michelson, Stephen. *Inequality*. New York: Basic Books, 1972.

Joseph, Keith, and Sumption, Jonathan. *Equality*. London: John Murray, 1979.
Jouvenel, Bertrand de. *The Ethics of Redistribution*. Cambridge: Cambridge University Press, 1952.
Koyré, Alexander. *From the Closed World to the Infinite Universe*. Baltimore: The Johns Hopkins University Press, 1957.
Kraditor, Aileen S. *The Ideas of the Woman's Suffrage Movement, 1890–1920*. New York: Columbia University Press, 1965.
Kuttner, Robert. *Revolt of the Haves: Tax Rebellions and Hard Times*. New York: Simon & Schuster, 1980.
———. *The Economic Illusion: False Choices Between Prosperity and Social Justice*. Boston: Houghton Mifflin, 1984.
———. "The Poverty of Economics." *The Atlantic Monthly* (February 1985): 174–84.
Laidler, Harry W. *History of Socialism*. New York: Thomas Y. Crowell, 1944.
Lakey, Sandford A. *Equality in Political Philosophy*. Cambridge: Harvard University Press, 1964.
Le Grand, Julian. *The Strategy of Equality: Redistribution and the Social Services*. London: George Allen & Unwin, 1982.
Lekachman, Robert. *Economists at Bay*. New York: McGraw-Hill, 1976.
———. *Greed Is Not Enough: Reaganomics*. New York: Pantheon Books, 1982.
Lemann, Nicolas. "The Origins of the Underclass." *The Atlantic Monthly* (June 1986): 54–68 and (July 1986): 231–5.
Lewis, Michael. *The Culture of Inequality*. Amherst: University of Massachusetts Press, 1978.
Lipset, Seymour Martin. *The First New Nation*. New York: Basic Books, 1963.
Lindbloom, Charles E. *Politics and Markets*. New York: Basic Books, 1977.
Lloyd, Arthur Young. *The Slavery Controversy*. Chapel Hill: University of North Carolina Press, 1939.
Lodge, George Cabot. *The New American Ideology*. New York: Alfred Knopf, 1975.
Lowell, Abbott Lawrence. *Essay on Government*. Boston: Houghton, Mifflin, 1889.
Lovejoy, Arthur O. *The Great Chain of Being*. Cambridge: Harvard University Press, 1936.
Mansfield, Edwin. *Economics*. 5th ed. New York: W. W. Norton, 1986.
Marty, Martin E. *Religion, Awakening and Revolution*. N. p.: McGrath Publishing Co., 1977.
May, Henry F. *Protestant Churches and Industrial America*. New York: Harper & Brothers, 1949.
McClosky, Herbert, and Zaller, John. *The American Ethos*. Cambridge: Harvard University Press, 1984.
McLoughlin, William G. *New England Dissent, 1630–1833*. Vol. I. Cambridge: Harvard University Press, 1971.
Murray, Charles. *Losing Ground: Social Policy, 1950–1980*. New York: Basic Books, 1984.
Myers, Henry Alonzo. *Are Men Equal?* New York: G. P. Putnam's Sons, 1945.
Nielsen, Kai. *Equality and Liberty*. Totowa, N. J.: Rowman & Allanheld, 1985.
Novak, Michael. *The American Vision*. Washington: American Enterprise Institute, 1979.

———. *The Spirit of Democratic Capitalism*. New York: Simon & Schuster, 1982.

Nozick, Robert. *Anarchy, State, and Utopia*. New York: Basic Books, 1974.

Okun, Arthur. *Equality and Efficiency: The Big Trade-off*. Washington: The Brookings Institution, 1975.

O'Neil, William L. *Everyone Was Brave*. Chicago: Quadrangle Books, 1969.

Oppenheim, Felix. "Egalitarianism as a Descriptive Concept." *American Philosophical Quarterly*, June 1970.

Parrington, Vernon Louis. *Main Currents in American Thought*. New York: Harcourt, Brace, 1930.

Paul, Jeffrey, ed. Reading Nozick. Totowa, N.J.: Rowman & Littlefield, 1981.

Pechman, Joseph A. *Setting National Priorities: The 1984 Budget*. Washington: The Brookings Institution, 1983.

———. *Who Paid the Taxes, 1966-1985?* Washington: The Brookings Institution, 1985.

Pechman, Joseph A., and Okner, Benjamin. *Who Bears the Tax Burden?* Washington: The Brookings Institution, 1974.

Pechman, Joseph A., and Timpane, Michael P., eds. *Work Incentives and Income Guarantees: The New Jersey Negative Income Tax Experiment*. Washington: The Brookings Institution, 1975.

Pennock, J. Roland, and Chapman, John W., eds. *Nomos IX: Equality*. New York: Atherton Press, 1967.

Phillips, Derek. *Equality, Justice and Rectification*. New York: Academic Press, 1979.

Piven, Frances Fox, and Cloward, Richard A. *The New Class War: Reagan's Attack on the Welfare State and Its Consequences*. New York: Pantheon Books, 1982.

Plattner, Marc. "The Welfare State Versus the Redistributive State." *The Public Interest* (Spring 1979): 28-58.

Polanyi, Karl. *The Great Transformation*. New York: Farrar & Rinehart, 1944.

Pole, J. R. *The Pursuit of Equality in America*. Berkeley: University of California Press, 1978.

Proceedings of the Aristotelian Society, 1955-56. London: Harrison & Sons, 1956.

The Public Interest, Spring 1986. A series of articles on social welfare programs.

Rawls, John. *A Theory of Justice*. Cambridge: Harvard University Press, 1971.

"Redefining the American Dilemma." *Time Magazine*, November 11, 1985, pp. 33-36.

Rees, John. *Equality*. New York: Praeger Publishers, 1971.

Robins, Philip K.; Spiegelman, Robert G.; Weiner, Samuel; and Bell, Joseph G. *The Guaranteed Annual Income: Evidence from a Social Experiment*. New York: Academic Press, 1980.

Ruffin, Roy J., and Gregory, Paul R. *Principles of Economics*. Glenview, Ill.: Scott, Foresman, 1983.

Ryan, William. *Blaming the Victim*. New York: Random House, 1971.

———. *Equality*. New York: Pantheon Books, 1981.

Schaefer, David Lewis, ed. *The New Egalitarianism*. Port Washington, N.Y.: Kennikat Press, 1979.

Sen, Amartya. *On Economic Inequality*. London: Clarendon Press, 1973.

Skurski, Roger, ed. *New Directions in Economic Justice*. Notre Dame: University of Notre Dame Press, 1983.

Smith, Adam. *An Inquiry into the Nature and Causes of the Wealth of Nations*

(1776). Indianapolis: Liberty Classics, 1976.
―――. *The Theory of Moral Sentiments* (1759). Indianapolis: Liberty Classics, 1976.
Smith, T. V. *The American Philosophy of Equality*. Chicago: University of Chicago Press, 1927.
Sochen, June. *Herstory: A Woman's View of American History*. New York: Alfred Publishing Co., 1974.
Sombart, Werner. *Why There Is No Socialism in the United States*. White Plains, N. Y.: Sharpe, 1976.
Sowell, Thomas. *Race and Economics*. New York: Longman, 1975.
―――. *Ethnic America*. New York: Basic Books, 1981.
―――. *The Economics and Politics of Race*. New York: William Morrow, 1983.
Statistical Abstract of the United States, 1986.
Steinfels, Peter. *The Neoconservatives*. New York: Simon & Schuster, 1979.
Sumner, William Graham. *What Social Classes Owe to Each Other*. New York: Harper & Brothers, 1883.
―――. *Folkways*. Boston: Ginn & Co., 1906.
Tawney, R. H. *Equality*. London: George Allen & Unwin, 1931.
―――. *Religion and the Rise of Capitalism*. London: J. Murray, 1936.
Thurow, Lester. *The Zero-Sum Society*. New York: Basic Books, 1980.
―――. *Dangerous Currents*. New York: Random House, 1983.
―――. *The Zero-Sum Solution: Building a World-Class American Economy*. New York: Simon & Schuster, 1985.
Tocqueville, Alexis de. *Democracy in America*. (1835–40) 2 vols. New York: Doubleday, 1969.
Troeltsch, Ernst. *The Social Teachings of the Christian Churches*. 2 vols. New York: The Macmillan Co., 1931.
Tufte, Edward R. *Political Control of the Economy*. Princeton: Princeton University Press, 1978.
Tullock, Gordon. *The Economics of Income Redistribution*. Boston: Kluwer-Nijhoff Publishing, 1983.
Verba, Sidney, and Orren, Gary R. *Equality in America: The View from the Top*. Cambridge: Harvard University Press, 1985.
Walzer, Michael. *Spheres of Justice*. New York: Basic Books, 1983.
Weber, Max. *Protestantism and the Spirit of Capitalism*. New York: Charles Scribner's Sons, 1930.
Westen, Peter. "The Concept of Equal Opportunity." *Ethics* (July 1985): 837–50.
Whitehead, Alfred North. *The Function of Reason*. Princeton: Princeton University Press, 1929.
―――. *Process and Reality*. New York: The Macmillan Co., 1929; Harper Torchbook, 1960.
―――. *Adventures of Ideas*. New York: The Macmillan Co., 1933; New York: Mentor Books, 1955.
―――. *Modes of Thought*. New York: The Macmillan Co., 1938.
Wieman, Henry Nelson. *The Source of Human Good*. Carbondale: Southern Illinois Press, 1945.
Wilber, Charles K., and Jameson, Kenneth P. *An Inquiry into the Poverty of Economics*. Notre Dame: University of Notre Dame, 1983.
Wilensky, Harold. *The Welfare State and Equality*. Berkeley: University of California Press, 1975.
Williams, Walter E. *The State Against Blacks*. New York: McGraw-Hill Book Co., 1982.

Williamson, Chilton. *American Suffrage: From Property to Democracy, 1760–1860*. Princeton: Princeton University Press, 1960.
Wilson, William J. *The Declining Significance of Race*. Chicago: University of Chicago Press, 1980.
Wogaman, Philip. *Guaranteed Annual Income: The Moral Issues*. Nashville: Abingdon Press, 1968.
———. *The Great Economics Debate*. Philadelphia: Westminster Press, 1977.

Index of Persons

A

Abernathy, George, 125
Alperovitz, Gar, 160, 162, 166, 167
Anthony, Susan B., 45, 49, 50, 60, 61
Appleby, Joyce Oldham, 160
Aristotle, 4, 5, 27, 39, 41, 144, 169
Auletta, Ken, 159, 164, 165, 166

B

Banfield, Edward, 45
Baumol, William J., 143, 161, 162, 163, 166
Beauchamp, Tom, 126, 127
Bedau, Hugo Adam, 27, 28
Beitzinger, A. J., 58
Bell, Daniel, 95, 97, 128, 160
Bellah, Robert N., 58, 95, 126, 160
Bellamy, Edward, 54, 62
Bentham, Jeremy, 92
Berger, Peter, 92
Berlin, Isaiah, 27, 28, 29
Binder, Alan S., 143, 161, 162, 163
Bird, Larry, 137, 138
Blackstone, William, 125, 126
Blocker, H. Gene, 97
Brandt, R. B., 27
Brown, Antoinette L., 48, 49
Browning, Edgar K., 166
Bryce, James, 55, 162
Bryson, Lyman, 58
Buhle, Mari Jo, 60, 61
Buhle, Paul, 60, 61
Butler, Nicolas Murray, 53, 62

C

Calhoun, John C., 42
Callicles, 1
Calvin, John, 31
Cauthen, Kenneth, 28, 59, 89, 126, 161
Chapman, Carrie, 45
Chapman, John W., 27, 29
Clark, J. B., 162
Clark, Kenneth, 152
Cloward, Richard A., 167
Cobb, John, Jr., 89, 160
Conway, Moncure Daniel, 43
Coser, Lewis A., 162
Croly, Herbert, 54, 62
Crosby, Richard W., 91

D

Darwin, Charles, 50–51
Delaney, Martin, 43
Depew, Chauncey, 52
Dewey, John, 54
Douglas, Stephen, 42
Douglass, Frederick, 43, 45
Dworkin, Gerald, 162

E

Eddis, William, 37
Edwards, Jonathan, 36
Elliot, E. N., 60
Ely, Richard T., 54

F

Faux, Jeff, 160, 162, 166, 167
Fitzhugh, George, 42, 160
Frankena, W. K., 27, 28, 30
Franklin, Benjamin, 58
Friedman, Milton, 160

G

Gage, Matilda Joslyn, 60
Galbraith, John Kenneth, 161
Gamwell, Franklin I., 89, 161
Gans, Herbert, 160
Garfinkel, Irwin, 163, 165
George, Henry, 54
Gilder, George, 163, 165, 166, 167
Gilligan, Carol, 98
Glazer, Nathan, 126
Greeley, Horace, 45
Green, T. H., 94–95
Gregory, Paul R., 143, 162, 163
Gross, Barry, 126
Gutman, Amy, 92, 127

H

Hadley, Arthur Twining, 53, 62
Harper, Ida Husted, 60
Harrington, Michael, 164, 165
Harrison, Lawrence, 127
Hartshorne, Charles, 64, 89
Haveman, Robert H., 163, 165
Hayek, F. A., 1, 30, 94, 160, 162, 171, 177
Heilbroner, Robert, 160
Heimert, Alan, 59
Heslep, Robert, 125
Hill, James J., 52
Hobbes, Thomas, 3, 34, 67, 90, 92
Hobhouse, L. T., 94–95
Hochschild, Jennifer, 177
Hofstadter, Richard, 61, 62
Hole, Judith, 60, 61
Hopkins, Charles Howard, 62
Howe, Irving, 162
Howe, Julia Ward, 61

I

Ignatieff, Michael, 166

J

Jackson, Andrew, 38
James, William, 54
Jameson, Kenneth P., 160, 161, 163
Jefferson, Thomas, 35, 37, 41, 58
Jencks, Christopher, 95, 127
Jesus, 10, 40, 76–77
Johnson, William R., 166
Justinian, 1

K

Kant, Immanuel, 92
Kemp, Jack, 165
Keynes, John Maynard, 129, 160, 176, 177
King, Martin Luther, Jr., 31, 100
Knight, F. H., 94
Koyré, Alexander, 58
Kraditor, Aileen, 60, 61
Kristol, Irving, 162
Kuttner, Robert, 28, 96, 129, 160, 161, 163, 164, 167

L

Laidlow, Harriet Burton, 48
Le Grand, Julian, 162
Leiden, Wolfgang von, 28
Lekachman, Robert, 129, 162, 164, 166, 167, 177
Lemann, Nicolas, 165, 166
Leontiff, Wassily, 161
Levine, Ellen, 60, 61
Levy, Frank, 167
Lewis, Oscar, 152
Lincoln, Abraham, 31, 43
Lipset, S. M., 3
Lloyd, Arthur Young, 60
Locke, John, 3, 34, 35, 37, 41, 90, 92, 132
Lodge, George Cabot, Jr., 90, 126
Long, Russell, 170
Loury, Glenn, 165
Lovejoy, Arthur O., 58
Lowell, Abbott Lawrence, 53, 62
Lowell, James Russell, 177
Lucas, J. R., 28

M

Malthus, Thomas, 52
Mansfield, Edward, 162, 163

Marty, Martin, 59
Mason, George, 34
May, Henry F., 62
McClosky, Herbert, 31, 61, 160
McKeon, Richard, 27, 169–170, 177
McLoughlin, William G., 59
Michel, Richard C., 167
Mill, John Stuart, 1, 92, 168, 169
Miller, Perry, 58, 59
Mises, Ludwig von, 94, 164
Montesquieu, Charles Louis, 35
Morris, Randall, 94
Mott, Lucretia, 45, 47, 48
Mumford, Lewis, 168
Murray, Charles, 167
Myers, Henry Alonzo, 60, 62

N

Nettleship, R. L., 95
Newton, Isaac, 31, 35
Nietzsche, Friedrich, 1, 42
Niles, Nathaniel, 36–37
Nozick, Robert, 30, 79–84, 95–98, 137, 161

O

Okun, Arthur, 28, 96, 166
O'Neil, William, 60, 61
Oppenheimer, Felix, 27, 28
Orren, Garry R., 27, 59, 62, 126, 128, 160, 177

P

Parrington, Vernon, 59
Paul, Alice, 50
Paul, Jeffrey, 97
Pechman, Joseph A., 166, 167
Pennock, J. Roland, 27, 29
Phillips, Derek, 97
Phillips, Wendell, 45
Plato, 27, 90
Plattner, Marc, 95, 97
Polanyi, Karl, 160, 164
Pole, J. R., 58, 59, 60, 61, 160
Priest, Josiah, 60
Proudhon, P.-J., 29

R

Rainborough, Colonel, 1
Rawls, John, 27, 29, 30, 79–86, 91, 92, 95–97, 126, 127, 128
Reagan, Ronald, 168, 169
Rees, John, 27, 28, 30
Riven, Frances Fox, 167
Robins, Philip K., 166
Rockefeller, John D., 52
Rose, Ernestine, 48, 49
Ross, Fred, 60
Rousseau, Jean-Jacques, 3, 27, 90, 92
Ruffin, Roy J., 143, 162, 163
Ryan, William, 90, 152, 164, 165

S

St. Paul, 1, 3, 76, 90, 140, 169, 173
St. Simon, 29
Samuelson, Paul, 162
Schaefer, David Lewis, 91, 126, 128
Schroeder, W. Widick, 89, 161
Schulman, Marshall, 142, 153
Sen, Amartya, 162
Shaw, Anna Howard, 45, 60
Shearman, Thomas, 51
Skidmore, Thomas, 38, 59
Skurski, Roger, 162
Smith, Adam, 34, 35, 58, 132
Smith, Elizabeth H., 97
Smith, Elizabeth Oakes, 49
Smith, T. V., 59, 60, 61
Sochen, June, 60, 61
Sombart, Werner, 51, 61
Sowell, Thomas, 127, 165
Spencer, Herbert, 52
Spencer, John, 161
Stanton, Elizabeth Cady, 45, 46, 47, 49, 50, 60, 61
Steinfel, Peter, 62
Stewart, Mary A., 45
Stone, Lucy, 44, 61
Sturm, Douglas, 89, 161
Sumner, William Graham, 52–53, 62

T

Tawney, R. H., 30, 129, 160, 171, 177
Thurow, Lester, 129, 159, 160, 164, 167

Index of Persons

Timpane, P. Michel, 166
Tilton, Theodore, 43
Tocqueville, Alexis de, 38, 59
Train, George, 45
Troeltsch, Ernst, 58
Tucker, Robert C., 29

V

Veblen, Thorstein, 54, 160
Verba, Sidney, 27, 59, 62, 126, 128, 160, 177
Vlastos, Gregory, 27, 28

W

Walzer, Michael, 28
Ward, Lester, 53–54
Watkins, J. W., 28
Weber, Max, 160
Weston, Peter, 124
Whitehead, Alfred North, 24, 30, 63, 87, 88, 89, 95, 138, 142, 152, 161, 175, 176, 177
Wieman, Henry Nelson, 30
Wilber, Charles K., 160, 161, 163
Williams, Walter E., 165
Williamson, Chilton, 59
Wilson, William J., 165
Winthrop, John, 1, 33, 170
Wollheim, Richard, 27

Z

Zaller, John, 31, 61, 160

Index of Subjects

A

Affirmative action, 116–117
American Revolution,
  and equality, 32–38
Anarchism, 9, 93

B

Bible, ix, 61
  and slavery, 39, 40, 41
  and women's movement, 46, 48–49

C

Calvinism. *See* Puritan thought
Capitalism, 31, 33–34, 42, 56, 71, 88, 92, 93, 132, 160
Christian natural ethics, ix
Common good, 19, 20, 21, 34, 36–37, 64, 65, 66, 67, 71, 73, 74, 77, 79, 87, 93, 94–95, 96, 97, 136, 141

D

Democracy, 31, 33, 34, 35, 36, 37, 42, 54, 68
Distribution of income, 142–144
Distribution of wealth, 144, 163

E

Earnings capacity, 145–146, 163, 164
Economic equality, 129–167, 169–177
Efficiency, 10, 78, 80, 95, 96, 117, 122, 130, 134, 140, 141, 167
Egalitarianism, 7–14, 66–71, 94, 97
  justification of, 23–26
  maximal, 13, 20–23

and the poor, 2, 21
and process philosophy, 24–26, 63–65
Emancipation Proclamation, 43
Enjoyment, 24–25, 64–65, 66, 74–77, 85
Equal Rights Amendment, 50
Equality
  and Christianity, 3, 33–34
  and envy, 1, 31, 52, 172, 176
  and excellence, 10, 119–120
  and impartiality, 3–4
  and liberty, 2–3, 10–11, 53–54, 56, 57, 58, 63–64, 72, 73–79
  and merit, 10, 52, 54, 77, 82, 84, 96, 141
  and need, 6, 10, 77, 85
  and rules, 29
  and Stoicism, 3
Equality of estimation, 55
Equality of opportunity, ix, 12, 20, 38, 52, 57, 68–70, 72, 77, 82, 92, 99–127, 129, 131, 136, 160, 171, 173, 174
Equality of result, ix, 3, 20, 38, 52, 55, 57, 68, 69, 72, 77, 131, 136, 137, 174
Equality principle, 66, 74
Eschatology, 92
Ethical theory, 4–25, 29, 64–65, 74–79, 83–86, 121–124, 131–142, 172–177
Ethics
  deontological, 10, 11, 25, 28, 121, 122, 123, 127
  teleological, 10, 11, 25, 28, 121, 122, 123

191

F

Family values and success, 119, 151–152, 153, 154, 165
Fifteenth Amendment, 43, 44
Freedom. *See* Liberty
Freedom principle, 66, 73, 74
Freedom of religion, 27
Full employment, 129, 130, 134, 142, 145–147, 162, 164, 174

G

Genetic inequality, 7–8, 27, 118
God, 1, 21, 24, 32–33, 35, 41, 46, 47, 48, 94, 162, 169
Great Awakening, 31, 36
Guaranteed minimal income, 77, 82, 120–121, 122, 136, 142, 163, 174

H

Happiness, 12–13, 20–26
Hierarchy, 32–33, 42, 90, 91, 92, 93
Historical consciousness, 35

I

Ideal types, 66, 71, 72, 74, 78–79, 90, 98
Impartiality, 5–6, 7, 12
Individual good, 64–68, 72, 73, 74, 79, 81, 87, 93, 94–95, 97, 136, 141
Individualism, 31, 34, 36–37, 55–56, 63, 65–71, 79, 84, 94, 132
Individuals, and society, 55–56, 64–66, 70–73, 74–77, 78, 79, 84–85, 90, 92, 109–111, 135, 140–141
Inequality
  as justifiable, 9–10, 27
  natural, 7
  as necessary, 8–9, 27
  social, 7
  as unavoidable, 7–8, 27
Inflation, 130, 132, 134, 146
Interdependence, 20, 21, 133–135, 140, 172–173

J

Justice, 4–6, 9–11, 12, 15, 18, 20, 21, 24, 26, 28, 29, 30, 44, 52–54, 57–58, 63–88, 105, 126, 141

L

Laissez-faire, 50–55, 159
Legal equality, 55
Libertarianism, 18, 21, 30, 50–55, 66–71, 79–82, 83, 84, 86, 88, 94, 97, 137–138, 171, 172
Liberty, 2–3, 10–11, 30, 31, 34, 37, 53, 56, 58, 63–65, 66, 69, 72, 73–79, 129, 131–132, 137–140, 141, 171, 173, 174, 177
Love, 20, 29, 34, 41, 42, 49, 84, 96, 97, 127

M

Marxism, 91, 98, 175
Military budget, 159

N

Natural inequality, 7–8, 41–42, 45, 52–53
Nature, law of, 1, 3, 17, 21, 31, 32–33, 34, 35, 36, 37, 41, 42, 46, 47–48, 59, 61, 169
Negative income tax, 120, 148–149, 154, 156, 164
Neo-classical economics, 138–139, 162
Neo-conservatives, 57
Nineteenth Amendment, 50

O

Order, and justice, 105

P

Person, definition of, 25–26
Political equality, 37, 56, 67

Polity principle, 66, 67, 74
Populism, 54
Post-Keynesian Institutionalism, 160
Poverty, 129, 142–144, 145, 149–156, 157, 173, 177
Power, 9, 33, 36, 59, 176
Preferential treatment, 103–123
Priority principles, 77–78
Process philosophy, x, 24–26, 63–65, 86–88, 89, 138
Progress, idea of, 31–32
Progressivism, 54
Puritan thought, 33, 35–37, 59

R

Race
    and class, 151
    and women's movement, 45
Rectification, 117, 122
    case against, 106–108
    case for, 108–111
Redistribution of income, 54, 132, 136, 138, 144, 169
Reverse discrimination, 77, 106
Religious equality, 34, 57
Rules, 5, 6, 7, 10, 13, 25, 29, 65, 91, 96, 97, 102, 103

S

Sexism, 3–4
Sixteenth Amendment, 54
Slavery, and equality, 38–44
Social Darwinism, 50–55
Social equality, 37–38, 55
Social nominalism, 66, 70, 74, 75, 81, 87, 88, 90, 92, 93, 94, 110–111, 126, 132, 135–136, 137, 172
Social organism. *See* Social realism
Social realism, 66, 71, 74–75, 81, 84, 85, 87, 90, 92, 93, 95, 110, 126, 136, 137
Socialism, 13, 42, 54, 61, 92, 174–175
Sociocracy, 54
Sociological principle, 66, 74, 90, 91
Sociology of knowledge, 98
State, role of, 21, 68, 70, 71, 72, 76, 80, 82, 93, 132, 133, 155, 171
Strong principle of equality, 13–14
Sufficient reason, 13
Suicide, 94
Supreme Court, 17, 43, 44

T

Tax expenditures, 158
Tax incidence, 166
Taxes, 54, 156–159, 167
Transfer payments, 157

U

Underclass, the, 149–156
Utility maximizing, 139, 161–162

V

Value principle, 66, 74, 91
Value theory, 24–25, 88, 174
Voting Rights Act, 43, 44

W

Weak principle of equality, 13–14
Welfare, and work, 146–147, 166
Welfare programs, 147–149, 150, 154, 164
Women's movement, 44–50
    and race, 45

X

Xenophobia, 51